Culture and Society

Culture and Society

An Introduction to Cultural Studies

David Oswell

SAGE Publications
London • Thousand Oaks • New Delhi

First published 2006

SAGE Publications Ltd
1 Oliver's Yard
55 City Road
London EC1Y ISP

SAGE Publications Inc.
2455 Teller Road
Thousand Oaks, California 91320

SAGE Publications India Pvt Ltd
B-42, Panchsheel Enclave
Post Box 4109
New Delhi 110 017

British Library Cataloguing in Publication data

A catalogue record for this book is available from the British Library

ISBN 0 7619 4268 8 978 0 7619 4268 9
ISBN 0 7619 4269 6 978 0 7619 4269 6

Library of Congress Control Number Available

Typeset by C&M Digitals (P) Ltd., Chennai, India
Printed on paper from sustainable resources
Printed and bound in Great Britain by Athenaeum Press, Gateshead

Contents

Acknowledgements

Thanks to Nick and Maria who helped enormously with the Brazilian music; to Eamonn, the heroic ideas pilot; to my three bright daughters; and to Marizi, who means more to me than any book could possibly fathom.

Thanks to Ofra Koffman for reading draft chapters and to Chris and Mila from Sage for, among other things, being so patient. Also thanks - over the years - for discussion and advice from Suki Ali, Brian Alleyne, Andrew Barry, Vikki Bell, Chetan Bhatt, Kirsten Campbell, James Donald, Paul Filmer, Mariam Fraser, Azzedine Hadour, Stuart Hall, Kevin Hetherington, Christine Hine, Ian Hutchby, Alan Irwin, Chris Jenks, Jenny Kitzinger, Scott Lash, Celia Lury, Michael Lynch, Kate Nash, Sean Nixon, Dick Pels, Laura Peters, Baukje Prins, Michael Pryke, Paul Rixon, Vic Seidler, Frederick Vandenberghe, Valerie Walkerdine and Steve Woolgar.

ONE Introduction: From the Beginning

In the south east of Brazil, in the state of Minas Gerais, in the small town of Ponte Nova beneath the mountains, a boy grows up in an Arab community, listening to the sound of Lebanese voices, singing the mass in an old, local Catholic church. In his youth he gets interested in jazz and bossa nova. In 1970, at the age of 24, João Bosco meets the carioca poet Aldir Blanc and they start playing samba, boleros, a mix of Latin, Caribbean and African music. One of the songs they create is a beautiful tune called 'O Mestre Sala dos Mares' (The Master of Ceremonies of the Seas) (1975). The song talks of a 'black navigator' visiting various ports. His audience – a fusion of cultures, 'races' and ethnicities – come alive in the music and dance of the carnival.

The song was originally written as a homage to the black sailor, João Candido, who led the Chibata rebellion (or the revolt against 'the whip') of 1910. Many of the sailors in the Brazilian navy were black, in contrast to the whiteness of the officer class. Candido led a mutiny against the maltreatment of the sailors and in particular against the severe beating of a friend on his ship, *Minais Gerais* (named after the state in which Bosco was to be born). The rebellion spread and Candido called on the Brazilian president and the naval establishment to cease using the chibata as a means of discipline. Fearing an attack on the republic, an amnesty was negotiated, but many of the sailors, once having given up their arms, were slaughtered and João Candido was exiled to the Amazon. He finally went crazy and died selling fish in Rio De Janeiro.

'O Mestre Sala dos Mares' was written by Bosco and Blanc during the dictatorship in Brazil. The original lyrics talked of the whip and the revolt and it was initially titled the 'Black Admiral'. But the Brazilian naval establishment were still smarting and the lyrics and title were censored. Words that easily signified the original event – such as 'revolt' and 'blood' – were replaced by the songwriters with ones that give the song a surreal tone: 'Glory to the pirates, the mulattos, the sereias, Glory to farofa, cachaça, the whales'. The song now talked of the orchestration of a carnival dance and the navigation of the sea. The black admiral, now referred to elliptically as the 'black navigator', directs the dancing at the carnival. The song – formed as it is through the overlapping genealogies of 'race', colonisation, enslavement, gender and sexuality – emerged at a politically turbulent time in contemporary Brazil and reminds us not to forget 'our history', a history that is hybrid, vibrant and formed in resistance. Culture matters.

One hundred and thirty-five years before, Frederick Douglass (who the cultural theorist Paul Gilroy states as having been known for talking 'sailor like an old salt' (1993a)) had been sailing with Irish crew on Baltimore Clippers and had given his first public abolitionist speech to a white audience in the late 1830s in the Athenaeum library in Nantucket, a largely Quaker dominated island, 24 miles off the coast of New England. From Nantucket, a fleet of more than 70 whaling ships sailed the Pacific and Atlantic Oceans, hunting the great mammals for blubber to process into oils for industry, cooking and lighting. In the late eighteenth and nineteenth centuries it was a major economy, not just for the island, but also for the north American and other outposts of an emerging network of industry and trade. In the late eighteenth century, the white colonisers drew on the native Wampanoag Indians as oarsmen for the boats, but by the nineteenth century the crew was more mixed with sailors from further afield, from Boston and other towns on the mainland. Nearly ten years before Douglass gave his speech, an almost all-black crew had returned in 1830 from a voyage of over 14 months with 2,280 barrels of oil and the local newspaper declared that it was the 'GREATEST VOYAGE EVER MADE' (Philbrick, 2001). Such a journey was to be compared with the earlier and more fateful one for which the island is now better known – the voyage of the *Essex*. The journey that took a mixed-race crew from the north American coast to the tip of the south Americas, to be rammed, west of the Galapagos and north of the Marquesas islands, by a sperm whale of biblical proportions. The largely white survivors, who made it back to safety, three months after the *Essex* had been sunk and after much hardship and cannibalism of their fellow crewmates, had some of their story told in various reports, newspaper articles and in Herman Melville's great US novel, *Moby Dick*. What is striking for us about this event is not only the horror and violence, but also the faith and hope that is encoded in such stories of different 'peoples', communities, species, materials, technologies, and journeys. Culture matters.

As I write the opening words to this book on culture, I'm listening to Bosco on my CD player, with a book about the history of the Nantucket whalers to one side and a copy of Gilroy's fabulous text, *The Black Atlantic* on the other. In the long history of the Atlantic and beyond, these peoples, arts and work are set in the context of slavery, the movement and settlement of Europeans and the colonisation of native American Indian lands, and the diaspora of peoples of African descent across a huge geography. A movement of women, men and children, ideas, arts and influences. A movement of cultures. And, although a numbers of threads link these stories together (empire, sailing, and the sea), their particular genealogies, in many ways, have little in common. Across the different peoples of Ponte Nova and Nantucket, across the different forms of expression from literature to song, and across the different religions, politics, daily struggles and imagined futures, we happily refer to particular styles of music, to the lived experiences of workers, and to the conflict between people as 'cultural'. Moreover, we use the term *culture* not only to refer to things different in form or distant in place, but also to events and happenings across large stretches of time. Thus, we quite happily refer to a song from the 1970s and a book from 1851 with the same term, 'culture'. I say this not in order to dismiss the term 'culture' as too broad and general to take account properly of all the detail and distinction across these different cases, but to stand back in amazement at how well the category 'culture' allows us to hold these differences up for inspection, without ever making the assumption that the differences are reducible to one and the same thing; the deaths of a boatload of black sailors is not the same as a story of a whale. Having said this though, we should be wary of assuming that the meaning of the term culture has itself remained constant over those 100 or so years. Just as the world changes over time and place, so too does the meaning of a word and the use to which it is put.

This said, we might also wonder whether 'culture' is not only a category or an idea, but also something substantive, something material. If we are to talk about the pleasures of listening to a song or the hardship of living in a whaling community as 'cultural', then do we mean that a culture is tangible, malleable and affective? In a very real sense, songs and stories only travel and find their way across space and time because they are carried alongside other materials. In the satchel of a solitary traveller or in the minds and bodies of masses of people forced to take flight, in the ordinary conversation across a telephone line or through the global distribution of a Bollywood blockbuster, across land, sea and air, in different forms and through different means, across a multiplicity of bodies, culture finds its way into different places over different times. Culture in all its flexibility allows us to think not just of the stuff that is carried but also all that goes on in the carrying.

This book is a book about *cultural matters*. It is a book about cultural matters in two senses: first, in the sense that it is concerned with questions about the materiality of culture, about its material practices, about the technologies that support it and shape it, about the forms and affects that any culture might have; and, secondly, it looks at why culture might be important in the shaping of our and other people's lives and at how culture has been valued in the academic study of culture, in particular in the discipline of cultural studies. But what, then, is culture? What is the matter of culture? And what kind of matter is the matter of culture? The English cultural critic, Raymond Williams, states boldly in his *Culture and Society* (1958) that 'the idea of culture, and the word itself in its general modern uses, came into English thinking in the period which we commonly describe as that of the Industrial Revolution'. A particular idea of culture emerges in relation to a series of related ideas about industry, democracy, class, and art. But to what does this idea refer? Williams argues that in the late eighteenth and early nineteenth centuries, the word 'culture' changes its meaning:

> Before this period, it had meant, primarily, the 'tending of natural growth', and then, by analogy, a process of human training. But this latter use, which had usually been a culture *of* something, was changed, in the nineteenth century, to *culture* as such, a thing in itself. It came to mean, first, 'a general state or habit of mind', having close relations with the idea of human perfection. Second, it came to mean 'the general state of intellectual development, in a society as a whole'. Third, it came to mean 'the general body of the arts'. Fourth, later in the century, it came to mean 'a whole way of life, material, intellectual and spiritual'. (1958: xvi)

A song by João Bosco or the abolitionist philosophy of Frederick Douglass might be understood through the first three types of culture to which Williams refers. These forms of culture refer to the arts and high cultural disciplines that are seen to cultivate the mind and the spirit, to lift oneself and society more generally above the quagmire of dereliction and depravity. Equally though, the peoples of Nantucket or Ponte Nova might be understood in the sense of culture as a 'whole way of life'. Thus we would understand a whaling community not simply according to the work that these people carried out, but according to how they lived more generally, including their forms of artistic expression as well as the ceremonies of marriage and kinship relations.

For Williams 'culture' in the nineteenth century takes up a privileged position of being able to document and bear witness to the changes in those other fields of industry, democracy, class and art. In that sense, culture takes on the capacity of being that which allows being to reflect and to be conscious of itself. Whether a television news programme or an advert on the subway or the statue of a political figure, culture is able to witness events and circumstances, changes and developments, lives and deaths in domains outside of itself. It makes possible a kind of reflection on the world. But in Williams' account, culture comes into being only inasmuch as it grows and changes from being a *being in process* to *being as a state*, as if the process of being, that we might ordinarily associate with the notion of growth, is not sufficiently indicative of solidity and materiality. It is as if culture as a process is not seen to sufficiently matter. Of concern, then, is that in foregrounding a culture of the late eighteenth and early nineteenth century as the matter of culture, we lose sight of culture in its more natural, organic, but also more technical and technological sense: namely, we lose sight of culture as growth and training. Culture could refer to the environment in which bees, oysters, fish, silk or bacteria might emerge and grow, but also to the growing itself, to the tending of the organisms, plants and animals, to their training and to their development. Culture refers to the close correlation between growth and government, in the sense that a parent governs the upbringing of their child. Such an idea of culture brings its meaning close to that of cultivation, to the cultivation of plants and animals and, by analogy, to the cultivation of manners and dress in humans. Just as the care and training of a field of wheat helps to produce a good yield, so it was thought, from the Romans onward, that humans could be equally cultivated.

Of course, by the end of *Culture and Society*, Williams has come full circle and suggests in response to the wound that is made upon society by industrial modernity that any sense of solidarity, of community and common culture must pay attention to its husbandry:

> Against this the idea of culture is necessary, as an idea of the tending of *natural* growth. To know, even in part, any group of living process, is to see and wonder at their extraordinary variety and complexity. To know, even in part, the life of man, is to see and wonder at its extraordinary multiplicity, its great fertility of value ... The tending is a common process, based on common decision, which then, within itself, comprehends the actual variations of life and growth. The natural growth and the tending are parts of a mutual process, guaranteed by the fundamental principle of equality of being. (1958: 337–8)

But instead of proposing culture as growth and government as a solution to the problem of division and inequality in modern society, we will, in this book, take it as our starting point. In that sense, when the literary critic, Terry Eagleton, reminds us that to talk of 'cultural materialism' is to present a tautology, we should not read either term as providing limits on the other (Eagleton, 2000). This book intends to avoid the Scylla of presuming that culture is reducible to, or determined by, matter and the Charybdis of taking matter as that fixed stuff of the world that can only be divided and shaped by an active culture.

That said, we should not then presume that the matter of culture – its being or its ontology, to put it more philosophically – is reducible to economic matter, to human bodily matter, or to lived experiential matter. If anything, the history of culture from the late eighteenth century onward tells us that, importantly, matters of culture are also spiritual. Most notably the English critic, poet, and schools administrator, Matthew Arnold says in his influential volume *Culture and Anarchy* (1960 [1869]) '*The kingdom of God is within you*; and culture, like manner, places human perfection in an *internal* condition, in the growth and predominance of our humanity proper, as distinguished from our animality' (1960: 47). For Arnold, culture is what is best, the ability to know what is best, the mental and spiritual application of what is best, and the pursuit of what is best. Such an understanding of culture as spiritual matter, read through the doctrine of Christian Anglican theology, reads the traits of industrial capitalism, whether in terms of the bourgeois striving for wealth or the harsh realities of poverty, as matter to be purged:

> Now, the use of culture is that it helps us, by means of its spiritual standard of perfection, to regard wealth as but machinery, and not only to say as a matter of words that we regard wealth as but machinery, but really to perceive and feel it is so. If it were not for this purging effect wrought upon our minds by culture, the whole world, the future as well as the present, would inevitably belong to the Philistines. (1960: 51–2)

For Arnold the spiritual matters of culture are posed against industry, machinery, and materialism:

> The idea of perfection as an *inward* condition of the mind and spirit is at variance with the mechanical and material civilisation ... Faith in machinery is ... our besetting danger ... as if it had a value in and for itself. What freedom but machinery? what is population but machinery? what is coal but machinery? what are railroads but machinery? what is wealth but machinery? what are, even, religious organisations but machinery? (1960: 49–50)

A theological division between soul and matter, between indivisible spirit and divisible matter, is presented, such that when life is reduced to mechanics it is only ever seen as instrumental. But for Arnold, culture as the inward perfection of the soul is matched by its more '*general* expansion of the human family', in terms of the capacity of culture to be constitutive of a humanity that is more than the individual, and by its '*harmonious* expansion of human nature', in terms of its ability 'for seeing more than one side of a thing' (1960: 49).

For some, such as the poet Samuel Taylor Coleridge, this spiritual aspect of culture is closely tied to a sensibility for the nation and for the tradition and progress of civilisation. Thus against the backdrop of a still-recent memory of the French Revolution of 1789, he says:

> [T]he objects and final intention of the whole order being these – preserve the stores, and to guard the treasures, of past civilisation, and thus to bind the present to the past; to perfect and add to the same, and thus to connect the present with the future; but especially to diffuse through the whole

> community, and to every native entitled to its laws and rights, that quantity and quality of knowledge which was indispensable both for understanding of those rights, and for the performance of the duties correspondent. (1972: 34)

Only if wisely guided and cultivated can a nation and civilisation grow. For Coleridge, writing before Arnold, an ecclesiastical language is used to describe the cultivation of a nation, but it is one that was intended to be stripped of its religion, such that any governing class cultivating the spirit of the nation was not of a religious, but a cultural, nature.

It is in the context of the French revolution that a range of philosophers and poets, writing before Arnold, help to give birth to a sense of culture as embodying the spirit of the people, namely a notion that the people are the primary site of cultural expression, a people of spirit and nation. This seemingly more modern definition can be seen clearly, nearly 100 years later, in its more solidified form in Edward Burnett Tylor's 1871 text *Primitive Culture*: 'Culture or Civilisation, taken in its wide ethnographic sense, is that complex whole which includes knowledge, belief, art, morals, law, custom, and any other capabilities and habits acquired by man as a member of society' (Tylor, 1874: 1, quoted in Bennett, 1998: 93; Kuper, 2000: 56). The anthropologist, Adam Kuper, refers to Tylor's work as nothing less than 'an intellectual revolution' (2000: 56), but although there is much agreement that Tylor's definition of culture leaves little that is not included under its wing, there is some dispute as to the role that Tylor plays in the long genealogy of modern culture. For example, the historian of anthropology, George Stocking had argued that Tylor's definition, in fact rested on Arnold's understanding of culture and civilisation: namely, far from putting into play a relativist understanding of different cultures (in the plural), Tylor had reduced culture to a single evolutionary and hierarchical model (i.e. to Culture in the singular) (Stocking, 1968). Thus we can clearly see this when Tylor states, with regard to the question of hierarchically organising different cultures across the globe, that: '[t]he educated world of Europe and America practically settles a standard by simply placing its own nations at one end of the social series and savage tribes at the other, arranging the rest of mankind between these limits according as they correspond more closely to savage or to cultured life' (Tylor, 1874: 26).

Tylor's relation, not just to Arnold, but to the Romantic tradition, is significant in terms of how we understand the notion that culture is a whole way of life. Williams, in 1958, clearly locates the emergence of this idea in the tradition of Coleridge and Carlyle:

> The sense of 'culture' as a 'whole way of life' has been most marked in twentieth-century anthropology and sociology ... The sense depends, in fact, on the literary tradition. The development of social anthropology has tended to inherit and substantiate the ways of looking at society and a common

> life which had earlier been wrought out from general experience of industrialism. The emphasis on a 'whole way of life' is continuous from Coleridge and Carlyle, but what was a personal assertion of value has become a general intellectual method. (1958: 232-3)

By and large though, most modern commentators, and Williams himself in his later works, refer to Tylor as the originator of culture in its anthropological sense. Thus, for example, even the poet and critic T.S. Eliot, in his *Notes Toward the Definition of Culture*, states that: 'the culture of the individual cannot be isolated from that of the group, and ... the culture of the group cannot be abstracted from that of the whole society; ... our notion of "perfection" must take all three sense of "culture" into account at once' (1948: 24). Moreover, he states that:

> I mean first of all what the anthropologists mean: the way of life of a particular people living together in one place. That culture is made visible in their arts, in their social system, in their habits and customs; in their religion. But these things added together do not constitute the culture ... a culture is more than the assemblage of its arts, customs, and religious beliefs. These things all act upon each other, and fully to understand one you have to understand all. (1948: 120)

As the cultural theorist Tony Bennett argues, the definition of culture proposed by Tylor is 'inescapably normative' (1998: 88). But a notion of the 'anthropological concept of culture' is normative, not only because of the way that Tylor provides a model of uneven comparison between different cultures, but also because of the way that a certain version of late nineteenth century anthropology is used to represent the whole of a discipline from then to now. In part, it is due to the uneasy history of the relation between anthropology, colonialism and a sense of culture as residing in the locale of a particular place (the 'tribe', the 'society', the 'nation', the 'people') that contemporary anthropology has become so reflexive and critical about itself as a discipline and about its understanding of culture (cf. Appadurai, 1996; Geertz, 1973; Hannerz, 1992; Rosaldo, 1993; Strathern, 1991, 1995).

Nevertheless, despite the sophistication of many contemporary anthropologists and cultural theorists as to the place and nature of culture, there is a residual normativity that runs throughout some debates about culture in the field of cultural studies and elsewhere. At too many times, the positive ascription of 'the anthropological concept' or the application of an 'ethnographic study' of culture brings with it the baggage of whole series of connotations about place, society and nation. Thus, if in this book I refer to 'the anthropological definition' it is not to reduce anthropology further to a normative understanding, but to foreground the problem of the often unwitting deployment of this late nineteenth century discourse. This is an issue for me because to a large extent this book concerns the attempt to deconstruct that understanding, to make connections from language and belief to physical materiality, but also to lift culture from the space of an enclosure and stretch it, warp it and twist it. The roots that ground oneself in culture and the routes that traverse that cultural identity mean that we can think about culture as more than simply bound within a single place. I, for example, live in London. If I think about the culture of London, I am forced to do more than look at what happens or has happened within a single geographical place and to do more than look at the people that occupy that particular territory. In order to understand the culture of those people who live in London, I have to look also to the connections that are made to peoples, communities, places, media and cultures across and outside of that particular geographical locale. Moreover, in doing so, we would be forced to rethink the idea that there was any single culture within London, that there was 'a whole way of life' that could be seen and studied. To study a culture, then, means not to analyse the habits, customs, beliefs, ideas and arts in an enclosed and isolated place, but to investigate the connections and disconnections, the circulations and movements, the ups and downs that make a culture a living culture above and beyond its singular location.

The study of culture over the last two centuries has been shaped by the disciplines of anthropology, literary studies and sociology, but also philosophy, art history, linguistics, media studies, psychoanalysis, politics and history to name but a few. Cultural studies – as that discipline that has 'culture' as its primary object of analysis – has been informed by these surrounding disciplines. Cultural studies is a field that is disciplined through its relatively short history by a focus on certain kinds of cultural theory, certain objects of study and certain kinds of method and methodology. To say this is not to claim that cultural studies is not thus interdisciplinary or is not formed by its surrounding and supportive disciplines, but that of necessity any knowledge and any field of knowledge is situated within particular contexts and forms of understanding. It is not that cultural studies is clearly distinguished from these other disciplines that consider the cultural, but that cultural studies is perhaps a favoured home for doing so. In many ways, cultural studies has taken a lead and has become a favoured site for thinking across these disciplinary spaces about historical and contemporary culture. Moreover, cultural studies is a frame within which one can consider the translations and cross-overs across objects of study, such as the relation between a novel and a television programme, or a film and genetic biology, or an airport and professional fashions, or a Latin text on military campaigns and nineteenth century painting.

By and large, the cross-overs that have contributed to the formation of cultural studies have been within the arts, humanities and human sciences. But more recent innovation in the discipline has led, in the context of the cultural, to translation between the humanities, social sciences and the physical and medical sciences. For example, recent research might consider the relations between a medical text, masculine practices of medicine and the emergence of medical diagnostics, or it might consider our understanding of the novelistic form and the impact of early twentieth century physics. Cultural studies has become a space for thinking about the economics of globalisation and the cultural fact of empire, for grappling with the relation between genetic technoscience and film culture, for mapping the physical connections between different identities in geographical space, and for imagining how objects might have something to say about the nature of culture. In this sense, cultural studies is one of the places in which it is possible to analyse the relations across the human and non-human, the technological and the organic, and the natural and artificial. Such work clearly questions any conventional understanding of the divisions between culture and nature, culture and technology, or culture and materiality.

In this book I try to give a sense of some of the main theoretical models for understanding recent developments in the field concerning culture and materiality, but I do so in the context of what many would see as the founding and longstanding debates and problems of cultural studies. In the opening three chapters I consider three areas of debate that have dominated the field, concerning the production of cultural meanings, the shaping of cultural meanings and identities within structures and institutions of power, and the valorisation of popular culture as a central stage in the organisation of modern societies. In chapter two, on semiotics, I look at the articulation of cultural signs: how cultures take on meaning and are thought to be structured like languages, how cultural expression is always in the context of social interaction and always in relation to an audience and how cultural signs are like machines that do things and that make connections not just to other cultural signs, or in the context of a single cultural system, but to other materialities in sometimes quite complex forms. Then in chapter three the question of power in the context of culture is considered: how culture is structured and formed in the context of relations of power and how culture assists in the exercise of power and control over others. Is culture a means of deceiving people, an ideology that helps to keep people in their place? Or is the relation between culture and power more ambivalent, and more open, oriented as much to the possibility of democracy and freedom as it is to control and domination? In chapter four, I look at the notion of popular culture in the history of cultural studies. I look at why it is important to study popular culture (in the sense that ordinary cultural forms and practices are as important to investigate as elite or high cultural forms and practices), but I also ask what we might mean by that category and whether it has any relevance for contemporary understandings of culture and cultural formations. My discussion in these opening chapters is intended to give the reader a good sense of some of the core debates in the field, but also to suggest the movement that debate might be taking: namely, in terms of a shift toward understanding cultural semiosis as both symbolic and material, understanding power as not only ideological but also more governmental and technical and understanding a sense of common culture as predicated less on a national people, than on a more dispersed multitude.

In the next four chapters, I look at four contemporary and central problem-spaces, or fields of questioning and investigation, in cultural studies: the problem of identity, the problem of body, the problem of economy and the problem of globalisation. The list is certainly not exhaustive, but it is suggestive of what may be seen as significant debates for us to consider now. These chapters build on the earlier chapters; they attempt to give the reader a strong grounding in what are the important aspects of these areas of debate; and they are intended to push you into thinking about these areas innovatively. Chapter five, on identity, then looks at questions of cultural identity in the writings of Homi Bhabha, Judith Butler and Stuart Hall concerning questions of cultural authority, performance, and diasporisation. But the chapter also discusses the problem of the subject in relation to an object world that is lived and organised through complex foldings and interaction. In chapter six, on the body, I consider culture, not in opposition to, but alongside nature and technology. Donna Haraway's understanding of the cyborg or Gilles Deleuze and Felix Guattari's thoughts on desiring-machines or Bruno Latour and Michel Callon's work on actor-networks all help us to rethink more classical conceptions of the body and natural organism. Moreover, it is through the work of Michel Foucault that we begin to understand how not only the body, but life itself has since the eighteenth century increasingly become a central focus of power and knowledge. Suffice it to say, this has major implications for how we think about culture. In the following chapter seven, on the economic, I look at how Marxist approaches to the relation between culture and economy were pursued in cultural studies in the 1970s and 1980s. But I also look to more recent work on how the economic is itself seen as a cultural phenomenon. To suggest that something seemingly so material as the economic can be thought of as cultural has profound consequences for how we understand the economic but also culture itself. And in the last chapter of this section, chapter eight, I look at the problem of globalisation. In the contemporary world it is hard not to see how cultural spaces are connected to other cultural spaces and infused by cultures from other places. Culture is increasingly circulated, stretched and warped. I look at this problem in terms of contemporary debate about changing economic, social, political and cultural conditions, in the context of the brute historical fact of empire, but I also urge a note of caution with regard to how to account for the scale of such a global problem. In the final chapter of the book, I conclude not only by attempting to bring together the various debates and arguments and schools of thought discussed in the book, but also by raising the question of how we might think about an ethics of cultural study. In doing so, we return to some of the core literature within the field, but read from a different angle. Across all of these chapters the relation between culture and matter and the question of the materiality of culture is a constant provocation: what is the matter of culture? How is culture material?

This book is one for students who are initially coming to the field, as much as it is one for those thinking about some key issues at more advanced stages in their thought. It is a book that is clearly theoretical. It is not a book about method or about how to research culture. It is a book of ideas about the nature of culture. This is an introductory book, but it is not meant to be an easy book to read - as if interesting ideas should be easily digested and consumed. But nor is it a difficult book as if good ideas were only ones that were incomprehensible or made incomprehensible through lack, rather than acquisition, of knowledge. The understanding of culture - no less than the mending of a car, working in a stock exchange, or caring for the plants in a garden - implies the need for a technical (i.e. theoretical) language. Any technical language, of necessity, marks a difference between the one who knows and the one who doesn't, between the professional and the lay person. Such ideas lie at the heart of cultural studies thinking, about popular culture and about democracy. But the point is not to make analysis accessible to the point of meaninglessness. Nor is the point to make this book a popular book, if by that I mean one read or capable of being read by all and anyone. Rather this book is intended as a point of translation between a discipline and field of study and those who are interested in these ideas and those who want to learn more. In many ways it is not intended to drag everyone in off the streets; it could not, nor should it try. It is a book in a sea of other books and writings about culture. It is hoped that anyone reading it will understand that to sail across the waves requires some training of how to handle a boat in the water; how one achieves that training is another matter, but for me this book in front of you is one form of that discipline.

TWO Semiosis: From Representation to Translation

When a man marches into a room wearing a military uniform and holding a rifle on his shoulder, we have a pretty good idea that this man is either a soldier or he is someone pretending to be a soldier. The man is dressed not only with the cloth, leather, buttons and shiny bits of metal, but with *signs*, entities that tell us something about the man, that signify to us and that allow us to make an interpretation. The combat fatigues, boots and rifle do not only signify the man, they also signify the community to which, not the man, but the signs belong. This said, within a single sign community or across different sign communities there may be not agreement as to the meaning of a sign, but disagreement and struggle. Does the uniform signify liberation or occupation, 'our side' or 'their side', peace or war? Moreover, a gun in the hands of a soldier is surely a sign, but its bullets do more than signify.

In the late nineteenth and early twentieth century, the US pragmatist philosopher Charles Sanders Peirce referred to the process of how signs are produced, interpreted and connected to things and to each other as *semiosis*. Peirce argues that a sign is something that stands for something to somebody in some respect or capacity (cf. Peirce, 1998: 13). For Peirce a sign is something that is interpreted (i.e. it has an interpretant that is attached to the sign) and is related to an object (i.e. that which the interpretant is about):

> [A] sign is anything, of whatsoever mode of being, which mediates between an object and interpretant; since it is both determined by the object *relatively to the interpretant*, and determines the interpretant *in reference to the object*, in such wise as to cause the interpretant to be determined by the object through the mediation of this 'sign'. The object and the interpretant are thus the two correlates of the sign; the one being antecedent, the other consequent of the sign. (1998: 410)

Although in many ways an oversimplification of Peirce's philosophy of signs, it can be argued that in some respects he is interested in the degree of motivation between an object, a sign and its interpretant (cf. Eco, 1976). In his science of signs, or semiotics, he makes a distinction between different kinds of semiotic relations according to, what we might understand as, the degree of motivation (cf. 1992: 5–7, 226–8; 1998: 410). First, at one end, he refers to the *symbol* that has no motivated relation to its object and interpretant over and above its conventional usage. In that sense, the symbolic designates a relation between object, sign and interpretant that is arbitrary. Secondly, Peirce talks of signs that are linked to the object through a sense of likeness. He refers to these signs as *icons*. Thus a photograph is iconic in the sense that the photograph is an exact resemblance of that which is represented; the icon is isomorphic of that which is represented. Finally, Peirce refers to signs that have a high degree of motivation as indices. An *index* is linked to its object through relations of contiguity: namely through closeness, connectedness or causality. The classic example, is that smoke is an index of fire (cf. Peirce, 1998: 4–10). The semiotic nature of the index has interested many from the ancient Stoics to those concerned with the development of medical semiotics (diagnostics) in the nineteenth century onward (cf. Eco, 1984). For example, medical science is able to methodically investigate the translation of signs and objects from symptoms such as sweating, high temperature, aching limbs, sore throat and coughing to the diagnosis of influenza. Or it is able to identify swelling and softness of surface tissue and diagnose internal bleeding. Sometimes the diagnosis names the collection of symptoms; sometimes it names the cause.

But much work on the semiotics of culture has been influenced, not only by Peirce, but by the early twentieth century Swiss linguist Ferdinand de Saussure of whom we will talk much more shortly. The semiotics of culture has focused, by and large, on the question of representation and on the sign as symbolic and, by and large, it has been highly critical of approaches that recognise the relative degree of motivation between signs and objects. Moreover, to a large extent in cultural studies, the world of signs as symbolic has been contrasted to a world of materiality; the former has been seen to be as constructive of and representative of that materiality. Thus, Stuart Hall states:

> According to this approach, we must not confuse the *material* world, where things and people exist, and the *symbolic* practices and processes through which representation, meaning and language operate. Constructivists do not deny the existence of the material world. However, it is not the material world which conveys meaning: it is the language system or whatever system we are using to represent our concepts. (1997a: 25)

Furthermore, it is within the symbolic that agency (namely, the capacity to do things) is made visible. Hall continues:

> It is social actors who use the conceptual systems of their culture and the linguistic and other representational systems to construct meaning, to make the world meaningful and to communicate about that world meaningfully to others. (1997a: 25)

The advantage of adopting such an approach that looks exclusively at symbolic relations between signs is that we can begin to understand the systematic nature of signification. Different dress codes, for example, are understood with reference to the system of dress codes as a whole. A person dressed as a soldier is differentiated from one dressed as a sailor and one dressed as a airwoman. The different colours of the uniforms (for example, green, white, blue) signify the differences between the different armed forces. It is not that the colour white necessarily signifies a sailor in the navy, but rather that the colour only signifies with reference to what it is not (i.e. to the system as a whole). One of the problems with such an approach though is that it is concerned with symbolic relations to the detriment of other types of semiotic relations. Thus, consider the following example: a young naval recruit is given a pair of heavy black boots that signify 'hard-wearing' and 'durable in all conditions'. But if the boots are slightly too big and are beginning to give the recruit blisters, they will nevertheless signify something very different to that recruit. The sign is not simply symbolic, but also indexical. The material discomfort caused by wearing the boot has a relation to the meaning that the 'boot' has for the recruit. Moreover, if the young recruit finds herself with other young recruits in a dark and dank room with a leaky roof and the recruit removes her boot to catch the raindrops dripping from the roof, then the boot will perhaps signify something different again to those other young sailors in this rain-sodden room. The other recruits might, for example, view the sailor as noble and kindly in offering her boot to catch the rain or they might, alternatively, think her foolish and rather stupid, as it will be her wearing a wet boot come morning. In this latter sense, then, the sign is used (over and above any symbolic or indexical meaning it might have) as a means of social interaction with others.

In the following pages I will look at the most important resources for understanding cultural semiosis. I will initially consider Saussure's ideas about the sign, about the linguistic system, and about how such a system is presumed to be commensurate with an enclosed linguistic community (namely, those who speak a common language). I will then look to the work of two Russians, a linguist, Valerian Voloshinov and a literary theorist, Mikhail Bakhtin, in order to understand semiotics in terms of social interaction or dialogue and to see how such approaches might help us to rethink questions about the ordering of society and language. Finally, I look to the works of a range of writers, including Ian Hunter, Ludwig Wittgenstein, Michel Foucault and Gilles Deleuze and Felix Guattari, who have found the notion of representation and the distinction between symbolic and material wanting. It is from this work that we get an understanding of semiosis as concerned with the possibility of translation across material differences and a more complex sense of the relations across social, semiotic and material spaces.

Language, Social Solidarity and Difference

At the beginning of the twentieth century Saussure was trying to understand language as a systemic whole, not reducible to the particular speech acts that give any language its texture. His major work, *Course in General Linguistics* (1915), was paradoxically compiled from student notes from a series of lectures he gave from 1906 to 1911. Although linguistics was the focus of his work, Saussure was attempting to formulate a general science of semiology (his term for the study of signs), that is a science not simply of written or oral language, but of gestural, visual and other languages as well. Central to this project was the notion that 'language is a social fact' (1974: 6). But such a simple turn of phrase, borrowed from the late nineteenth century French sociologist Emile Durkheim, masks the complexity of establishing language as a system.

There are clear parallels between the work of Saussure and others, such as Durkheim, in establishing a form of social science in the context of a series of questions about solidarity and structure. Briefly, Durkheim distinguishes between the different forms of solidarity that underpin pre-modern and modern societies. He privileges a notion of society that is comprised of social facts and collective representations. For Durkheim, the collective consciousness of a society – the shared ideas, values and norms of a community – refers to the collective condition of human social experience and not simply to the sum of individual elements (1982). The analysis of Durkheim's is but one in a longer lineage of thought from the late eighteenth and early nineteenth centuries concerning the nature of social solidarity. At that time, after the French and North American revolutions, the growth of the sovereignty and rights of the individual are conjoined with the development of the idea of 'society' as a domain of association and community, such that the latter could be posed as a domain independent of direct government by the state: namely, as a domain whose rules were seen to be immanent to itself (cf. Donzelot, 1991; Wagner, 2001a, b). In a very literal sense, these thinkers were concerned with questions as to how a society could hold together in the absence of direct monarchical and ecclesiastical rule. For these thinkers, human beings were seen to have a sociality or solidarity that is pre-individual, one that is immanent to the very structure of society. The problem for us today is that this way of making social order intelligible seems to make the structure of society co-extensive with the territorial boundaries of the nation-state.

It is Saussure, in the early twentieth century, who understands this pre-individual solidarity in terms of the notion of a linguistic community, such that what holds the collective together are not people, but the linguistic system. But let us start at the beginning with the sign. For Saussure, verbal language is made up of a series of sounds that are perceived by the ear. A series of acoustical impressions are produced by the vocal organs that are understood as meaningful sounds. These meaningful sounds are known as *phonemes* and are to be distinguished from grunts or other noises that we would not assume to be part of a linguistic system. For example, the phonemes 'c', 'a' and 't' can be placed together to form a larger meaningful unit referred to as a sound-image or *signifier*. Phonemes are not really meaningful on their own, but when combined with other phonemes they can produce units that are meaningful. 'C', as a phoneme, on its own does not have any meaning, but it does in combination. For Saussure, 'auditory impressions exist unconsciously' (1974: 38). Before a sound is uttered, both speaker and hearer have reference to a system of phonemes that when assembled in particular ways are able to produce meaning. But the collection of phonemes, put together to produce a sound-image, are not simply physiological. They are put together in order to produce meaning and hence, for Saussure, are also psychological. The sound-images are articulated with units of meaning or *signifieds*. Thus 'cat' refers to a fluffy animal with four paws, whiskers, who purrs, eats fish and gets chased by dogs. Signifiers are attached to signifieds according to a *code* and together they comprise a *sign* (Barthes, 1968).

Later semiologists, such as Barthes, have looked at how the units of meaning that are coded (or articulated) with signifiers are of two types. The literal meaning attached to a signifier is known as the *denotation*. Thus the denotation of 'cat' includes the definition we might read in a dictionary, such as 'a small domesticated quadruped' (Concise Oxford English Dictionary, 1964: 186). The second type of signified refers to the wider associative or symbolic meaning that might be attached to a signifier; this is known as the *connotation* (Barthes, 1968, 1973). Thus 'cat', in patriarchal contexts, can also be associated with femininity. Cats are seen as feminine creatures, sleek, sexy, wily and independent. Barthes talks about connotative meaning as ideological (1973).

Both signifiers and signifieds have meaning only inasmuch as they are constructed within systems of difference. In this sense, Saussure and his followers argue that signifiers and signifieds are not defined positively, but only negatively in terms of what they are not. Moreover, the relation between signifiers is not motivated by the object or referent itself. The signifier 'cat' does not have a natural relation to the fluffy animal. Rather the relation between signifier and signified is arbitrary, although many commentators argue that the relation is actually conventional (cf. Eco, 1976). From this we can gather that signification is purely formal; it is not based on the substantive quality of the world.

For Saussure, individual speech acts, or *parole*, are only possible because of the structure, or system, of language, or *langue*. Thus, the speech act, 'This is my cat', spoken by Mrs Pommefritter at 4.23 in the afternoon on 4 May 1969 in a police station in London, makes sense not because Mrs Pommefritter has a private language known only to herself, but because the signifiers and their grammatical, or syntactical, composition refer to a public system of language. Individual speech acts only make sense in relation to a general system of codification or language. Although the relation between the signifier 'cat' and the signified of 'a fluffy quadruped' is itself arbitrary inasmuch as any signifier could have been used, the signifier that is actually used needs to be one that is used by a whole community of speakers and not Mrs Pommefritter alone. Whereas speech acts are made by individuals in particular circumstances, language as a system is collective. Saussure argues that for language to be social the sign must be arbitrary in nature:

> The arbitrary nature of the sign explains ... why the social fact alone can create a linguistic system. The community is necessary if values that owe their existence solely to usage and general acceptance are to be set up; by himself the individual is incapable of fixing a single value. (1974: 113)

Language is constituted as a 'sort of contract signed by the members of a community' (1974: 14) and although the mass of individual speech acts are heterogeneous (i.e. many and different), the linguistic system itself is homogenous (i.e. one and the same) and can be understood and analysed separately from those speech acts. Language has a life of its own. It is a system, a social institution and a product of its own history. Saussure refers to language as an 'organism' (1974: 20). Thus, although linguistic systems are related to the ethnography and culture of a nation, to political and social history, to social institutions (such as the church, the school and so on) and to changing geographies (i.e. in terms of migrating populations and so on), language is itself, according to Saussure, a separate and distinct entity. For Saussure, then, language is social inasmuch as '[i]ts social nature is one of its inner characteristics' (1974: 77); it is coextensive with its community of speakers, although not reducible to any one speech act by any one of those speakers.

This said, Saussure's understanding of language is somewhat paradoxical. The articulation of signifier and signified meet in the mind of the speaker or listener: language 'is a system of signs in which the only essential thing is the union of meanings and sound-images, and in which both parts of the sign are psychological' (1974: 15). Linguistic phenomena 'are realities that have their seat in the brain' (1974: 15). But no one human mind contains within it the structure of language itself. The system of language is only found in the collective mind. Saussure states:

> If we could embrace the sum of word-images stored in the minds of all individuals, we could identify the social bond that constitutes language. It is a storehouse filled by the members of a given community through their active use of speaking, a grammatical system that has a potential existence in each brain, or, more specifically, in the brains of a group of individuals. For language is not complete in any speaker; it exists perfectly only within a collectivity. (1974: 14)

Thus although signification, the combination of signifier and signified, is made possible in the mind, this psychological fact is itself a consequence of the system of language, not the individual. In this sense, language is, to borrow from Durkheim, the site of a 'collective consciousness'. Individual speech acts are accidental, not necessary aspects of language.

For Saussure, language is a space of social solidarity. But Saussure adds a different dimension. The system of language is commensurate with the community of speakers of that language and the linguistic actions of individuals are secondary to the primacy of the linguistic organism. Moreover, linguistic solidarity is produced through the mechanisms of language. Saussure talks of *associative* and *syntagmatic solidarities*: '[t]he set of phonic and conceptual differences that constitutes language results from two types of comparisons; the relations are sometimes associative, sometimes syntagmatic' (1974: 127). Associative solidarities refer to those groupings according to common meaning. Thus 'cat', 'dog', 'guinea pig' are associated according to the common paradigm of domestic pets. Associative relations are also known (following the work of the linguist Roman Jakobson) as paradigmatic relations. These relations are, according to Saussure dependent on the memory function of the brain: namely, the brain is able to store a series of common terms, any one of which may be pulled out and placed in a particular linguistic utterance such as 'The cat is sitting on the mat' or 'The dog is sitting on the mat'. These relations are defined as *in absentia* because as one term is used so all the other terms in the storehouse are not used. In contrast, syntagmatic solidarities are defined as *in praesentia* and refer to groupings of signifiers that are present at the same time. Syntagmatic relations refer to the combination of terms standing next to each other. These are linear relations as in the grammatical combination of words in a well-formed sentence, 'The dog eats biscuits'. 'Dog' and 'eats' have no relation of common meaning. Their only relation is due to their being placed next to each other in the forming of a grammatical sentence.

Language, for Saussure then, is not only a system of differences, but also the site of solidarities:

> In language everything boils down to differences but also groupings. The mechanism of language, which consists of the interplay of successive terms, resembles the operation of a machine in which the parts have a reciprocating function even though they are arranged in a single dimension. (1974: 128)

Although the difference machine construes the relation between signifier and signified as arbitrary, the arbitrariness is by degree: '[b]etween the two extremes – a minimum of organization and a minimum of arbitrariness – we find all possible varieties' (1974: 133). Thus the degree of motivation of the signifier and signified (i.e. the degree of stickiness, perhaps, between word and meaning) is explained by the syntagmatic and associative solidarities. Saussure avoids commenting directly on the full sociological implications of his science of semiology and he keeps within the limits of linguistics. Thus the full import of his analysis of linguistic solidarity and differentiation is never discussed in terms of, for example, social and cultural differentiation. These types of analysis would need to be left to later sociological, anthropological and cultural studies researchers.

Nevertheless, Saussure's comments on language, ethnicity and national boundaries are revealing. For Saussure any boundary between two languages is conventional. Moreover, he states that:

> [A]brupt transitions from one language to another are common, due to circumstances that have destroyed imperceptible transitions. The most disruptive force is the shifting of populations. Nations have always shuttled back and forth. Their migrations, multiplied throughout the centuries, have wrought confusion everywhere, and at many points all trace of linguistic transition has been wiped out. (1974: 204)

Saussure continues by taking the example of the family of Indo-European languages: Slavic overlaps with Iranian and Germanic languages; German links Slavic and Celtic; Celtic is related to Italic; and Italic is between Celtic and Greek. Peoples migrate and settle; they cross territories; languages travel and change. Here the marks of national difference are not territorial; they are linguistic: '[t]he culture of a nation exerts an influence on its language, and the language, on the other hand, is largely responsible for the nation' (1974: 20). Moreover, if we include rites, customs and everyday practices within the broad spectrum of semiological data, the differentiation of nations becomes more enclosed. Saussure talks about ethnic unity in terms of the 'multiple relations of religion, civilization, common defense, etc., which spring up even among nations of different races and in the absence of any political bond'

(1974: 223). It is this ethnic unity that has a mutual relation with linguistic system:

> The social bond tends to create linguistic community and probably imposes certain traits on the common idiom; conversely, linguistic community is to some extent responsible for ethnic unity. In general, ethnic unity always suffices to explain linguistic community. (1974: 223)

The correlation of language and ethnicity is resonant of the cultural relativism of the late nineteenth and early twentieth centuries. It is a form of cultural relativism that is immanent to the development of the discipline of anthropology in the late nineteenth century, but also to discussions of culture well into the twentieth century (cf. Kuper, 2000).

In Saussure, then, we see how the systemic nature of language is closely correlated with ethnicity and national culture, on the one hand, and with the community of speakers and their social solidarity, on the other. The boundedness of language is thus the boundedness of society, but also the boundedness of a nation. In this light, the simple ethnographic examples that mark the English word 'cat' from the French 'chat' or the different ways of saying snow in Inuit language or the difference between how the Welsh and the English mark out colour differences between grey, green and blue are more insidious. 'Cat' and 'chat', not only refer to two different ways of pointing to the same fluffy animal with pointy ears, but also reference the difference between two languages, two societies, two peoples, two ethnicities and two nations. For Saussure the differences have no bearing on race. Linguistic systems are not analogues of racial types (1974: 222). Nevertheless, the correspondence between language and ethnicity, on the one hand, and the strict differences (however overlapping) between national languages (as the tracing of communities of speakers), on the other, serves well to deliver the same certainties and the same purification of space that racial difference has historically been so good at delivering. As Michael Hardt and Antonio Negri state, with reference to the equivalence between people, nation and racial dominance: '[t]he identity of the people was constructed on an imaginary plane that hid and/or eliminated differences, and this corresponded on the practical plane to racial subordination and social purification' (2000: 103). But instead of a purification that disavows or represses difference, the solidarity that is constructed within Saussurian linguistics is such that it is a necessary correlative. For Saussure, solidarity is predicated not on a shared set of meanings, beliefs or ideas, but on a community of differences.

The most trenchant critique of Saussurian linguistics, from within cultural theory, has come from the work of the French philosopher, Jacques Derrida. At one level, it might seem that the work of Derrida is appropriate for the undoing of the closure of the bounded space of social solidarity and the linguistic system and to some extent this would be true. Derrida has shown how the system of differences that constitute a language are not fixed. A signifier does not simply refer to a signified that sits in the head of the speaker or listener. The idea or concept of a fluffy, four-legged purring animal does not in any way complete the signifier 'cat'. On the contrary, Derrida argues, the meaning of a term is always displaced along the chain of possible meanings. The signified is always deferred. There is no 'transcendental signified', to use a phrase deployed by Derrida, no meaning that halts the flow of meaning, that stops the play of signification. We can think of the example of looking up the word 'cat' in a dictionary. Instead of giving us something substantive, the dictionary passes us on to other words and other meanings, that we then look up and so on and so on. In this sense, language is not only a system of differences in which signs *differ* from each other, but also meanings are constantly *deferred*. Signs are differentiated from each other on a spatial plane, but also meaning is endlessly deferred on a temporal plane. The signifier is never finally stitched to the signified. The term Derrida coins to name such a process is not difference (with an 'e'), but *differance* (with an 'a'). For Derrida the silent 'a' is such that it cannot be heard in the consciousness of individuals, but only in writing (1978a). Derrida talks not of signs (based on the sound-image), but of 'grams' (or written traces) and refers to his philosophy of signification as 'grammatology' (1976). Thus, Derrida's critique – that he calls deconstruction – is posed not only against the notion that meaning is fixed, but also against the notion that any such meaning might find itself in the mind of the speaker or listener. In this sense, Derrida is explicitly deconstructing the residual psychologism of Saussurian semiology and of the science of signs more generally (1976). No meaning ever appears as a presence present to consciousness. Thus, although we might think that a 'cat' in English and a 'chat' in French refer to the same fluffy signified and that translation across the two languages is a possibility, we would, according to Derrida, be very mistaken. Any attempt at translation is a transformation. The meaning of 'cat' cannot simply be transported. It is constituted within a system of differences and the endless play within that system. Any sign does not transparently represent a world outside of itself; rather a language is constitutive of that unsettled reality.

Although Derrida's deconstruction of Saussurian semiology is certainly inviting and takes us some way toward understanding some major problems, it nevertheless has its own problems. First, Derrida's critique is predicated on a prioritisation of the formal qualities of the sign that are foregrounded by Saussure (i.e. that both signifier and signified neither relate directly to physical sound itself nor to any referents in the world). Derrida states that 'by de-substantializing both the signified content and the "expressive substance" – which therefore is no longer in a privileged or exclusive way phonic – by making linguistics a division of general semiology, Saussure powerfully contributed to turning against the metaphysical tradition the concept of the sign that he borrowed from it' (Derrida, 1987: 18). Thus, in order to make way for a general semiology, and also for a Derridean grammatology, the sign must be de-substantialised. It must be stripped of its materiality and its particularity. In this sense, it is only the form of the phoneme that must be carried from speech to writing to gestural semiotics and so on, not the privilege of speech itself. But the bind in which Derrida is caught is precisely that even though translation at the level of the signified is ruled out of court, it nevertheless slips back in at the level of the formal quality of the sign itself (and whether we call it sign or gram makes no real difference). It is important, as we shall see later in this chapter, not only to substantialise the sign, but also make it thoroughly particular. Speech is different from writing which is different in turn from other semiotic systems, but this does not disavow the possibility of translation, on the contrary it is what makes translation both possible and necessary.

Secondly, although deconstruction displaces the presence of consciousness and any external agency that might serve to anchor meaning, it prioritises *differance* as *systematic* (1978a, 1978b, 1987). Derrida allows for meaning to be traced throughout the dictionary, as it were, but the world of *differance* is limited to that dictionary, limited to the sociality of language as the constitutive limits of solidarity. In this sense at least, Derrida stays within the problematic of solidarity and difference. The deconstruction of closure is only skin deep. If solidarity is unbounded, then the reason for difference is taken away. It is not for no reason that deconstruction is a precise form of critique that identifies a binary, identifies the relations of dominance and suplementarity, and reverses the value of the polarity, in such a way as not simply to prioritise the supplement as a new dominant, but to problematise the logic of dominance itself. For example, if we take the binary citizen/soldier, we would ordinarily assume that in times of normalcy 'citizen' is the dominant term and that 'soldier' only identifies those particular citizens who are trained by the military for warfare. In this sense, any meaning of the category 'soldier' is secondary to the meaning of 'citizen', inasmuch as a soldier fights for the population of a given state, namely for the whole society of citizens. Soldiers are citizens first, soldiers second. Soldiers are only seen to fight at exceptional times, such that the normal is seen as a state of peace and the abnormal a state of war. Any deconstruction of this relation between citizen and soldier, of this relation between dominant and supplement, might in the first instance reverse the logic of the discourse and argue that any 'peace' is only made possible through the violence of the state. The state, as that which holds the legitimate means of force, constructs a population as citizens only inasmuch as those citizens are made equal under the common rule of law. Moreover, the territory of any particular state is only so because it has been accrued over centuries of warfare. In this sense, peace is only the temporary outcome of a perpetual state of war. Or to put it more lyrically, we constantly fight for peace. In addition, any citizen's allegiance to the nation-state implies their implicit willingness to fight in the defence of that nation; equally though, as if the reverse of that contract, the state is able to call-up, or enforce, that individual to fight. In contrast, those who do not pledge allegiance to the nation-state and who resist the force of that state are, in effect, soldiers in citizen's clothing: terrorists by any other name. Isn't the 'war on terror' an acceptance of this perverse logic, that all social existence is dictated by the logic of war?

If we accept this analysis - if only for the purpose of an example - then we can see how the deconstruction of the difference between soldier and citizen does not simply reverse the polarity of the terms (i.e. soldiers are 'normal' and citizens are 'abnormal'), but leads to an undermining of the logic of the binary construction itself: in Orwellian 'doublethink', peace is war. Deconstruction is an energy efficient critique as it relies on adding nothing except the terms within the system present. But it does *always presuppose the system* and the slippage that occurs as a result of deconstruction is *always within the system*: if the slippage were to slip outside the system it would be spillage or drainage, not destabilisation.

Utterances, Dialogue and Heterogeneity

In contrast to, and in criticism of, the Saussurian model, the work of a group of writers, living under the Stalinist regime in the Soviet Union, construed the sociality of language in a manner that foregrounded not the homogeneity of the system, but the heterogeneity of the utterances. A series of works written variously under the names of Valerian Nikolaevich Voloshinov, Pavel Nikolaevich Medvedev and Mikhail Mikhailovich Bakhtin were written from the 1920s to the early 1970s. These men were a group of intellectuals, friends and writers; the authorship of their various works is disputed; but there is some suggestion that the major works were written by one man, Bakhtin. As with the anecdote concerning Saussure's great text (namely that it was never written by him but from his students' notes), the story of Bakhtin, not being one person but many, has a familiar echo. The story stands as an allegory of the works themselves, a series of works that deal with the heterogeneity of language, not its stifling uniformity; with the vibrancy of language, not the submission of the written word to the authority of the master's monologic voice. Whatever the truth of authorship, the writings of Voloshinov and Bakhtin in particular allow us to look at lived culture as composed of many voices, speaking together, contesting each other, creative and vibrant. It is because of this understanding of the vibrancy of language, of a sense of speech as social interaction, that these writers have come to the fore in recent discussion about culture and language across a range of the humanities and social science disciplines.

It is with the *utterance*, or the particular speech act, that Voloshinov prefaces his major work titled *Marxism and the Philosophy of Language* (1973 [1929]). Thus, whereas Saussure looks to the structure of language as *langue* or as 'ready-made code', Voloshinov looks to *parole,* not as an individual expression, but as a social act in relation to others, as 'living speech'. Voloshinov typifies the social psychology that is resonant of Saussure as 'metaphysical', 'mythic', concerning the 'collective soul', 'collective inner psyche' and the 'spirit of the people' (1973: 19). Voloshinov instead looks at the performance of *discourse* in specific social situations. His starting point is that the 'word' is defined not in terms of its 'purity', but in terms of its 'social ubiquity' (1973: 19). The sign is everywhere. Social struggle, change and interaction resonate in the sign itself; the sign becomes an index of social change. It is not something that is conjoined – in terms of its formal and meaningful element – in the mind of the speaker or listener; it only has a life inasmuch as it is externalised in a social world and inasmuch as it is an index of the importance attached to certain things, meanings and events: namely, within the 'social purview of the given time period and the given social group' (1973: 21):

> Every sign, as we know it, is a construct between socially organized persons in the process of their interaction. Therefore, the forms of signs are conditioned above all by the social organization of the participants involved and also by the immediate conditions of their interaction. When these forms change, so does sign ... Only so approached can the problem of the relationship between sign and existence find its concrete expression; only then will the process of the causal shaping of the sign by existence stand out as a process of genuine existence-to-sign transit, of genuine dialectical refraction of existence in the sign. (Voloshinov, 1973: 21)

In Voloshinov's discussion, the sign is spread across a community of speakers and listeners. But, although there are some similarities with Saussure inasmuch as this community is not typified by its sameness but by its difference, for Voloshinov the sign community is one divided by social class. For Saussure the sign community is coextensive with the system and the sign is meaningful only in relation to the system, but for Voloshinov the sign community is a site of struggle and the sign is always divided through that struggle. Every sign does not so much reflect social existence; it *refracts* it. The sign is a vital and dynamic entity; it is defined by its '*multiaccentuality*':

> Class does not coincide with the sign community, i.e., with the community, which is the totality of users of the same set of signs for ideological communication. Thus various different classes will use one and the same language. As a result, differently oriented accents intersect in every ideological sign. Sign becomes an arena of the class struggle. (1973: 23)

For Voloshinov, the ruling class attempts to close down this multiaccentuality, to close down the class struggle over the sign and to impose a single uniform set of meanings. To a large extent these attempts are foiled by the vibrancy of discourse itself, by its necessary interactivity: '[t]he sign is a creation between individuals, a creation within a social milieu' (1973: 22). Every sign has two faces; it is Janus-faced; it looks from one side of an interaction to the other: from inside one person to outside that person, but also from one person to another.

Expressive theories of language make a distinction between the inner expression and the outer objectification or externalisation of that expression. In this sense, language is the externalisation of intentions and meanings of an individual. For Voloshinov, such a theory of language, disavows the necessity of outward objectification; every expression must, of necessity, be expressed; it must be verbalised or materialised through a shared language; and in order for it to be intelligible to others as well as oneself it must be constructed in a series of signs that are common to oneself and others. Moreover, for Voloshinov, it is the outward expression that organises the experience of the individual, not the other way around. Whereas for Saussure, the sociality of the expression is returned to the systemic nature of language (i.e. language as a system is a social fact), for Voloshinov the sociality of expression is analysed in terms of the necessary *addressivity* of the utterance; '[*t*]*he word is oriented toward an addressee*, toward *who* that address might be' (1973: 85). Even on those occasions when we talk to ourselves inside our heads or when we write those secret words in our diaries or we make comments to ourselves on post-it notes, we are talking to others, albeit others imagined, rather than externalised in actual persons standing in front of us or at the other end of a telephone: '[e]ach person's inner world and thought has its stabilized *social audience* that comprises the environment in which reasons, motives, values, and so on are fashioned' (1973: 86). Thus Voloshinov argues:

> Orientation of the word toward the addressee has an extremely high significance. In point of fact, *word is a two-sided act*. It is determined equally by *whose* word it is and *for whom* it is meant. As word, it is precisely *the product of the reciprocal relationship between speaker and listener, addresser and addressee*. Each and every word expresses the 'one' in relation to the 'other'. I give myself verbal

> shape from another's point of view, ultimately from the point of view of the community to which I belong. A word is a bridge thrown between myself and another. If one end of the bridge depends on me, then the other depends on my addressee. A word is territory shared by both addresser and addressee, by the speaker and his interlocutor. (1973: 86)

Every utterance is always, of necessity, *oriented toward an other*. In this orientation, in this address to another, the sign is intoned in certain kinds of ways; it is valued in particular ways. The sign is always weighted or accented in the moment of address.

Every utterance, then, is constituted as an interaction; it is, of necessity, social; '[*t*]*he immediate social situation and the broader social milieu wholly determine – and determine from within, so to speak – the structure of an utterance*' (1973: 86). An utterance is not only addressed to an other, but also within a field of utterances: 'determined by the whole aggregate of conditions under which any given community of speakers operates' (1973: 93). When speaking to another person our language is always infused with the protocols and customs that exist prior to our interaction. Every utterance is always inscribed within a broader *dialogic* or *intertextual* field. When we meet and address a friend, we might reach out our hand or embrace them or kiss them on both cheeks. We might ask how they are and how they have been. We might sit and drink coffee and talk about family and friends. Each utterance draws on a broader field of utterances and thus constructs each interaction within a broader set of *speech genres*, those familiar repeated forms of interaction: the greeting, the social talk, the requests for food and so on: '[t]he outwardly actualized utterance is an island rising from the boundless sea of inner speech; the dimensions and forms of this island are determined by the particular *situation* of the utterance and its *audience*' (1973: 96).

Equally though each interaction is about something. Each interaction has a *theme* or an *object*. But the object of discourse is not something that exists external to that discourse, to that interaction; it is not a 'referent', the object of a proposition; it is more broadly – and here again Voloshinov strikes a chord with Saussure – the meaning or meanings that come to bear on any interaction. In this sense, a discourse does not reflect an external object; it organises it, transforms it and refracts it (cf. Todorov, 1984: 55). In the relay of words, in the borrowings of used utterances, in the orientation of oneself to another, the object is touched; it cannot help but be infused by those movements.

Although it might seem easier for us to tie utterances down to a fixed set of codes, in doing so we only focus on the *given* and ignore the *creative* aspect of any utterance. Whereas the former refers to the reiterative aspect of language, that Saussure identifies in the system or that is articulated in the code, the latter refers to that which is novel in any utterance, the fact that it is not simply a repetition of something already said before:

> The *given* and the *created* in the verbal utterance. The utterance is never the simple reflection or the expression of something that pre-exists it, is given and ready. It always creates something that had not been before, that is absolutely new and is nonreiterative, and that, moreover, always has a relation to value. (Bakhtin quoted in Todorov, 1984: 50)

The particularity or singularity of the utterance, its creativity, is a consequence of its sociality, its embeddedness within a social situation or its field of enunciation. Any utterance is always particular to a situation: to a particular space and time, a particular object of dialogue and a particular relation between interlocutors and the event (cf. Todorov, 1984: 42). Thus the 'utterance *as a whole*' refers to both the verbal and extraverbal elements of any utterance (Voloshinov, 1973: 96). The event is always original.

To a large extent, when Voloshinov, but also Bakhtin and others, talk about utterances they are referring to speech acts or speech performances. To a large extent dialogue is conceived only as verbal interaction. And yet, they also talk of dialogue to mean other forms of performance or interaction – although they have a tendency to reduce such performances to the model of speech – and other forms of dialogue that are not simply face-to-face. A book written for an audience, printed and read, then criticised in the press, constitutes a form of dialogue between author and her or his readership (cf. Voloshinov, 1973: 95). The discussion of the voices in texts, rather than just verbal utterances, comes to the fore in the work of Bakhtin on the novel, rather than Voloshinov on ideology. For Bakhtin, the novel is made up of many voices and cannot be reduced to the voice of the author. This is discussed most notably in his work on Dostoyevsky (translated as *Problems of Dostoevsky's Poetics*, 1984) and more general writings on the novel (collected in the translation *The Dialogic Imagination*, 1981). In the terms already used above, when a speaker produces an utterance, that utterance is not the property of the speaker; it belongs also to the listener, but equally to the voices of those past utterances that make up the broader dialogic or intertextual field. For example, when I say to my lover 'I love you', although I feel these words and so does my partner, I hardly have a right to their originality. Their meaning is dependent on all the contexts in which these words have been uttered. In this sense, the 'I' of the utterance refers to me, the speaker, but is also constructed within the utterance itself. In the utterance an image of the speaker, the utterer, is thus created, an image that owes as much (if not more) to those prior voices and utterances than to me myself (cf. Barthes, 1990). Bakhtin refers to this interaction as a 'three-role drama' (quoted in Todorov, 1984: 52). The drama of these voices in any utterance is what Bakhtin refers to as dialogic. In utterances that are more cluttered and complex, such as a theatrical play, a television programme or a novel, the number of voices proliferate and we might talk about this in terms of the *polyphony*, not of the utterance, but of the *text*. In Bakhtin's discussion of the novel, he talks about the direct speech of the author (the authorial voice that might guide us through a story), the represented speech of the characters (characters in a novel that speak independently of, and sometimes in another world to, the author) and the doubly-oriented or double-voiced speech (such that when an author deploys a character that speaks both for her or him, but also for another). As the text becomes more consciously dialogic and more explicitly polyphonic, pulling away from, but also criticising, the centralising power of the author, the text becomes more self-reflexive, more aware of its status as writing. Bakhtin talks about this in terms of the *heteroglossia* of the text:

> Along with the internal contradictions of the object itself, the prose writer comes to discover as well the social heteroglossia that *surrounds* the object, the Tower of Babel confusion of languages that goes on around any object. The dialectics of the object are interwoven with the social dialogue surrounding it. For the prose writer, the object is a condensation of heterological voices among which his own voice must also resound; these voices create the background necessary for his own voice, without which his literary nuances would not be perceived, and without which they 'do not sound'. (1981: 91–2)

In such an analysis, we might begin to question whether it is correct to talk about utterances rather than texts. In many ways the dialogism explicit in a novel is less about a particular verbal interaction (as supposed by the notion of utterance) and more a space of such interaction. A text is, in some ways, such a space. Julia Kristeva, the psychoanalytic critic who brought Bakhtin's work over to the West from the Soviet Union in the late 1960s, uses just such a metaphor as the text and it is she who coins the term *intertextuality* to capture the meaning of Bakhtin's notion of dialogism. She says: '[t]he text is ... a permutation of texts, an intertextuality: in the space of a given text, several utterances, taken from other texts, intersect and neutralize one another' (Kristeva, 1982: 36). Moreover, every text is a creation precisely because it draws on the resources of other texts. In the making of a text, those other texts are transformed: '[i]n its structures, writing reads another writing, reads itself and constructs itself through a process of destructive genesis' (Kristeva, 1982: 77). Although Kristeva was instrumental in bringing Bakhtin to the attention of Western critics, she provides a reading of his work that synthesises his ideas within a formalist, post-Saussurian and post-Lacanian problematic (which is discussed in chapter five). In many ways the shift from interpersonal interaction to novels leads to an attempt to provide a space for the polyphony of voices, but to frame these voices within the 'text' leads only to these voices being submerged within a system of differance; they become systematised (cf. Billig, 1997; Holquist 1990).

The writings of Voloshinov and Bakhtin are fruitful, not only for the analysis of speech acts and texts, but also for more cultural and sociological questions concerning power and democracy and it is in this respect that I want to mark a very deep difference from Saussure and post-Saussurian cultural thought. Bakhtin talks about the diversity of discursive types within any social community. Not only are there a plurality of utterances, but also a plurality (although limited in number) of speech genres (for example, talking as a lecturer, speaking to your mother face-to-face, talking to a lover on the telephone and so on). Bakhtin refers to this diversity as *heterology*. The notion of heterology joins closely with the notion of heteroglossia, which refers to the diversity of languages (in Bakhtin's sense). In sociological and cultural terms, these notions are important as they help to explain how everyday social and cultural life is not simply rich, detailed and diverse, but also counterposed to countervailing forces that attempt to close down this diversity and difference. Bakhtin talks about these forces in terms of the centripetal force of power and authority, centralising culture and the centrifugal force of linguistic and social diversity, the heterology and heteroglossia of the quotidian:

> The category of common language is the theoretical expression of historical processes of linguistic unification and centralization, the expression of the centripetal forces of the language. The common language is never given but in fact always ordained, and at every moment of the life of the language it is opposed to genuine heterology. But at the same time, it is perfectly real as a force that overcomes this heterology; imposes certain limits upon it; guarantees a maximum of mutual comprehension; and becomes crystallized in the real, though relative, unity of spoken (daily) and literary language, of 'correct language'. (1984: 83–4)

For Bakhtin centripetal forces are monologic. They attempt to speak with one voice, to speak only with the voice of authority and to authorise only those who speak with such a voice. These centralising forces would thus prefer a world of mimics to a world of difference. In this sense, any attempt to speak for 'society', 'community', 'culture' or 'nation' as if with one voice must be viewed with some scepticism. Any such monologism needs to be revealed as but one voice among many: namely, put in its dialogical context. For Bakhtin, then, there is no collapse of the semiological onto the space of social solidarity and national culture. Such a collapse constitutes a form of monological closure, a form of authority that attempts to reduce the heteroglossia of utterances to a single voice:

> Verbal and ideological decentring occurs only when a national culture sheds its closure and its self-sufficiency, when it becomes conscious of itself as only *one* among other cultures and languages. This new awareness will then sap the roots of the mythological sense of language, based on the notion of an absolute fusion of ideological meaning with language. (Bakhtin quoted in Todorov, 1984: 66–7)

Any attempt to speak for the nation, for the society, for the culture closes down the polyphony of voices and attempts to disavow the ambivalence and hybridity within the voice. In this sense, Bakhtin's understanding of dialogism and the necessary hybridity of dialogism (cf. Bhabha, 1996) is more than a notion of a democratic society made up of a diversity of voices or different cultures. For Bakhtin every voice, every 'culture' is not - or contains the possibility of not being - one voice or one culture; every voice, every culture contains within it a drama of voices, both present, past and future. The opening of the social into a heteroglossic space means opening up that space to the potential disruption of social order, to the overturning of hierarchies, to the constant questioning of authority, to what Bakhtin (1968) also refers to as the *carnivalesque* (the topsy-turvy world where the low become high).

Bakhtin provides an account of semiological interaction or dialogue that avoids, and provides a critique of, the collapse that is evident in Saussure and some post-Saussurian semiology: namely, the collapse of linguistic system, social solidarity, national culture and people. Any attempt to talk about 'society', in this sense as a social totality, as a whole system, is a form of monologism; it constitutes the reduction of the social to one particular version of it and it denies the constant creation and invention that is evident in everyday interaction. Moreover, any talk of a system of differences within which meaning is formed, however localised, merely prioritises one voice that speaks for that system, that says what that system is and how the differences are thus formed. This is all well and good, but Bakhtin lets such a monologism in from below. For Bakhtin, society is not a system, but a series of interactions, in the first instance, between two people; it is a notion of society that is based on a primary *intersubjectivity*. This interaction prioritises face-to-face talk as the model of all communication and discourse; all other forms of discourse and interaction are reduced to this interpersonal and intersubjective model and herein lies the problem. Thus, a model that makes visible social and cultural plurality is itself based on a reduction to a single model. This paradox certainly marks a progress on Saussure's understanding of language and society, but it also demonstrates the problem of modelling the social even one that is reflexive.

Rhizomes and Translation Across Material Difference

The move toward understanding language as a series of particulars, rather than as one thing governed by universal rules (whether the grammar of the code or of discursive social interaction), has been made in a number of recent accounts that draw variously on Ludwig Wittgenstein's ordinary language philosophy, Michel Foucault's notion of a discursive formation and Gilles Deleuze and Felix Guattari's thinking about multiplicitous organisation.

Some of these accounts suggest a move beyond the analysis of semiosis as a relation between symbolic and material, or as one that is principally concerned with 'representation', to one that begins to comprehend the translation across material difference. Ian Hunter in his article 'After representation' (1984) takes to task the post-Saussurian critique of language as transparent and of the role of signifying systems in the differentiation of matter and experience. Language does not simply represent a world that is pre-existent. Language does not simply name objects or states of affairs in the world. Language is not a transparent analogue of the world. But, Hunter argues, a post-Saussurian cultural analysis – that sees language as necessarily opaque and as constructive of the meanings of objects and experiences – is equally problematic. In particular, Hunter takes to task the analysis of colour differentiation in Catherine Belsey's *Critical Practice* (1980).

Belsey claims that different linguistic systems produce different ways of organising colour differentiations. Thus the Welsh term 'glas', that is literally translated as 'blue' would include the colours green and grey as identified by an English speaker. Moreover, the English 'grey' might cover both the Welsh 'glas' and 'llwyd' (literally translated as brown) (Belsey, 1980: 39). The undifferentiated continuum of colour experience – from one end of the spectrum to the other – is divided up differently in different languages. There is no natural experience of individual colours. Colour differentiation is a consequence of language. Belsey argues that any particular system of colour differentiation in any particular language is but one way of dividing the continuum among a number of possible ways. In contrast to this form of structural analysis, Hunter draws on the work of Ludwig Wittgenstein (1958, 1977, 1980) and his understanding of colour description. Wittgenstein does not return to a notion that colour names correspond to individualised pre-existent units of experience, but he does discuss colour naming in terms of very localised sets of practices. If someone refers to a 'reddish yellow', I can point to that colour and I can have an image of that colour in my head. If, however, someone refers to 'bluish yellow', I cannot do the same. Wittgenstein analyses this example in terms of the way that my understanding of a colour is not predicated on a system of cultural differences, but on particular *techniques* of choosing a colour. The apparatuses that we have ready to hand to refer to these colours include, for example, the colour wheel, the graduated palette and the rainbow. In these apparatuses red and yellow stand next to each other, but blue and yellow do not; hence we cannot have a bluish yellow. As Hunter explains:

> In Wittgenstein's example, then, the point is not that we cannot 'imagine' or *experience* bluish yellow, not that our *language* occludes some possible part of a colour continuum. Rather, it is that we happen not to posses a *technique* or *apparatus* that would permit us to engage in a particular set of

> activities. That we happen not to possess this technique or apparatus does not mean that our (or anyone's) organisation of colours is incomplete, or forms only part of 'all the possible organisations contained in the continuum'. The reason being that capacities for identifying colours and understanding the meaning of colour terms are local accomplishments resulting from the practical deployment of technologies such as that of the colour sample. Differences in colour concepts must not be traced to different divisions of a continuum of experience of 'chain of meaning', but to the differences in available technologies or 'language-games'. (1984: 419)

Different colour concepts are consequences of different *social technologies*. These technologies are built up, according to Hunter, in a piecemeal fashion and they find their conditions of existence not in a universal language, but in very particularised practices, institutions and discourses (such as schools, scientific laboratories, ophthalmic practices, families and so on).

This understanding of discourse and social technology draws not just from Wittgenstein, but also from the work of Michel Foucault. Foucault's work has been used widely within cultural studies, primarily to look at the relations of discourse, power and selfhood, but his analysis of discourse has been widely misinterpreted within the context of a post-Saussurian semiology, of which Foucault was insistently critical. Although for Foucault a central category in his theoretical toolbox is that of discourse as a field of statements, his discussion does not take the route of understanding such a notion in terms of meaning being predicated on a universal system of language. Moreover, Foucault does not reduce the statement to intersubjective social interaction. The statement, for Foucault, is not a bridge between two people. Foucault argues that the statement is: 'a function of existence that properly belongs to signs and on the basis of which one may then decide, through analysis or intuition, whether or not they "make sense", according to what rule they follow one another or are juxtaposed, of what they are the sign, and what sort of act is carried out by their formulation (oral or written)' (1972: 86–7). A statement, then, although it involves signs, is a function; it is defined by its use. Moreover, statements are organised not on the basis of their meaning, but according to their dispersion and regularity, namely, their discursive formation:

> The fact of its belonging to a discursive formation and the laws that govern it are one and the same thing; this is not paradoxical since the discursive formation is characterized not by principles of construction but by a dispersion of fact, since for statements it is not a condition of possibility but a law of coexistence, and since statements are not interchangeable elements but groups characterized by their modality of existence. (Foucault, 1972: 116).

A discursive formation identifies a series of statements found next to each other, in a particular form of organisation, such that we can talk about things in certain kinds of ways, at certain historical periods and in certain social and geographical spaces. A discursive formation does not identify a law that exists outside of time and space; it does not refer to a condition of possibility, but to a condition of existence. It is defined or constituted only by the elements present within itself. It is no more and no less than this. The Foucauldian notion of discourse is set against an understanding of statements, or signs, that refer back to a general code or intersubjective iteration because such conditions frame a discursive organisation outside of particular social and historical occasions. Thus, although Foucault's notion of discursive formation looks like a more historical and socially specific version of Saussure's *langue* (or a signifying practice), it is no such thing. In this sense, language does not have a general grammar nor does it contain certain rules with regard to its capacity to represent and construct an external reality. Discourse is between words and things; it is the term we use to describe the organisation of both words and things. Language itself is thus a much more piecemeal affair.

However, as Wittgenstein says: '[t]o obey a rule, to make a report, to give an order, to play a game of chess, are *customs* (uses, institutions)' (Wittgenstein, 1958: 81). It is not as if there is language on one side and the external material world on the other, as if the latter were a continuous stream of matter or *hyle*, only divided or constructed by the rules and differentiations of language and the symbolic. Such an understanding of the world is one construed through a logic of representation, whereby the sign that stands in for that which is absent is an analogue of that absent thing. In this sense, language is seen to constitute the classificatory system that includes all classifications, the class of all classes: namely, within its definition all of the world exists. Nothing escapes its boundaries; nothing escapes the borders of its territory; it is society, the people, but also the world. It is the measure of all things and within it all things are measured, sized, fitted and organised. As others have noted, this problem of the one class and the many particulars is a problem of epistemology: namely, a problem of how we construct a way of knowing things. Representation names not the only way of knowing things, but just one particular way of doing so and one that has a long and troubled history from the ancient Greek philosopher Plato onwards.

One of the ways of trying to think outside of this problem of representation has come from the work of the philosopher Gilles Deleuze and the radical anti-psychiatrist Felix Guattari. In particular, they present a notion of the *rhizome* as a figure for understanding the complexity of relations that get simplified in the notion of representation (e.g. the analogical relation between a present sign and that which is represented or between the symbolic and the material). A rhizome refers literally (from the ancient Greek *rhizōma*) to the rooting structures of vegetal matter. But in the hands of Deleuze and Guattari it takes the form of a set of principles for understanding semiosis. First, they talk about the rhizome in terms of its connectedness and heterogeneity: 'any point on a rhizome can be connected to any other, and must be ... [S]emiotic chains of every kind are connected in it according to very diverse modes of encoding, chains that are biological, political, economic, etc.... [N]o radical separation can be established between the regimes of signs and their objects' (1983a: 11). Thus, unlike the models of Saussure and Bakhtin, language is neither an enclosed system of signifiers and signifieds nor a field of utterances, semiotics is about the connections between what are traditionally thought of as linguistic and non-linguistic, but also across signifying and a-signifying material (i.e. material that does not signify). For example, a series of connections might be made across the letters on the surface of a typewriter keyboard, the hardware in a computer, the word-processing software and the final manuscript that might be produced. The letters on the keyboard would not ordinarily be seen to be signifying material; they do not in and of themselves have meaning. But they do, nevertheless, allow connections to be made. In addition, Deleuze and Guattari multiply what might ordinarily be seen as a division between material and symbolic; they talk instead about specific regimes such as the biological, the economic, the political and so on. In doing so they do not assume that the connections made in any one field or regime are similar in any way to the connections made in another regime. Moreover, connections are made across these regimes.

Secondly, they talk about the rhizome as being a multiplicity. A multiplicity is neither the one nor the many, both of which suggest some kind of identity or resemblance between the entities. For example, Bakhtin's understanding of sociality as being made up of utterances, makes the move toward understanding society not as one thing, but as many things, many utterances. Nevertheless, in saying that society is made up of many utterances, Bakhtin has reduced society to the logic of the utterance (i.e. to one thing). The utterance becomes the measure of all things. So in talking about the rhizome as a multiplicity, Deleuze and Guattari are trying to talk about the way in which connections across entities are about different things of different kinds being assembled in such a way that those things cannot be reduced to any one thing. For example, at the end of a trip around the aisles of a supermarket my trolley is filled with lots of items, such as wine, bread, cheese, biscuits, vegetables and so on. I could reduce all those items to a single measure (or paradigm) and refer to the objects as 'my weekly shopping'. But equally I could try to account for those items in all their diversity and thus try not to reduce a bottle of Chateauneuf du Pape to a lump of Cheddar cheese. Both these items are qualitatively and materially very different - wine and cheese - and the point is to take account of all the items while at the same time accounting for all their differences. There are different units of measure. And hence this understanding of difference is very different from that of Derrida, who accepts a fundamental ambivalence at the heart of the sign, but nevertheless reduces the play of difference to the measure of the gram (or the deconstructed sign).

Thirdly, a rhizome can be cut or broken up at any point. Moreover, at each break or rupture the sides of the break do not sit opposite each other, each mapping each other, each mimicking each other. Deleuze and Guattari refer to the example of a colony of ants that we might attempt to disperse by knocking down their ant-hill and divide by putting something in between them. The ants divide up, but constantly attempt to reconstitute themselves over the divide in multiform ways. The lines or breaks between entities are more like stretchings and criss-crossings and Deleuze and Guattari talk about this in terms of 'lines of flight' or 'becomings'. Thus, if we take our example of the signifier 'cat', the idea of a cat we have in our heads (the signified) and the actual fluffy animal that purrs (the referent) then each part is made of different material (phonemes, mental images, and different types of organic matter). The phonemes do not resemble the thoughts in my head nor the fur, skin, bones and flesh of the actual cat. This is an assemblage of different types of materials: '[t]here is neither imitation nor resemblance, but an explosion of two heterogeneous series in a line of flight consisting of a common rhizome that can no longer be attributed nor made subject to any signifier at all' (Deleuze and Guattari, 1983a: 20). The passage from signifier to signified to actual cat marks a passage across different materials. Instead of a resemblance or representation, then, Deleuze and Guattari use a geographical analogy to talk about the way in which there is a process of territorialisation and deterritorialisation. The movement from one thing to another, the process of becoming, is understood as an expansion or reduction of respective territories. The phonemes, thoughts, and actual cat are linked, but in the passage from signifier to actual cat the phonemes have become deterritorialised and reterritorialised as actual cat. From phonemes to actual cat we see a process of becoming. As Deleuze and Guattari say: '[d]ependent on a binary logic, mimicry is a poor concept when applied to phenomena of a totally different order' (1983a: 22). Phonemes, thought and actual cat have 'a-parallel evolution'; they change together differently.

Fourthly, Deleuze and Guattari refer to the rhizome as a map – not in the sense that a map supposedly represents a real territory, an exact simulation of the real – but in the sense that a map enables one to move through territories, to find new architectural sites, to meet new people, to travel to different places. In that sense, it is a way of 'establishing contact with the real experimentally': '[t]he map is open, connectable in all its dimensions, and capable of being dismantled; it is reversible, and susceptible to constant modification' (1983a: 25, 26). The map is performative and in that sense it has a lot in common with Bakhtin's notion of the utterance as creative. The rhizome is not a code; it is something that produces change through bringing different things together; it is literally inventive (i.e. a coming together as well as a making new).

Finally, a rhizome is made up of lines, such that there are no fixed points or positions: 'the rhizome is made only of lines: lines of segmentation and stratification as dimensions, but also lines of flight or of deterritorialisation as the maximal dimension according to which, by following it, the multiplicity changes its nature and metamorphoses' (1983a: 48). There are no points of advantage or perspective from which one can stand and take account of the rhizome as a whole. Such a total picture can never be taken. It is like a labyrinth from the inside; we can try to imagine the picture, so we can solve the puzzle and get out; but we can never step above the series of routes to see where we are going. It is only known through a series of local connections; we are necessarily short-sighted in the rhizome. Moreover, it is not that there is an outside nor even an inside as such parameters, such boundaries, would establish the shape of the rhizome. If we take the example of a spider's web, does it make sense to talk about that series of weavings as having an inside and an outside. Is that point near the centre of the web, but not on a thread, somewhere between two threads, inside or outside the web? Equally though, just as there are no points of perspective or fixed positions, there is no centre; the rhizome is de-centred. Again, we don't need to assume that this is somehow a complex idea to grasp: does a car have a centre? Is it the engine? Or maybe the front seat? Sometimes such questions that we are so used to in the social and cultural sciences – such as those concerning fixedness, centredness and so on – make no sense outside those disciplines.

The notion of the rhizome, then, helps us to understand the problem of semiosis differently from that of a traditional model of representation. It implies that there is not a space that can be designated as language or the symbolic or the space of meaning and another space called matter, an undifferentiated *hyle*, as if *hyle* were an originary presence; as if one class of things called 'signifiers' represented (either actively constructing or passively naming) another class of material objects and states of affairs in the world. The rhizome is the class which includes itself as a class. Matter is within semiosis every step of the way; not as one thing, but as many things differently; it is constitutive of the organisation of organisation. The rhizome is, according to the Italian semiotician Umberto Eco, a type of encyclopaedia:

> If the so-called universals, or metatheoretical constructs, that work as markers within a dictionary-like representation are mere linguistic labels that cover more synthetic properties, an encyclopedia-like

> representation assumes that the representation of the content takes place only by means of *interpretants*, in a process of unlimited semiosis. These interpretants being in their turn interpretable, there is no bidimensional tree able to represent the global semantic competence of a given culture. Such a global representation is only a semiotic postulate, a regulative idea, and takes the format of a multidimensional network. (1984: 68)

The rhizome is a regulative idea that helps us to think about multiplicity and to think about the materiality of semiosis. It helps us to think beyond two types of space, two types of solidarity that mirror each other in analogical repetition: the symbolic and the material. Part of the problem, then, is that we work with an assumption that we can only mix like with like and that one system of resemblances forms one sphere that collapses onto another system of analogues. The diagram that we use to think about semiosis is thus part of the problem. We think of bounded wholes, spheres, with insides and outsides, rather than series, complex series, not of entities that resemble each other, but series of items that are defined by their singularity: namely their incommensurability. A series of singularities thus poses the question, not of communication (the passage of like with like), but of translation across material difference. As John Rajchman suggests in his discussion of Deleuze's semiotics: '[t]he components of a multiplicity, unlike the members of a set, must be indefinite or vague, matching with the "vagabond" manner in which a multiplicity is constructed; and the problem in Deleuze's logic then becomes how to repeat "free differences" in complex wholes that don't reduce what makes them differences, how to connect "singularities" in a "plan of consistency" that preserves what makes them singular' (Rajchman, 2000: 55).

There is certainly a danger, as Nick Couldry warns, of a faddish version of complexity and connectionism that 'simply repeats what we already know (things are complex and interrelated) without beginning to explain *what sort* of order cultures involve, and where and on what scale we should look for it' (2000: 94). But in many ways the work of Deleuze and others returns us to some of the central questions of semiotics: namely, what is the nature of the sign; how is it related to other signs and things; and how might we sensibly demarcate lines of division between different forms of semiosis. Such work helps us to think not about chaos, but about the ordering of semiosis. In this respect it would be foolish to think that it is possible simply to move on from Saussure's analysis of the symbolic and semiological solidarity or from Bakhtin's understanding of dialogic relations that construe the social as a heterogeneous space. Whatever the difficulties with both these approaches, they do nevertheless present extremely productive models for understanding culture as semiosis and the relation between sign and community. In many ways the Saussurian system, in positing a universal form to language (i.e. in terms of its constituent parts and its mechanisms of combination and association), makes possible an understanding of different particular languages and cultures. Language as a system, inasmuch as it provides a grid or a table, makes possible the comparison of linguistic, semiological and cultural systems and thus makes possible a form of cultural relativism. Different cultures can be compared, according to their different semiological worlds, because semiology is predicated as a universal system. The one thing that different cultures have in common is the system of semiology. In contrast, Bakhtin's dialogism makes possible an ambivalence and hybridity within the authorial voice and thus questions the positing of such a universal system; it makes possible a form of reflexivity that particularises the account as well as the object under study (i.e. the linguistic system or the culture). Where both of these models come unstuck though is in their understanding of semiological relations as primarily relations between humans within, or across, particular speech communities. The move that is made in more recent work suggests that semiosis is neither enclosed within particular communities nor is it limited to exchanges between humans. Equally though, it is not possible to pose a single model of semiosis as representative of all semiotic activity. It is possible for cultural researchers to investigate translations across material difference, not by reducing the entities under investigation to a single system or model of the utterance, but by acknowledging the singularity of the entities. In such an analysis the rhizome - as the figure of such multiplicity - does not become a wild card, the figure of complexity and chaos, but the initial point of understanding complex cultural ordering. The question becomes one of how bridges are constructed and how translations are made possible across such hybrid series (cf. Latour, 1993).

Chapter Summary

- Cultural studies has traditionally drawn on Saussure's systematic analysis of signs and meaning and understood semiosis in terms of the representation of material relations through the symbolic.
- But Saussure's semiology is problematic because:
    - it conceives of significations within an enclosed system and;
    - the system of signs and differences is seen to be co-extensive with society and nation.
- Derrida's deconstruction of Saussure is still caught within the logic of the symbolic and system.
- Voloshinov and Bakhtin provide a model of sign production that is more reflexive and that questions the relations between language, ethnos and nation. The Voloshinov and Bakhtin model is typified by:

- its focus on particular utterances, not linguistic systems
- its dialogic and highly contextual nature
- semiosis predicated on model of intersubjective social interaction.

- More recent theories have been keen to move away from foundational models (either systemic or intersubjective) and to understand semiosis as particular, complex and heterogeneous. These theories (derived from Wittgenstein, Peirce, Foucault and Deleuze) understand semiosis as particular not universal, indexical not symbolic, and thus not comprehensible through a division between the symbolic and the material.

THREE Power: From Ideology to Government

It might not seem readily apparent that power has anything to do with culture. The singing of a song, the watching of a television programme, the writing of a novel do not in and of themselves necessarily assume an invitation to think of power. Equally, the analysis of the lived cultural experiences of particular groups of people can be conducted with no reference at all to questions of force, domination and exclusion. And yet, to a large extent cultural studies has insisted that power is central to understanding culture. Why might this be so? Before immediately thinking of capitalist conspiracies or invisible controlling agents or sophisticated surveillance technologies or 'fascist insects preying on the life of the people', we need only to realise that the most mundane experiences and forms of expression involve decisions being made, actions taken and outcomes realised. The simple act of transmitting a song on the radio implies that one particular song has been chosen rather than another. Sometimes such a choice is fairly innocuous, Kylie Minogue rather than Madonna. But what if the radio only played Kylie and Madonna, but not Diana Ross and J Lo? Is this a decision based on musical style or on 'race'? Is this a question of choice or power? In its crudest sense 'power' refers to how the actions of one being are influenced by another. It concerns the capacity to act on the actions of others. And it is often said to involve the capacity of some to mobilise others such that the interests of some are served rather than others (Lukes, 1974). Clearly, in the context of systematic, regularised and structural forms of dominance, repression, abuse, and exclusion, the question of the relation between culture and power becomes highly significant. But what role might culture play in this? Does culture have particular capacities that other media don't have? Can we talk about cultural power as a distinct form of power? Is the distribution of cultural resources significant in the weighting across a population of other resources, such as economic, political and social? If someone has more and better 'culture', do they also have more money and better education? Do organisations gain more economic or political power by way of mobilising their cultural power (e.g. through the media, public relations, and advertising)? Equally though, some might argue that culture has no relation to power and that culture is simply the expression of individuals with no direct ability to shape the opinions of others nor to do those others harm. But such a view might be forgetful of the power of words and ideas, of stories and imagination, of passion and experience in the building of worlds, worlds that include some but exclude others, that congratulate some but disparage others and that allow some to accumulate great symbolic, cultural and economic wealth and for others to have very little.

Much discussion of these issues in cultural studies has focused on the relation between culture and the dominant social and political institutions that support and reproduce structural inequalities. Thus, much of the context for this discussion has been the nation-state, liberal-democratic forms of polity and capitalism. Importantly, power has been understood inasmuch as it is seen to encode and be encoded within cultural meaning. Initially, the question of ideology, understood primarily through the ideas of two Marxists, Louis Althusser and Antonio Gramsci, dominated the early debates in cultural studies in the 1970s and 1980s. Cultural forms, and particularly popular cultural forms, were seen as key sites of ideological struggle. Consent to dominant regimes of class, 'raced' and gendered power was seen to be gained and maintained through the articulation of cultural meaning. By the mid-1980s the discussion had turned away from a politics of suspicion and resistance to dominant social structures to a revaluation of democracy and a demand for social and cultural diversity. Although power was still seen to be closely tied to cultural meaning, the politics had shifted away from a focus on closure to one of openness. Also in the 1980s and 1990s, the work of Michel Foucault on power, knowledge and governmentality helped to reshape the field of study in such a way that the State was re-introduced into the debate, but only inasmuch as it was completely re-formed from its earlier manifestation in 1970s Marxist cultural and political theory. At the time that cultural studies was reviewing the relation between culture and government, social and cultural theory more generally was beginning to understand the productivity of power in advanced liberal and biopolitical culture. Moreover, serious questions as to the locus of power within the domain of the nation-state have become ever apparent.

Hegemony, Ideology and the State

Much theorising and discussion of power in the discipline of cultural studies has been in the context of Marxist and post-Marxist theory. As with many other disciplines in the social and human sciences in the 1970s, Marxism provided a central ground for debate. The legacy of these debates in cultural studies has been far reaching and long-standing and although many of the terms of this debate now seem antiquated, the underlying questions and issues are perennial and deserve to be considered however simple or old-fashioned or 'political' they might seem. Antonio Gramsci and Louis Althusser figure largely in these debates.

While a prisoner in Italy, between 1926 and 1937 under Benito Mussolini's fascist rule, Antonio Gramsci wrote what are now known as his 'prison note-books', a series of writings on Italian history, economic and social organisation, and political rule. Gramsci had been a political activist involved in various strikes and the organisation of workers' councils in Turin. He established the weekly journal *L'Ordine Nuovo* (the New Order) in 1919, was involved in the founding of the Italian Communist Party in 1921, and became the leader of that party in 1924. He died in 1937, three days after being released from prison. During his time in prison, Gramsci saw the defeat of left-wing political parties and organisations in the face of a growing fascism in terms of an enduring problem within Marxist theory, namely the problem of 'economism' and the attendant failure to account for the agency of individuals and social groups. Put crudely, economism made the assumption that the economic order determined the social, cultural and political order and, moreover, that the economic could be known through a Marxist positivist science. If capitalism was going to collapse, then it would be due to economic determinations and not to do with the political activities of individuals and organisations. Thus, at a time when Gramsci had thought it imperative to campaign and struggle against the fascist encroachment on Italian politics in the 1920s and 1930s, there were writers, such as Bukharin and ideologues of the Soviet Communist Party, who cautioned against interfering with the wheels of history. Gramsci drew upon the work of Vladimir Ilyich Lenin who had argued that in order to bring down the Tsarist regime in Russia in the early twentieth century, the working class needed to construct an alliance with the peasants. Only if the working class developed a political leadership of the majority classes in Russia could the old regime be toppled (Lenin, 1969).

The 1970s were a time of much political turmoil in the form of anti-colonial, feminist, 'black', lesbian and gay, workerist and student struggles and protests. Gramsci provided a context for understanding these struggles in terms of the formation of alliances across different groupings and for understanding these struggles as ideological in a deeply cultural sense. In Gramsci's writings the concept of leadership or *hegemony* becomes of central importance for understanding both the means of overthrowing bourgeois liberal democracy by the working class and a form of analysis of its continuation and forms of rule. Any class, he argued, is unable to rule or command the running of society and the State on its own. The condition of rule is that it is done through the necessity of consent and through forming alliances. A class is only able to take up or maintain a position as a ruling class, if it is able to form and secure alliances with other classes and class fractions in such a way that supports its rule (Gramsci, 1978: 443). But hegemony is not only about the mobilisation of classes and class fractions into a unity; it is concerned with the mobilisation of both classes and other social, political, military and economic forces (cf. Gramsci, 1971: 180–5). In this sense, an analysis of the relations of forces in any situation must bring into consideration not just social actors – such as particular classes or class fractions – but also other actors such as media power, military strength, policing capacity, and so on (1971: 167). Although Gramsci is critical of what he sees as the mechanistic dogma of some earlier Marxist writings on the relation between economic base and ideological superstructure, his own analysis is heavily indebted to a mechanistic philosophy inasmuch as society is conceived in terms of the relation and balance between forces. In this sense, hegemony aims toward a state of equilibrium:

> [T]he dominant group is coordinated concretely with the general interests of the subordinate groups, and the life of the State is conceived of as a continuous process of formation and superseding of unstable equilibria (on the juridical plane) between the interests of the fundamental group and those subordinate groups – equilibria in which the interests of the dominant group prevail, but only up to a certain point. (1971: 182)

Gramsci conceives the State in an extensive way, to include both the state in the limited sense of governmental and political institutions (such as the judiciary, executive, and legislature) as well as civil society (i.e. private institutions such as the media, church, family and so on). Gramsci argues that there are two types of power that operate within the State, each roughly correlated with political and civil society: coercive power (domination) and directive power (hegemony) (1971: 12; cf. Merrington, 1978; Simon, 1982). For Gramsci, then, culture – and importantly the popular culture of the nation – comes under the rubric of the modern State and is identified as a central aspect of hegemonic struggle. In order to maintain control in a society, a ruling group needs not only to control governmental and political institutions, but also to have hegemonic direction of civil society:

> [T]he supremacy of a social group manifests itself in two ways, as 'domination' and as 'intellectual and moral leadership'. A social group dominates antagonistic groups, which it tends to 'liquidate', or to subjugate perhaps even by armed force; it leads kindred and allied groups. A social group can, and indeed must, already exercise 'leadership' before winning governmental power (this indeed is

> one of the principal conditions for the winning of such power); it subsequently becomes dominant when it exercises power, but even if it holds it firmly in its grasp, it must continue to 'lead' as well. (1971: 57–8)

Hegemony, then, is not domination; it is not a physical or repressive force. It works through consensus, through gaining the consent of the people over which leadership is sought. If there is a breakdown in the relations of consent, then there is a crisis of authority: '[i]f the ruling class has lost its consensus, i.e. is no longer "leading" but only "dominant", exercising coercive force alone, this means precisely that the great masses have become detached from their traditional ideologies, and no longer believe what they used to believe previously' (Gramsci, 1971: 275–6). A class or social group is able to become hegemonic inasmuch as it is able to build a series of alliances. These alliances are formed through consent, not through physical force, repression or violence. And that which cements the alliances is ideological. Gramsci understands the cementing of alliances not through some rational process, but through culture. He talks about engaging with the people at the level of culture, particularly the culture of the 'national-popular': namely, those largely unconscious day-to-day traditions, customs and habits that ground the popular culture of a nation.

It is this relation between hegemony and ideology that has provided a central focus for cultural studies. For example, in a criticism of the dominant ideology thesis – that presumes that the dominated classes are duped, or in a state of false consciousness, and simply imbibe the ideas and practices of the ruling class – Tony Bennett argues that bourgeois hegemony does not simply subsume, or impose bourgeois values and ideas on working-class culture, but rather bourgeois culture and ideology has to be *articulated* (or linked) with working-class culture:

> As a consequence of its accommodating elements of opposing class cultures, 'bourgeois culture' ceases to be purely or entirely bourgeois. It becomes, instead, a mobile combination of cultural and ideological elements derived from different class locations which are, but only provisionally and for the duration of a specific historical conjuncture, affiliated to bourgeois values, interests and objectives. (Bennett, 1986a: xv)

In this sense, ideologies are never pure; they are always, of necessity, negotiated. In order to persuade others to consent to the ideas and practices of one group, the ideas and practices of that group need to demonstrate that they also represent the interests of the persuaded group. Following Gramsci, cultural studies scholars have shown that the domain in which this negotiation takes place is the domain of common sense, in the realm of meaning and sensibility that is most ordinary and that is able to appeal across classes.

Stuart Hall and his colleagues in their detailed analysis of the moral panic surrounding the construction of the 'black mugger' in the 1970s, used the notion of hegemony to show how the dominant ideology of 'law and order' gained popular consent (Hall et al., 1978). They show how the post-war social democratic consensus in the UK began to fracture in the 1970s under the strain of a revivified political militancy and the increasingly visible contradictions of global capitalism. As the signs of crisis began to show, the Conservative Government of the day (under the premiership of Edward Heath) moved closer to a neo-liberal politics at the same time as it embraced an increasing authoritarianism. An ideological consensus was constructed through an increasing fear of crime and a racism directed at the UK's black population. The 'black mugger' formed a condensation of these concerns and enabled the development of an 'authoritarian populism' which, in 1979, provided the platform for the onset of Thatcherism. The ground upon which that ideological struggle was seen to be fought was that of common sense: that was the language of the press and the television media; that was the language of ordinary people; and that was the language that needed to be engaged with in order to bring about progressive social change.

In Gramsci's writings, common sense is talked about as superstitious, traditional, folkish and spontaneous. It is understood as fragmented and incoherent and it is understood in contrast to the unity and coherence of ideology:

> Common sense is not a single unique conception, identical in time and space. It is the 'folklore' of philosophy, and, like folklore, it takes countless different forms. Its most fundamental characteristic is that it is a conception which, even in the brain of one individual, is fragmentary, incoherent and inconsequential, in conformity with the social and cultural position of those masses whose philosophy it is. At those times in history when a homogenous social group is brought into being, there comes into being also, in opposition to common sense, a homogenous - in other words coherent and systematic - philosophy. (1971: 419)

In this sense, common sense is not only the ground upon which ideological battles are fought, it is also that which needs to be contested and brought to bear under the weight of critical consciousness. Gramsci distinguishes between a passionate sensibility and a coherent conception of the world, between common sense and good sense. In order to change people's minds and conduct, common sense must not be foregone in favour of an arid knowledge, rather it must be carried over, as it is that passion that forms the connection between the leaders and those who are led:

> One cannot make politics-history without this passion, without this sentimental connection between intellectuals and the people-nation. In the absence of such a nexus the relations between the

> intellectual and the people-nation are, or are reduced to, relationships of a purely bureaucratic and formal order; the intellectuals become a caste, or a priesthood. (1971: 418)

In many ways Gramsci is also trying to deconstruct the distinction between knowing and feeling that more traditionally has been understood in hierarchical political (i.e. between ruler and ruled) and philosophical (i.e. between mind and body) terms. For Gramsci the transition from a state of incoherence to coherence, from common sense to good sense, is seen as dialectical, inherently progressive, and is closely tied to an understanding of the transition from a sensibility for the 'simple' to a state of knowledge: '[o]nly then can there take place an exchange of individual elements between the rulers and ruled, leaders and led, and can the shared life be realised which alone is a social force – with the creation of the "historical bloc"' (1971: 418). The transformation of the people into a condition of knowing, though, is understood by Gramsci in different ways and he makes constant comparisons between Marxism and Catholicism and the priesthood in terms of the way in which relations of expertise (those who know and those who don't really know) are maintained. For Gramsci, the Catholic church is one of the main cultural institutions used to explain hegemony, but it is also to be distinguished from Marxism that, in contrast, builds upon the simple and transforms it from common sense into good sense; and it does so in a way that begins to dissolve relations of power internal to the construction of knowledge. For Gramsci, then, hegemony is centrally about ethics, education and leadership because it is about raising the knowledge and status of the people, leading them to 'a higher conception of life' and ending the relations of power that have dogged their lives for so long (1971: 332–3). By and large, cultural studies has focused on Gramsci's understanding of hegemony as a strategic balance of forces, a series of struggles and negotiations between classes on the field of culture, rather than focus on his more dialectical and ethical sense of hegemony and cultural development.

The other main resource for thinking about ideology, culture and power in cultural studies in the 1970s and early 1980s was the work of the French Marxist, Louis Althusser. In contrast to Gramsci's dialectical sense of political and cultural agency and his keenness to synthesise theory and practice, science and common sense, intellectuals and the people, Althusser, writing about 30 years later, was eager to mark the break between Marxist science and common sense ideology. In a criticism of what he sees as Gramsci's 'historicism' – namely, a form of theory that is never able to break out of the impasse of history and ideology – Althusser lauds the theoretical knowledge of structure. Althusser was working in the context of 1960s Paris, a time of social and political reflection after the liberation from Nazi German occupation during the Second World War, the anti-colonial struggles in Algeria, and the upheavals of the events of 1968 when student radicals and other political groups turned the city upside down with occupations, teach-ins and barricades across the streets. But Althusser was also writing in the context of the existentialism and social theory of Simone de Beauvoir, Jean-Paul Sartre and Raymond Aron and more particularly in the context of the historical epistemology of Gaston Bachelard, Georges Canguilhem and, latterly, Michel Foucault. The importance of these later writers cannot be stressed enough, as Althusser's concern is really with epistemology not with practical or contemporary politics. Although a member of the French Communist Party, he had very little to say on the atrocities committed by Stalin despite the Twentieth Congress of the Soviet Communist party in 1956 condemning the dogmatism and political 'errors' of Stalin. Althusser is centrally concerned with understanding Marx's work (*Capital* in particular) as scientific (how this might be done and the implications in doing so). The French tradition of historical epistemology provided Althusser with a conceptual context for understanding that scientific knowledge was not reducible to ideology – as it had been understood, to some extent, in the work of Gramsci, for whom there is no clear differentiation between science, religion and ideology (i.e. all talked about in terms of a 'common conception of the world') or as it was to be construed in the work of many more 'post-modern' cultural theorists who failed to identify the epistemological singularity of particular discursive practices (i.e. such that everything is social construction and relative). For Althusser, scientific knowledge is that which marks a break – an epistemological break – with ideology. This break is both historical (inasmuch as science is predicated on a progression from the historically prior ideologies) and theoretical (inasmuch as science, as a theoretical practice, cannot be reduced to the processes of history). Science, as Marxist science (based on the logic of *Capital*), stands outside history.

Thus, in contrast to Gramsci, Althusser's Marxism (influenced also as it was by the Lenin of *The State and Revolution* (1965 [1917]) is deeply anti-populist and anti-popular. Althusser was nevertheless a brilliant philosopher and his theoretical writings have been deeply influential in our understanding of ideology in terms of the construction of the subject. Althusser makes a contrast between the *concrete individual* and the *ideological subject* (1969, 1971; Althusses and Balibar, 1979). Whereas the former is that which exists in an undifferentiated form prior to society and the symbolic, the latter is that unity which is an ideological fabrication. Althusser conceives of agency only at the level of structure; individuals don't have any active part to play in history or society. For Althusser, concrete individuals are only the supports (a translation from the German term, *Träger*, used by Marx and Engels) for the determinations and overdeterminations at the level of structure. He argues in *Reading Capital* that:

> [T]he structure of the relations of production determines the *places* and *functions* occupied and adopted by the agents of production, who are never anything more than the occupants of these places, insofar as they are the 'supports' (*Träger*) of these functions. The true 'subjects' (in the sense of constitutive subjects of the process) are therefore not these occupants or functionaries, are not, despite all appearances, the 'obviousness' of the 'given' of naive anthropology, 'concrete individuals', 'real men' - but *the definition and distribution of these places and functions. The true 'subjects' are these definers and distributors: the relations of production* (and political and ideological social relations). But since these are 'relations', they cannot be thought within the category *subject*. (Althusser and Balibar, 1979: 180)

Althusser's development of the Marxist notion of *Träger* rightly opens up the question of structural relations, agency and subjectivity as a pivotal problematic. In many ways, one of the great strengths of Gramsci's analysis of the mechanics of power was that it conceives of the problem of ideology, not simply in terms of subjectivity (e.g. bourgeois subjectivity or proletarian subjectivity), but in the relations across class alliances and negotiations. Althusser understands the subject to be very much in tension with the relationality of structure, but he never adequately resolves that problem.

Althusser's theory of the ideological subject is more fully, but perhaps less adequately, explored in his essay 'Ideology and the ideological state apparatuses' (1971). In this essay Althusser raises the simple yet important question regarding the need for any social formation not only to produce, but to reproduce itself. He states that a social formation needs to reproduce both the productive forces (i.e. technology, knowledge, labour) and the existing relations of production (i.e. the class relations between the bourgeoisie and the working class). It does so, Althusser argues, by the exercise of State power through the Repressive and Ideological State Apparatuses. This scheme broadly corresponds with Gramsci's understanding of the State as both political and civil. The Repressive State Apparatus (RSA) refers to the government, the army, police, courts, prisons and so on: namely those institutions that have at their disposal the means of incarceration, punishment and violence. In contrast, the Ideological State Apparatuses (ISA) refer to the churches, schools, universities, family, law, political parties, the media, and culture. As with Gramsci, Althusser gives particular importance in modern societies to the role of education: 'it is by an apprenticeship in a variety of know-how wrapped up in the massive inculcation of the ideology of the ruling class that the *relations of production* in a capitalist social formation ... are largely reproduced' (1971: 156). For Althusser, educational institutions work, to put it crudely, to produce managers, on the one hand, and shop-assistants, factory workers, call-centre employees and so on, on the other. Educational institutions can be seen to be more closely directed by the State, but other institutions are much less obviously so. Nevertheless, for Althusser, as for Gramsci, private or civil institutions, such as the media and churches and so on, are seen as State apparatuses inasmuch as the distinction between public and private is seen to be one that emerges within bourgeois law and inasmuch as these private institutions are seen to support the continuation of bourgeois rule and the State as the purveyor of the status quo. Schools, churches, media and other institutions, thus, are seen collectively to support and provide the conditions for the reproduction of capitalism. But, Althusser argues, whereas the RSA is relatively centralised through the administration and control under party political leadership, the ISAs are 'multiple, distinct, "relatively autonomous" and capable of providing an objective field of contradictions'. The ISAs are held together by 'the ruling ideology, the ideology of the ruling class' (Althusser, 1971: 149). The ISAs, then, are one of the means through which a social formation reproduces itself, but are themselves held together, and given a function, by ideology. These institutions are not neutral, but necessarily political in Althusser's understanding: '*no class can hold State power over a long period without at the same time exercising its hegemony over and in the State Ideological Apparatuses*' (1971: 146). However, whereas Gramsci understands this problematic in terms of the strategic game of building hegemonic alliances and articulations, Althusser looks to the structural and constitutive role of ideology.

When Althusser talks of ideology, he distinguishes between *specific* ideologies and ideology *in general*. It is the latter that provides him with a theoretical understanding of the State and of the reproduction of the forces and relations of production. In order to understand Althusser's theory of ideology it is important to understand why it is not a theory of specific ideologies. For Althusser, specific ideologies (such as nationalism, patriarchalism, libertarianism) are constructed within history and they can only be understood with reference to their social and historical context: namely with reference to their relation to their location within the social formation and the economic base. Any understanding of specific ideologies necessarily refers us to more than those ideologies themselves, to what lies outside, and determining, of them (1971: 159). Althusser argues, if we are to have a theory of ideology in general, then we must propose that ideology cannot be understood at the level of the particular. For Althusser, *ideology has no history*. This is not because ideology is like a dream, a pure fantasy (although it does sometimes have those qualities), but because 'it is endowed with a structure and a functioning such as to make it a non-historical reality, i.e. an *omni-historical* reality, in the sense in which that structure and functioning are immutable, present in the same form throughout what we can call history' (1971: 161). A theory of ideology in general is thus the abstraction of the particular examples of ideologies. According to Althusser a theory of ideology is scientific inasmuch as it raises the descriptive to the level of the theoretical. Ideology has no history because it is the object of theoretical knowledge and its truth, as it were, is related to that body of knowledge and not directly to the empirical ideologies in particular. Althusser attempts to provide a Marxist scientific account of ideology. Science is an understanding, not of particular facts, but of the structure of those facts and that structure is necessarily a theoretical abstraction. It is only because of this that a science has any explanatory power.

What then is the structure of ideology? Althusser argues that the structure of ideology can be understood according to two main features: first, that ideology concerns the positioning of a subject and, second, that ideology has a material, not ideational, existence. In the first instance, Althusser states that '[i]deology represents the imaginary relationship of individuals to their real conditions of existence' (1971: 162). Ideology is not simply an illusion, myth or false consciousness. Ideology is not an imaginary representation that represents the world. It is not a relationship between a representation and the world (i.e. in terms of its truth or falsity, its imaginariness or verisimilitude), rather it is, for Althusser, a relation between a subject and its real conditions of existence (such that those conditions are shaped, for example, by the relations between capital and labour in a capitalist mode of production). It is the imaginary nature of this relation that is of significance:

> [I]t is not their real conditions of existence, their real world that 'men' 'represent to themselves' in ideology, but above all it is their relation to those conditions of existence which is represented to them there ... it is the *imaginary nature of this relation* which underlies all the imaginary distortion that we can observe ... in all ideology. (1971: 164)

This imaginary relation concerns the constitution of the subject as an ideological subject. But this is not to suggest that ideology is somehow not material. Althusser argues that, in the second instance, ideology has a material existence. Ideology cannot be reduced to a notion of ideas as ideal or spiritual entities. Ideology is embedded in rituals, institutions and material practices: 'an ideology always exists in an apparatus, and its practice, or practices' (1971: 166). Clearly the materiality of an ideology is not the same as the materiality of a paving stone or a traffic light, but it is nevertheless material. Thus, Althusser states that for a subject: '*his ideas are his material actions inserted into material practices governed by material rituals which are themselves defined by the material ideological apparatus from which derive the ideas of that subject*' (1971: 169). Ideology, then, concerns the ordering of material practice and the constitution of a subject. Ideology works inasmuch as it works on subjects.

Ideology constitutes concrete individuals as subjects. The subject appears as something that is obvious - eternal and common sense - but this obviousness of the subject is one of the primary ideological effects. We readily recognise ourselves as subjects: namely as subjects with agency, freedom and responsibility.

Althusser refers to the way that we are hooked into ideology through the notion of *interpellation*. We recognise ourselves in ideological practices - such that that recognition is an imaginary relation between us and the world (e.g. predicated on a notion that we are free to choose) - as an automatic reaction. He gives an example of a policeman calling in the street, 'Hey you'; we immediately turn around as if we are the one being called. Cultural studies scholars have looked at the mechanism of interpellation across a range of practices such as advertising, film and other media. An advertisement, for example, talks to 'you' directly as if the 'you' it was addressing was not a general 'you', but 'you' in particular, you reading the advertisement. For Althusser, ideological recognition is also a mis-recognition, inasmuch as that which is ignored or misrecognised is one's real position within the relations of production (i.e. relations of class). Moreover, Althusser argues that, inasmuch as we are always caught in this interpellation by ideology, we are *always already* in ideology. There is no escape. Althusser argues that even at birth we are interpellated by ideology as individuals. For example, when a baby is born those around it want to give it a name based on its family and sex. It is always already caught in the ideological practices of patrilineage and family system. In this sense, although concrete individuals exist prior to ideology, they do so only in an abstract way, as there can be no individual that is not caught in the practices of ideology. In that sense, also, ideology is everywhere and eternal: 'ideology has always-already interpellated individuals as subjects' (1971: 175).

Despite the sophistication of Althusser's theory, there are clearly some problems. On the one hand, there are a series of problems regarding his understanding of the transformation from concrete individual to ideological subject. Althusser sees the task of ideology is to produce a unitary subject, but if this is so, how are we to understand the concrete individual unless as a prior unitary individual? The designation of something as 'individual' presumes that it can be individuated: namely, that it can be distinguished from others. Moreover, if ideology works through (mis)recognition, then surely the concrete individual that is interpellated is an agent with the capacity for recognition (cf. Hirst, 1976)? In many ways, the concrete individual is only ever a shadow of the ideological subject: the mechanism of interpellation is never able to reach outside of ideological circularity. A theory of ideology in general - one that is eternal and that has no outside - is unable to explain reproduction (a question about identity over time) and interpellation (a problem about the incorporation of something outside into something inside). It is not possible to explain the continuity of a structure with recourse to a structure that is continuous. On the other hand, there are related problems regarding the political implications of Althusser's theory on the grounds that it provides no place for human agency and no place for an epistemological subject that precedes its ideological construction (cf. Thompson, 1978). Thus, Althusser provides a theory of ideological subject positioning, but doesn't account for how that subject might be able to act in relation to or against such structural relations: how, for example, in Althusser's account, can subjects be political and change things? This seems to be at odds with Althusser's notion that State power can be taken by a particular class or that the ISAs are controlled by a bourgeois ideology or that history is the history of class struggle. If ideology is a structure and if ideology is outside of history, then there is no place for agency at all: all is an effect of structure. Moreover, although Althusser gives an account of Marxist science, such that science is clearly distinguished from ideology, he does not provide an adequate account of how we might be positioned as knowing, rather than unknowing, subjects nor how we might progress from one to the other nor even how we might be able to act on social and political knowledge. These are big political problems, not least because much of European political thought has presumed the importance of political subjects as having both agency and the capacity for distinguishing between knowledge and propaganda: hence, the notion that democracy is founded on the principle of citizens having information and knowledge about the society within which they live and the capacity to act upon that knowledge (e.g. in voting for certain parties at elections, holding demonstrations, etc.).

Discourse and Radical Democracy

It is significant that the first significant political theory to be adopted within cultural studies after the heyday of these earlier Maxists was one that drew upon Althusser and Gramsci as major theoretical resources, but did so in a way that figured 'democracy' as a major political ideal. Ernesto Laclau and Chantal Mouffe in their highly influential book, *Hegemony and Socialist Strategy* (1985), radically rethink the Gramscian notion of hegemony within the context of post-structuralist theory and a radical democratic politics. They provide a genealogy of the concept of hegemony and argue that it introduces a logic of the social which is incompatible with the basic categories of Marxist theory (inasmuch as it moves beyond a relation between the economic and relations of class). In this sense, they also move well beyond the Gramscian notion of strategic alliances and the importance of ideology in the cementing of such negotiated blocs. All social relations are seen to be necessarily overdetermined. Although a large part of their argument is weighted to a deconstructive history of traditional Marxist theory, the value of Laclau and Mouffe's argument concerns their understanding of the significance of new social movements in late modern cultural politics, of the discursive, differential and antagonistic nature of all social positions and of the ideal of a radical democratic politics.

Let's start by working through an example. In 1997 an Eastern European woman from Poland is working illegally in London as a domestic cleaner and a waitress. Her children, whom she sees only twice a year, are left behind in Poland looked after by the husband. Her name is Magda. A Marxist, such as Althusser, might want to argue that Magda is ideologically positioned or interpellated within particular capitalist relations of exploitation. Her positionality, as 'cleaner', is reproduced through various ideological structures (educational, legal, cultural). But the ISAs construct her positioning only to the extent that she is positioned within (and has an imaginary relation to) the economic structure of contemporary capitalism. A radical feminist might argue that Magda is equally caught within ideology, not so much with regard to capital, but to patriarchy. Magda is constructed in a position of oppression with regard to the patriarchal structure of the family and within the patriarchal-capitalist positioning of woman as servicing the needs of men and industry (as with nurses, shop assistants, secretaries, etc.). A liberal capitalist might argue that Magda is an individual, who, although facing certain constraints, is able to make free choices, based on her conscious free will, regarding her life and work. She is a woman who has freely chosen to come to London to work according to the pull of higher wages. Thus, even though Magda is a cleaner, she gets more in London than she would in Krakow as a trainee management consultant for which she was in training.

The point I want to make here is not that any one of these descriptions is either right or wrong (i.e. in the sense of being judged according to their relation to an objective world upon which a 'truth' can be delivered), but that each of these descriptions is in themselves not exhaustive. In terms of the question of Magda's relation to social power, not one of these descriptions (regarding relations of exploitation, relations of oppression, ideology of free will) is adequate in and of themselves. This inadequacy is not just because migrant and service industry labour poses a problem for traditional Marxist definitions of labour and understandings of the relations of production (in the sense that Magda is not technically 'working class') nor because the familial relations of Magda are, if anything reversed, such that the husband is at home looking after the children and the mother is in the public sphere of work nor because the dreams of living in London (part of the 'capitalist West') has constituted a part of her unconscious for such a long time. Rather the inadequacy is quite simply that any discursive positioning of the subject is not exhaustive. The discursive positioning of Magda is exceeded (in terms of her positionality across a range of discourses) and overdetermined (in terms of the necessary openness and relationality across these discourses). Moreover, it is not that Magda is defined by her structural or objective position in society and that ideology or discourse merely discovers, defines, or conceals that position. Let's look at this in more detail.

According to Laclau and Mouffe our subjectivity is not defined through our structural or objective relation to society or biology. It is not that we have a structural position as 'man' or 'woman', 'black' or 'white' and so on, and cultural discourses then describe or add texture to that fundamental positioning. All subject positions are constructed - at root - within and through discourse. There is no lived experience, for example, that can be said to ground our 'identity' over and above the construction of that lived experience through discourse. Laclau and Mouffe draw upon post-Saussurian semiotics to understand identity as discursively constructed within a system of differences. The relations between things are seen as socially constructed: 'every object is constituted as an object of discourse, insofar as no object is given outside every discursive condition of emergence' (1985: 107). As with Althusser's and Gramsci's accounts of ideology, Laclau and Mouffe make the claim that discourse is not 'mental' or 'ideational', but 'material' and they argue that discourse cannot be reduced to the linguistic inasmuch as it includes both linguistic and non-linguistic materials. As when a builder builds a home, words are used, but also bricks are passed and laid: '[t]he linguistic and non-linguistic elements are not merely juxtaposed, but constitute a differential and structured system of positions - that is, a discourse' (1985: 108). For Laclau and Mouffe, these different material elements are put together, or articulated, into a meaningful whole (albeit partially so): namely, a discourse. In this sense, we are born with certain bodies, thrown into particular social and economic situations, and live our lives through a range of different events and circumstances, but all of this, the collection of different moments, is only made meaningful through discourse, not because any element has meaning in and of itself.

Thus, for Magda, in the late twentieth and early twenty-first century, the discourse of 'Eastern European migrant as social problem' constructs her (as a subject) in relation to other elements: the asylum seeker, the scrounger, the hordes of people entering the UK through the channel tunnel, criminal gangs and prostitution, and so on. Such a discourse was clearly a problem for Magda, who although illegally resident and working in the UK before Poland's entry into the EU (and before acceptance of her permit to work in the UK), is neither criminal in a broader social sense nor typified by these nationalistic and xenophobic constructions. Nevertheless, this is how she is typified; this is how some of her employers think of her; this explains some of the looks she gets when her 'foreign' accent is heard at the shop counter. Magda's voice, her place of birth and nationality, and her travelling to the UK to work are made to signify – to represent – only through their relation with other signs and objects. They don't have any 'natural' or fixed or essential signification. Laclau and Mouffe argue that, as the meaning of any one element is its relation to other elements within the discursive system; if the system is closed and fixed, so too will the meaning of those individual elements. These elements will take on a necessary character. Of necessity, in this closed system, Magda's voice, her nationality and so on would represent the stigma of migration. But Laclau and Mouffe argue that such a closed system is a logical and actual impossibility: 'no discursive formation is a sutured totality and the transformation of the elements into moments is never complete' (1985: 106–7).

As the transition from elements outside any discursive system to moments inside such a system is 'never entirely fulfilled' (1985: 110), no discourse nor articulation is ever completely stitched together, or sutured, as a unity. All discourses and articulations are necessarily open ended or fuzzy. And thus, also, all identities within these discursive formations are open ended and fuzzy as well: 'there is no identity which can ever be fully constituted' (1985: 111) because all identities are relational, dependent on the system of difference within which they reside. If the discursive system is open, so must the identities be unstable. Here, for Laclau and Mouffe, is 'a decisive point' in their argument: '[t]he incomplete character of every totality necessarily leads to abandon, as a terrain of analysis, the premise of *"society"* as a sutured and self-defined totality' (1985: 111). There is no underlying principle or form or system that might be seen to constitute 'society' as an object of theoretical discourse. In contrast to earlier theoretical models (such as the Althusserian or the Gramscian), Laclau and Mouffe presume that subjectivity and the social are intimately tied together and that their fixity or non-fixity cannot be rooted ultimately in a foundational base or social order. The social is made up of many discourses, just as the subject is positioned or interpellated by many discourses; no one discourse can sum up the social; no one discourse can sum up the subject; both subject and social are open and overdetermined. The necessary openness of any discourse is seen as itself constitutive of discursive positionalities and formations.

If this is so, as Laclau and Mouffe argue, then any attempt to stitch together an identity implies the movement of power. The exercise of power implies the 'effort' to articulate elements into a discursive totality and the 'attempt to dominate the field of discursivity' (1985: 112). Laclau and Mouffe talk about articulation in terms of hegemony. However, unlike Gramsci's conception of hegemony in relation to class division and struggle within industrial capitalism and in relation to alliances across different classes in the form of a historical bloc, Laclau and Mouffe understand hegemony as a purely discursive endeavour. For Laclau and Mouffe 'society' does not sit outside of an identity determining it; rather the social is understood as that which is formed through articulation or discursive association. Moreover, it is because these social relations are always partial that hegemony is possible. There is never a fixed identity, complete closure, or total control precisely because hegemony refers to the process of struggle. The social, for Laclau and Mouffe, is always overdetermined and is never 'identical to itself' (1985: 113).

In this sense, then, any antagonism between classes or identities is not understood with reference to an underlying biology or economy or cultural fixity, but within the field of the discursive itself. Class, gender, sexuality, 'race' and ethnicity don't have any essential identity and meaning. The exercise of power implies the attempt to construct lines of inclusion and exclusion, to articulate one identity with another, but also to separate one identity from its other and to separate one image of society from its other:

> [I]f we maintain our conception of the social as a non-sutured space, as a field in which all positivity is metaphorical and subvertible, then there is no way of referring the *negation* of an objective position to an underlying positivity - be it causal or of another type - which would account for it. Antagonism as the negation of a given order is, quite simply, the limit of that order, and not the moment of a broader totality in relation to which the two poles of the antagonism would constitute differential - i.e. objective - partial instances ... The limit of the social must be given within the social itself as something subverting it, destroying its ambition to constitute a full presence. (1985: 126–7)

Antagonism is thus both internal and external to the social: '[s]trictly speaking, antagonisms are not *internal* but *external* to society; or rather, they constitute the limits of society, the latter's impossibility of fully constituting itself' (1985: 125). Antagonism represents the necessary 'limits of every objectivity' (1985: 125). As the constitutive outside of any discursive, social, or identity formation, antagonism thus marks the failure of language as a system of differences. It is the limit, to use Kristeva's term, as 'abject', that which is thrown beyond the realm of the symbolic (Kristeva, 1984b). Identity is, thus, formed on a series of exclusions, foreclosures and repressions.

For example, xenophobic and racist discourses circulate widely in the UK concerning the small influx of Eastern European migrants. Various headlines and lead stories in the UK press, as in other media, narrate the migrants as a flood breaking down the barriers of English national identity. This is a narrative of self and other, of England and its others; a story that has been played out before with different characters, but with a similar plot. But a xenophobic identity cannot be made positively, only negatively against its others. Although a xenophobic discourse may construct certain motifs as representative of a true Englishness – a land of Tebbits and Hobbits, of cricket and warm beer, of King Arthur and joyful children playing Robin Hood under the watchful eye of mother (thoroughly modern in a trite conservative kind of way) – the authority of this representation is far from secure. This discourse of Englishness is formed through a negation and repression of its others, those identities and discourses it feeds on and dispels at the same time. Those others – those exterior identities – form, in Laclau and Mouffe's terms, a 'constitutive outside'. Identity is relational; self-identity is relational; it is both self and other, such that the identity of one depends on the identity of the other. In this sense, the figure of Magda can be seen as the constitutive outside of a xenophobic English identity. The outside of any identity or discourse, though, is not non-discursive; it is constituted within the social terrain or 'field of discursivity' (i.e. the totality of possible discourses, which in Laclau and Mouffe's (1985: 113) account has a horizon of infinity).

How then do these highly theoretical arguments about discourse, subjectivity and the social relate to radical democracy? Some might argue that, in deconstructing both system and subject, social totality and individual agent, Laclau and Mouffe have no recourse to any authoritative trope of social justice, namely that through the recognition of the pain and suffering of others, we might be able to stand up against oppression, exploitation and domination. With no recourse to the humanist subject how can Laclau and Mouffe appeal to our sense of politics and social justice? Laclau and Mouffe make a distinction between the following: relations of subordination (i.e. when an agent is subjected to the decisions of another, as with an employee/employer relation); relations of oppression (i.e. when a relation of subordination has become antagonistic); and relations of domination (i.e. when a relation of subordination is considered illegitimate or wrong from the perspective of an agent external to that relation). A relation of subordination cannot in and of itself be a relation of oppression or domination just because it maps a differential or hierarchical relation between agents. It is only when the subordinate relation is subverted that a relation of oppression can be made visible. Thus, according to Laclau and Mouffe, 'slave' does not designate, in and of itself, a relation of oppression; it is only when this relation is made visible through a discourse of human rights that that relation becomes antagonistic and understood as oppression. It is only when a discourse exterior to that relation (as a third party) becomes articulated with that relation, does that relation become disclosed in a new light; that disclosure is formed through a relation of *equivalence*. For example, when a discourse concerning the rights of man (a discourse that became prevalent in the European Enlightenment in the late eighteenth century) was transposed to Haiti and deployed against the French 'masters' by the black revolutionary leader Toussaint L'Ouverture, an equivalence was articulated between the white French and the Haitian black French. The rights of black Caribbeans were now seen as having an identity common to those of the white French imperialists, on the grounds that the black Haitians were themselves French citizens and hence should be treated accordingly. Similarly, 'black', 'woman', 'lesbian and gay' and so on are not necessarily 'political' categories; they have to be made so; they have to be mobilised as such; they have to be articulated within hegemonic and counter-hegemonic struggle.

It is thus not on the basis of an essential 'humanity' that democracy and rights can gain a foothold on our political being; it is, on the contrary, as a result of the openness of all identities and the openness of all relations that the relation between 'master' and 'slave' can be surpassed. As Judith Butler has said, in relation to Laclau and Mouffe's analysis:

> The incompletion of every ideological formulation is central to the radical democratic project's notion of political futurity. The subjection of every ideological formation to a *re*articulation of these linkages constitutes the temporal order of democracy as an incalculable future, leaving open the production of new subject-positions, new political signifiers, and new linkages to become the rallying points for politicization. (1993: 193)

The possibility of constituting equivalences across social and discursive relations marks the possibility of a radical democracy.

Laclau and Mouffe's analysis of the discursive positioning of the subject, hegemonic articulation and radical democracy is one that underpins, or at least connects with, a number of arguments in cultural studies concerning power, identity and difference. Laclau and Mouffe should be applauded for helping us understand this problematic and for providing a theory of the subject and the social that underscores the necessity of a multi-cultural and democratic polity. And yet, we should be hesitant about any claim that the turn to discourse has 'enlarged' our understanding of political relations (i.e. not limited to the economic or the biological). Although it might be true that – as a consequence of the turn to political culture and to an understanding of the politics of culture – we now have a richer sense of politics, we should be circumspect as to what this might mean. In place of a multiplicity of different forms of understanding and of the difficulty of translating across different accounts, the turn to discourse has flattened much complexity to a primarily linguistic, post-Saussurian model. Whereas, for example, in Wittgenstein's thinking the analysis of 'language games' (as discussed in the previous chapter) is relatively opaque and any relation across social practice is relatively indeterminate, Laclau and Mouffe reduce analysis of this social terrain to a model of discursive relations (i.e. as understood in terms of metaphor, metonymy, difference and system). If difference itself is only constituted *within* a discursive system, then we are not able, in Laclau and Mouffe's model, to account for difference *between* the system and its outside. Laclau and Mouffe's model itself becomes unstuck. If the difference between one discursive system and another is itself discursive, then all difference is discursive. Moreover, even though the field of discourse might be infinitely variable, it is nevertheless, of necessity, constituted as a discursive totality. If, however, the difference between one discursive system and another is not discursive, then it is a difference that is constituted as more than formal. It is a difference of substance. Sticks and stones do break bones, whatever names they are called. It might be argued, then, that Laclau and Mouffe's analysis disavows the complex ontologies (the multiplicity of substance) that comprise social relationality and reduces all social practice to a formal equivalence. Even the relation between the discursive and non-discursive is understood in terms of a formal equivalence. Laclau and Mouffe's analysis provides us, for example, with an understanding of how the signifier 'woman' might be open and overdetermined (as a site of contestation and struggle), but it says nothing as to why the contestation over this particular signifier might have more significance than a discussion over whether someone likes their pasta overcooked or *al dente*. This is partly a question of the value attached to certain differences. Some differences matter, others don't. But it is also an issue of difference being constituted through more than the discursive. A rose smells sweet whatever its name. Any analysis of the contingency of the social and the discursive can be accounted for only with reference to something more than a formal equivalence, namely to a substantial difference as the measure of indeterminacy. Laclau and Mouffe in attempting to produce a general theory of the political end up by constructing a single currency of exchange: the discursive.

Moreover, this raises a problem with how we are to understand the relation between hegemonic power and the discursive. How are we to understand the power to form identities and differences between subject positions? How are we to understand this power with regard to the field of discursivity? Is hegemonic power internal or external to the realm of the discursive? Is hegemonic power immanent to or transcendent of the discursive? If the former, then power is reducible to the discursive: namely, power is defined only by its formal, rather than substantive capacity. If the latter, then we return to the problem of a power prior to and foundational of social relations. In part, these problems reside in the fact that although Laclau and

Mouffe call on the work of Foucault in their analysis, they align Foucault's understanding of discourse with a post-Saussurian understanding of linguistic system, rather than with a concern about the problem of organisation. In the next section we explore this further in the context of Foucault's notion of government.

Culture and Governmentality

Michel Foucault was a French historian of ideas, writing on the margins of philosophy, history and politics from the 1960s to his death in 1984. His intellectual work crosses areas of study from madness, medicine, the human sciences, sexuality, discipline and forms of political reason. These were far from distanced, objective studies of the past, but were detailed interventions that helped to elucidate contemporary social reality and to shape a politics therein. Foucault referred to his histories as genealogies or 'histories of the present'. They were histories intended to reveal lineages, but also breaks that upset the present. Central to his writing has been the question of power in relation to the self, to knowledge, and to technologies of government. In some ways though, it is an understanding of Foucault as a theorist of discourse that has gained most currency in cultural studies and cultural theory. But it is this image of Foucault's work that is most problematic and has led to some of his more apposite work being obscured. It is important, then, to understand some of the main themes of Foucault's writing in terms of a series of questions about power and organisation, such that what people say (i.e. discourse) has a significance, but not one that overshadows the nature of other important elements.

In a response to a paper on Foucault's conception of discourse (at a conference on Foucault's work in 1988 in Paris four years after his death) Paul Veyne, historian and friend of Foucault, saw no expediency in the term 'discourse' anymore:

> Why should it be that Foucault used this word rather than words like 'practices', 'archives' or 'presuppositions' to designate this thing in which we are to recognise positive finitude or rarefaction? Maybe he was just sensitive to the linguistic fashion in France at the time, and there is nothing more to it than that. (1992: 116)

Although many others in the 1970s, 1980s and 1990s had fetishised 'discourse' to the detriment of broader and yet also more specific understandings of the relations between power and culture, Foucault was never that attached to the movement. Even at the height of his interest (one year after the publication of *The Archaeology of Knowledge* (1972 [1969 in the original French]), his most extensive discussion of the methodology of the discursive), his investment is evident in a discussion of the philosophy of Gilles Deleuze:

> The univocity of being, its singleness of expression, is paradoxically the principal condition which permits difference to escape the domination of identity, which frees it from the law of the Same as a simple opposition within conceptual elements. Being can express itself in the same way, because difference is no longer submitted to the prior reduction of categories; because it is not distributed inside a diversity that can always be perceived; because it is not organized in a conceptual hierarchy of species and genus. Being is that which is always said of difference; it is the *Recurrence* of difference. (1977a: 192)

This is a difficult quote, but it is worthwhile reading it a few times. It is because things in the world constantly insist that they are different – or persist in being different – that things generally cannot be reduced to a single measure. A bottle of wine and a lump of cheese are both items of food, perhaps bought from a local shop, but they are not the same. Equally, their difference is not that a bottle of wine is the opposite of a lump of cheese: the one is not the negation of the other. If anything, then, the analysis of discursive formations was for Foucault not a means of reducing 'being' to a single model, but to think about being differently; namely, as an innovation in thought, an experimentation, an undoing of power through understanding the singularity of power in specific situations or events.

In many ways, the turn to discourse has become a distraction. Originally a means to a particular understanding of the contingency of the social and of social relationality, it has too easily become, as we saw with Laclau and Mouffe, the measure of that relationality. In many ways also, despite its brilliance, *The Archaeology of Knowledge* (1972) was, in some ways, forced upon Foucault, as a form of explanation for his earlier 'archaeological' works on madness, medicine and the human sciences; it forced his hand regarding that tension across these different types of material practice and across different problem-spaces. The elaboration of 'discourse' was not something to which he returned. Even in *The History of Sexuality, Volume I* (1979), although he talked at length on the discourse of sexuality, 'discourse' had by then lost its primacy as a singular term for explaining the problem of organisation. Discourse had come to mean the organisation of 'talk', not the organisation of organisation. The discursive had become secondary to the strategic and tactical:

> Discourses are tactical elements or blocks operating in the field of force relations; there can exist different and even contradictory discourses within the same strategy; they can, on the contrary, circulate without changing their form from one strategy to another, opposing strategy. We must not expect the discourses on sex to tell us, above all, what strategy they derive from, or what moral divisions they accompany, or what ideology – dominant or dominated – they represent; rather we must question them

> on the two levels of their tactical productivity (what reciprocal effects of power and knowledge they ensure) and their strategical integration (what conjunction and what force relationship make their utilization necessary in a given episode of the various confrontations that occur). (1979: 102)

In this formulation, Foucault doesn't make a claim for the constitutive power of discourse. On the contrary, discourse is but one form of element among many, across which an apparatus (*dispositif*) takes shape. He defines 'apparatus' accordingly: first, it is 'a thoroughly heterogeneous ensemble', including in some instances 'discourses, institutions, architectural forms, regulatory decisions, laws, administrative measures, scientific statements, philosophical, moral and philanthropic propositions – in short, the said as much as the unsaid'; secondly, any element is not fixed and can change its function, meaning and position, in the sense that 'a discourse can figure at one time as the programme of an institution and at another it can function as a means of justifying or masking a practice which itself remains silent'; thirdly, it is 'the system of relations that can be established between these elements'; fourthly, it is defined in terms of its relation within a field of force relations; fifthly, within these force relations the apparatus takes on a strategic function, for example, in the control of an unruly population and the socialisation of that population into a functioning economy; and sixthly, its formation is always premised on an experimentation and innovation, never a repetition of the same (Foucault, 1979: 92–3, 1980: 194–5; Deleuze, 1992). The apparatus is not defined by something external to it; it is not made intelligible with reference to one particular logic or model; rather the organisation of the apparatus is immanent to itself; it is 'the multiplicity of force relations immanent in the sphere in which they operate and which constitute their own organization' (Foucault, 1979: 92). The apparatus is not external to power; it is the shape and organisation of power; it is the singularity, or specificity, of power. Importantly, in Foucault's work, the variables that constitute the multiplicity of the apparatus and of power are always weighted within the specificity and singularity of the empirical and the historical, at least in their genealogical form. Power is a deeply empirical and substantial matter; it has existence. Thus, Foucault's analysis of power moves well beyond the legacy of the structure of class in Gramsci's and Althusser's analyses, but also beyond Laclau and Mouffe's analysis of hegemony as constituted within the horizon of the discursive. For Foucault, there is neither a pre-existent class nor structural inequality that frames modern power nor is there a single measure (such as 'discourse') for understanding its operation.

In Foucault's *Discipline and Punish* (1977b) and *History of Sexuality: Volume I* (1979), much stress was laid on the micro-political aspect of power, to the extent that many critics asked what had happened to the state. In a series of lectures and writings in the late 1970s and early 1980s, Foucault began to orient his thought to such concerns, not by addressing the question of the state directly, but by talking in more singular terms about the forms of power and knowledge that congregate around and support the state. In a lecture in 1978, Foucault traces a genealogy of what he terms 'governmentality', namely a rationality or mentality of government. His argument in this essay covers a period from the sixteenth to nineteenth centuries, a period that saw the emergence and development of the modern state. Foucault looks, not at the growth of the state into a bureaucratic welfarist machine, but at the shifts in European thought and practice that made possible such a centralised administrative apparatus. Foucault documents a shift from forms of rule in the *ancien regime* that took the shape of systems of alliances across kinship, household and estate to forms of government for the good of both individual and population from the eighteenth century onward. In the *ancien regime* the family provided the model of rule, such that systems of alliance and exchange linked noble families together and within such families the *pater familias* ruled not just his immediate family, but his extended family and those of his household and estate, including servants, clients and workers. In contrast, from the eighteenth century onward, the population as a whole becomes the object of government. From this time on we see the emergence of a whole series of knowledges and technologies for governing national populations. Notably, statistical knowledge is able to provide an understanding of the totality of the population and to figure it as a quantifiable entity. Statistics, as a science of the state, is deployed in relation to the population, such that the population is seen to have its own regularities (rates of births, deaths, diseases, cycles of growth, and so on) (cf. Hacking, 1991). Statistics becomes used both as a means of analysing the habits and forms of conduct, laws and regularities of a population living within a territory and as a means of government (Foucault, 1981: 252). Moreover, at this time the population is seen as directly related to the economic (in terms of the generation of wealth, spirals of labour and so on). The economic is now seen as a distinct entity, having its own laws and forms of management, separate from the family and closely aligned to the population. Thus, Foucault talks of how, in the eighteenth century, the family shifts its function from a model of government to an object and instrument of government: 'the family considered as an element internal to population, and as a fundamental instrument in its government' (1991: 99).

More generally though, in the context of what Foucault refers to as bio-power, individuals and populations are governed increasingly from the eighteenth century according to their well-being, their welfare and their life. The objects, instruments and rationalities of government that grow and develop in support of these objectives also support and facilitate the extensive networks of power that connect state, individuals and populations (Donzelot, 1979; Foucault, 1980, 1981; Gordon, 1991; Pasquino, 1991). Foucault is careful not to conflate governmentality with state power and he defines government accordingly:

> 'Government' [in the sixteenth century] did not refer only to political structures or to the management of states; rather it designated the way in which the conduct of individuals or of groups might be directed: the government of children, of souls, of communities, of families, of the sick ... To govern, in this sense, is to structure the possible field of action of others. (1982: 221)

Government, then, is not one directly related to the power of the state or social structure nor to a counter-power of the individual, but to forms of power – for there are many types of power – that spread across many and diverse forms of social, political and cultural life. For Foucault this notion of government is to be understood quite simply in terms of the phrase 'the conduct of conduct'. Government refers to a set of practices, or actions, that are concerned with, and focused upon, the actions of oneself and others. But what are not specified in advance, a priori, are the agents, objects, and means of government. For Foucault these are all open questions; or rather they are only circumscribed within the limits of history.

Foucault himself never wrote about culture in and of itself and yet his work on the emergence of modern forms of power has been seen as centrally important for understanding the close correlation between culture and government from the eighteenth century onward. Foucault's genealogical discussion of government is significant for us because it provides the ground for an understanding of 'culture', not as a social universal (i.e. as something that is endemic to all societies, in the sense that all societies can be defined by their particular traditions, beliefs, ideas and semiotics) nor as a particular expression of the individual (i.e. in the sense of artistic genius, creative labour and so on), but as the object and means of regulation. An understanding of the historical and contemporary relevancy of the 'cultural' to government has been pursued in the writings of a group of academics, initially located in Australia in the early 1990s. The shift that was forged by these writers was to move from an understanding of a relation between culture and politics to one between culture and policy and from a general form of resistance to power to specific engagements with particular institutional and discursive forms of government. To this effect, the most programmatic of statements comes from Tony Bennett in his paper 'Putting policy into cultural studies' (1992a). Bennett looks to Raymond Williams' uncovering of the different definitions of culture – as a way of life, as the works and practices of artists, and as the process of intellectual, spiritual and aesthetic development – in the context of the industrial revolution and increasing demands for democracy

(Williams, 1958, 1965). But instead of agreeing with Williams' account, Bennett seeks to display more visibly the problematic of government in terms of the relation between culture and conduct. He argues that:

> Williams ... misses one of the most distinctive aspects of the late eighteenth and nineteenth century transformations in which the changing and conflicting semantic destinies of 'culture' are implicated. This consists in the emergence of new fields of social management in which culture is figured forth as both the *object* and the *instrument* of government: its object or target insofar as the term refers to the morals, manners, and ways of life of subordinate social strata; its instrument insofar as it is culture in its more restricted sense - the domain of artistic and intellectual activities - that is to supply the means of governmental intervention in and regulation of culture as the domain of morals, manners, codes of conduct, etc. (1992a: 26)

Understanding this series of connections allows Bennett to see the relation between culture as aesthetic practice and culture as way of life not as oppositional to each other, or such that the valorisation of the latter is held up against the elitism of the former, but rather in terms of their often mutual deployment and organisation within a field of government. Thus, instead of assuming that 'lived culture' and 'artistic genius' have some existence, in a realist sense, in the external world, Bennett takes the view that these entities only have an existence as categories, or objects of knowledge, or discursive techniques that are applied to individuals and populations in order to expose those individuals and populations as entities capable of being governed in a particular kind of way (i.e. as cultural). In Bennett's view, the idea that a lived culture exists out there in some tangible sense of being able to go and live in it (i.e. in the anthropological sense of living within a culture) is a fiction, an invention designed in order to make people and things manageable and orderable. Similarly, artistic genius or creative labour is not seen to reside in the mind of an individual or in a particular way of working, rather it too is a fiction, designed in order to assume that those capacities and dispositions can be developed in people and, in thus doing so, those people can be made better either in an educational, spiritual or economic way.

In this sense, for example, the rate of fire arms offences in urban areas might be seen not in economic terms as a problem of the availability of weapons due to the opening of national borders, but as constructed in cultural terms as a problem of 'gun culture'. In urban areas across the UK, Europe and the US, 'gun culture' is seen to be a problem. It is often constructed as a particular 'racial' and ethnic problem associated with non-white peoples, in the UK predominantly 'black' Jamaican, in the US, African-American, in France, North African. In the US and UK, it is also widely associated with types of music and lifestyle, for example, the 'bling-bling' style and hip-hop music. It is seen as emerging from particular cultural geographies: in the UK, the street, in the US, the ghetto, in France, *la banlieue*. These are cultural spaces in the sense that people come from the 'street'; they are loyal to the 'street'; their communities are formed in the 'street'. Moreover, this type of 'culture' is seen as a culture that produces a certain version of hyper-masculinity (and in that sense, also draws on the long lineage of racial stereotyping of young black males). As a cultural problem, then, it takes a particular form and thus also is seen to require certain forms of cultural intervention: how to attract young black men to a different culture with different aspirations and ways of living; how to get hip-hop artists to sing about different things; how to get young people off the street; how to get more young black men into learning, art, and schooling. In this sense, take the award winning British artist, Dizzee Rascal, who has been presented as a young black male who could have ended up in a life of crime were it not for his devoted school teacher who turned him onto making music rather than simply listening to it. Now the Rascal is held up as a success story, a moral example of the power of art to turn young people into heroes. Such racialised stories, then, can be seen as exemplary of the governmental effects of culture – as both the means and the end – and they can be seen to have a clear genealogical history (cf. Hunter, 1988a, b).

Bennett argues that the emergence of 'culture' 'is perhaps best thought of as a part of that process of the increasing governmentalization of social life characteristic of the early modern period which Foucault and others have referred to by the notion of *police*' (Bennett, 1992a: 26–7). In tying the emergence of culture in its modern sense to the development of the 'police' – in the sense of policing manners and conduct, but also of policy-making – Bennett makes the argument that in the eighteenth century we see the use of culture as an element in the thinking of government, in its rationality, applied strategically not just to the elite, but to the population as a whole. He argues that, in the Enlightenment period, artistic and intellectual practices can properly be thought of in relation to their being instruments of government and policing with regard to the population, as defined through its cultural being (i.e. its composition through culture as a particular form of living). Culture is understood, not as symbolic, but as administrative. Culture, in this sense, takes on a 'civilising' function in a much broader way than conceived by Elias (1994). In accepting culture in its Foucauldian guise – namely as defined through its relation to power as positive and productive, as micro-physical, as technical, as formed through the conduit of specific institutional and state agencies and centres of calculation (but not dominated by a mythical and unitary state agency or centre of reason) and as defined, not in terms of it forming the *prima causa* of government, but through its effects – Bennett takes us a long way from Williams and from many contemporary cultural theorists who readily understand culture as a social fact, as transhistorical and universal. As Bennett lucidly states:

> [C]ulture might be thought of, and its emergence accounted for ... as a particular surface of social management. This would involve a theoretical procedure different from those which seek to arrive at some transhistorical construction of the specificity of culture: as a particular level of social formations ... or as the domain of signifying practices, or as both lived cultures and textual practices and their interrelations. In their stead we would enjoin the need to think of culture as a historically produced surface of social regulation whose distinctiveness is to be identified and accounted for in terms of (i) the specific types of attributes and forms of conduct that are established as its targets, (ii) the techniques that are proposed for the maintenance or transformation of such attributes or forms of conduct, (iii) the assembly of such techniques into particular programs of government, and (iv) the inscription of such programs into the operative procedures of specific cultural technologies. (1992a: 26–7)

This, as Ian Hunter has declared, means putting limits on what we mean by 'culture' (1988b) and it means becoming more reflexive with regard to the place of cultural studies and other cultural sciences in the production and regulation of culture. It has also meant for some (Bennett, 1992a, b, 1998; Cunningham, 1992) that we should start engaging with power (or as Bennett hyperbolically put it, start 'talking to the ISAs'), engage in the policy process (rather than just produce critique), train cultural technicians (not critics), accept social democracy (and ditch the revolution), and forego any a priori political standpoints or strategies (i.e. don't privilege generalised and universal anti-racist, pro-feminist, etc., struggles, but identify a politics specific to particular institutions, such that what is political may not be defined in the first instance by those fundamental sociological categories of class, gender, sexuality, 'race' and ethnicity). Such a declared position has not been accepted easily within cultural studies (cf. Ang, 1992; O'Regan, 1992).

This said, before concluding, it's worth raising a different line of criticism, one maybe more sympathetic to the project, but more divergent in terms of its implications. In Bennett's essay 'Useful culture' (1992b), he is at pains to stress that he does not want to contest the history of Williams' account of the development of 'culture'; he only wants to question the implications of that history. Thus he says:

> I do not ... wish to question Williams's reading of the line of descent from Coleridge and Newman to Arnold and thence to Leavis. What I do want to question, however, is the assumption ... that an adequate definition of culture can be derived from such an analysis. (1992b: 396)

This is surprising not least because Williams offers a highly selective account of the history of culture, a journey from Coleridge to Leavis, from Romantic aesthetics to early twentieth century literary criticism. It is an account that is firmly located in the English national imaginary (cf. Gilroy, 1993b). Moreover, it is not an account that we see paralleled, say, in the sociological history offered by Elias (1994) or by the various anthropological genealogies of Stocking or Kroeber and Kluckholm (cf. Kuper, 2000). Moreover, given, as Bennett argues, we should look to the relation between culture, government and conduct, then one might have expected a different list of names, dates and historical problems (cf. Hunter, 1988a).

Cultural studies has traditionally looked at the relation between culture and people (as we will see in the following chapter). Culture has been understood either as a popular culture in contrast to high culture or as the lived experience of the people. For Bennett these categories and distinctions are important in telling a history of culture and power such that the lived experience of a nation becomes the object of power. But in many ways he is too quick to assume that the categories of 'the people' and 'the population' (as discussed by Foucault) can be elided, the former shadowing and providing the means of governing the latter. Unless one treats the two in a realist sense (i.e. that both terms refer to the same entity) or unless there are historical and empirical grounds for their correlation (and it is difficult to see, from the evidence presented, how they can be correlated) then we have to assume that both categories refer to different unrelated entities. Although a population can be said to have its own regularities (cycles of growth, birth rates, death rates, fertility rates, state of health, patterns of diet, habitation and so on) it is far from clear whether the same is true of 'culture'. This is not to say, necessarily, that culture is not caught up in the question of government, but maybe not quite in the way that Bennett makes the argument. As Foucault says quite clearly, '[g]overnments perceived that they were not dealing simply with subjects, or even with a "people", but with a "population", with its own specific phenomena and its peculiar variables' (Foucault, 1979: 25). The government of culture has been to a certain extent about the management of people, but to what extent is the people coextensive with the population? Popular culture, national culture, but population culture? To a large extent, 'culture' in both its aesthetic and anthropological sense has been resistant to any notion of it being quantifiable and intelligible through statistical knowledge. Only in recent years has culture been thought of in such a way, and then primarily in response to the need to make culture work for the economy. If, however, it is correct to talk of population culture, then we would need to know how the population was able to be conceived and acted on as a qualitative phenomenon. In this sense, then, we need to know more specifically not only what place government plays in the history of culture, but also what place culture plays in the history of government. Such a genealogy must do more than apply 'governmentality' as if it were a concept that could be deployed universally without an understanding of the singularity of its history.

If we accept that there is a history to be told of the relation between government and culture, then to what extent has this relation undergone changes as a consequence of shifts at the levels of both culture and government? It is something of an irony that at the moment when there are calls for putting limits on the definition and application of 'culture', 'culture' is more widely discussed, distributed and deployed than ever before. More or less everything has now become opened up to the cultural; everything can be viewed and analysed as cultural; everything – from shopping to gene transplantation, from the environment to space exploration, from computing to virtual sex – can be, and has been, seen to be a cultural construction and hence fit for cultural analysis. Moreover, this expansion of the cultural is much broader than that defined within the discipline and expertise of cultural studies, or even of the cultural sciences in the academy generally. It occurs across a whole range of professions and practices, including advertising, management consultants, economists, environmentalists and others. Given this indubitable phenomenon, any call to look at the singularity of the 'cultural' within the specificity of its institutional and practical milieu might be said to miss the fact of its dispersion, the equivalences across the differences.

We might also note some significant changes in the forms of government in late modernity that might be seen to impact upon the cultural, concerning, for example, the predominance of advanced liberalism, the underwhelming of the national as a central locus of power, and the growth and shifting dynamics of bio-power. First, Nikolas Rose, in his discussion of late modern governmentalities, identifies a significant shift in governmental technologies toward forms of advanced liberalism. Drawing from liberal and neo-liberal philosophies, from forms of consumerism, from therapeutic lifestyles, from new market technologies (e.g. concerning niche markets, etc.) and so on, Rose marks a shift in the way that we govern ourselves and others toward forms of government that are centrally pre-occupied with the self and forms of liberty. He talks importantly of power and government not as working against our freedom (or agency), but *through* it. In this sense, power is not opposed to freedom, rather freedom is the means for its continuation and extension (Rose, 1989, 1992a, b, 1993). Secondly, it has been a focus of major comment and research that the locus of the state, as correlated with the nation and its sovereignty, has been under question and threat for some time. Major governmental policy decisions are made at a supra-national level in relation to other nation-states or regional agencies or international agencies and in the framework of international laws and treaties. But equally, communication, interaction and decision-making are taking place across sub-national agencies within and across nation-states. Importantly also is the role played by transnational capital in late modern government. All this suggests that governmentality is now not simply a game of state or a matter of reasons of state concerned with a population historically defined within the territory of the nation. Thirdly, Foucault talks about the emergence of the population and forms of modern government in terms of bio-power. As we will see in chapter six, the question of bio-power is discussed in broader terms than that of the government of the social and political life of the population and implies the government of biological existence. In work that comes out of the cultural studies of science, these questions have been pushed and investigated in relation to, for example, issues of fertility and gene transplantation (Franklin, 2003a, b, Franklin and Roberts, 2001). In a paper on global nature and genetics Sarah Franklin puts her finger on the pulse:

> We are currently witnessing the emergence of a new genomic governmentality - the regulation and surveillance of technologically assisted genealogy. This is necessitated by the removal of the genomes of plants, animals and humans from the template of natural history that once secured their borders, and their re-animation as forms of corporate capital, in the context of a legal vacuum. This dual imperative, to take evolution in one hand and to govern it with the other, is a defining paradox of global nature, global culture. (2000: 188)

It is not the place to explore these issues here, but they become major points of discussion and elaboration in later chapters.

These issues concerning different types of government are interesting in themselves, but they should also act as provocations for thinking about new forms of relation between government and culture. Rather than simply reduce culture to government, they should also provoke us to think about cultures of government. If we only see culture as a 'surface of social regulation', then we lose any sense of how culture might be constitutive of our governmental thinking. In the correlation of culture and government, Bennett tends to collapse the former into the latter. In many ways though, Foucault - in talking about the discourses and practices of government - raises government to the level of culture. Although, as we've already stated, Foucault never discussed 'culture' as such, it could be argued that he implicitly treats government as a cultural object and opens government to the possibility of cultural analysis. The problem with Foucault is that he treats this culture in a very limited sense. He looks at the history of governmentality as a history of texts and documents and as an elite practice. What he doesn't do is to look at its enduring and changing cultural formation in a richer more detailed sense of culture as thought, but also artistic practice, semiosis, and lived culture. This space of the 'culture of government' is clearly open for new research. For example, what comprises the cultural practices of the World Trade Organization or the United Nations? What cultural resources do Whitehouse officials draw on in their day-to-day iterations of policy making? What common cultures (e.g. sport, art, food, taste and dress) are shared by heads of state and government leaders from across the globe? What about the culture of scientists? Does governmental science and technology policy reflect a common culture or a shared language between scientists and government decision-makers?

In some ways all the theoretical perspectives that we've considered over this chapter have a common problem with regard to the question of the relation between culture and power: namely, there is a tendency to import a pre-existing political analysis of power (whether Marxist, post-Marxist or Foucauldian) and to fit 'culture' within that model. In many ways these models presume that a distribution of resources precedes culture in the sense that culture simply firms-up existing structures of power. It is easy to conflate culture with the ideological or to assume that discourse is the same as culture or to see 'culture' as yet another effect of regimes of modern government. Certainly, such moves have their rewards, but we should also guard against them and instead think about what more such theories need to say in order to accommodate the detail and the complexity of what we know about culture. It is only by beginning to make this kind of step that we might begin to think about whether there is something distinct about 'cultural power' that is different from other kinds of power and whether the history of the relation between culture and power as briefly mapped out in this chapter from Gramsci to Foucault is actually an important genealogy in the history of cultural power. These are important questions and ones not easily resolved.

Chapter Summary

- One of the defining features of cultural studies has been an investigation of the relation between culture and power.
- An important strand of this has been to look at meaning and power in terms of the concept of ideology. The work of Antonio Gramsci and Louis Althusser has been central to this investigation.
- Gramsci understands power in terms of the state, which includes both political and civil institutions and practices.
  - A ruling class is seen to dominate society through its control of the state and through both coercion and leadership.
  - For Gramsci, no class can control the state without leading the people (i.e. through ideological, moral and cultural means).
  - Gramsci understands the politics of rule in terms of the balance of forces in society; a class can only rule through building an alliance of classes and forces; it does this through ideologically cementing them together.

  - Hegemony implies the ideological and cultural cementing of classes into a ruling bloc, but the direction of this leadership is such that it must combine both political goals and the common sense of the people, and it must offer the possibility of leading the people to a better life.

- Althusser also presents a theory of ideology.
  - He is interested in how a society divided by class can be reproduced: namely, how concrete individuals can be made to take up certain positions within established relations of power.
  - Althusser also talks of the state as repressive and ideological and has a similarly expansive definition to include both political and civil institutions.
  - Ideology works by interpellating individuals and turning them into ideological subjects whose relation to their real conditions of existence (i.e. the relations of power that govern their existence) is imaginary.

- In the context of a series of questions about cultural diversity, democracy and political change, Laclau and Mouffe draw on Gramsci, Althusser, and post-structural theory to understand how subjects are discursively constructed within relations of power and how such constructions allow the possibility of radical change.
  - Subjects are constituted in discourse, but the construction is never 'sutured' or sealed as such; through the mobilisation of different discourses and through making equivalences across discourses, power relations can be revealed, contested and changed.
  - Rather than understanding power and subjectivity in terms of a foundational biological or social order (e.g. with regard to class, race, ethnicity, gender and sexuality), Laclau and Mouffe argue that it is only because there is no foundation to either the social or the subject that radical democratic change is possible.

- Foucault, rather than subsuming relations of power to discourse, looks at discourse as only one element within an apparatus of power and organisation.
  - Although the notion of the apparatus has allowed cultural studies scholars to look at the micro-physics of power, it has also allowed them to consider the relations across macro- and micro-arrangements. Foucault has understood these arrangements in terms of the notion of governmentality.
  - Work on the relation between culture and government has argued that rather than see culture everywhere, it is important to place limits on culture and to look at how it specifically becomes a problem of government in specific contexts. Thus 'culture' is something that is invented as a particular problematic of rule and order.
  - In this framework, culture (in both its aesthetic and anthropological senses) is understood as both an object and instrument of government deployed in relation to individuals and the population.

- Contemporary questions about culture and government need to be reviewed in the context of changes toward advanced liberal government, globalisation and the growth of bio-powers.

FOUR Popular Culture: From People to Multitude

The discipline of cultural studies, in its relatively short history, has been concerned to a large extent with popular culture: namely, a form of culture that today carries the connotations of entertainment rather than high art, of ordinariness rather than eliteness, of standardisation rather than individuality, and of commercialism rather than community. Much interest in cultural studies has been predicated on a foregrounding and valorisation of popular culture as a sociological and anthropological, rather than an aesthetic, phenomenon. By and large, cultural studies has not sought to judge the artistic or moral value of popular culture, but to understand its social formation. Although some might claim that such culture can be typified by its simplicity, most academic investigation of the matter has indicated the complexity of the phenomenon. Thus, many texts on the topic remind us that any definition of popular culture is met with a residual difficulty. Moreover, many contemporary texts suggest that popular culture, far from having any fixed and solid definition, is an 'empty conceptual category', one defined only inasmuch as it is constructed within competing theoretical parameters and frameworks or inasmuch as it is shaped through the broader context of particular discursive oppositions (Storey, 1993; Strinati, 1995). This is undoubtedly correct, but if we also trace the genealogies through some of the different theoretical frameworks and through some of the broader discursive contexts, we can see the outline of a problematic concerning, not surprisingly, a question of the sovereignty of a nation-people. Raymond Williams notes an aspect of this problematic as follows:

> Popular was being seen from the point of view of the people rather than from those seeking favour or power over them. Yet the earlier sense had not died. Popular culture was not identified by the people but by others, and it still carries two older senses: inferior kinds of work (cf. popular literature, popular press as distinguished from quality press); and work deliberately setting out to win favour (popular journalism as distinguished from democratic journalism or popular entertainment); as well as the more modern sense of well-liked by many people, with which, of course, in many cases, the

> earlier senses overlap. The recent sense of popular culture as the culture actually made by people for themselves is different from all these; it is often displaced to the past as folk culture but it is also an important modern emphasis. (1976: 199)

Williams, here, refers to five ways of thinking about popular culture: a notion of popular culture as framed within a structural relation of power between ruling class and the people; an understanding of popular culture as a marker of bad taste and poor quality within the field of cultural distinction; a notion of popular culture as populist in the sense that it is used as a means of ideological persuasion; a notion of popular culture as popular in quantitative terms; and finally a notion of popular culture as that which is made through the craftwork of the people. In their different ways these different definitions index a series of questions and concerns, not just about a culture *of* and *for* the people, but about the authenticity, control and representation of that culture.

A concept of 'the people' has been defined, in its history within political theory and philosophy, by Hobbes, Rousseau, Locke and others, as that population which lives within territorial boundaries and which has a central role in the rule or sovereignty of itself and of things that happen in that land. Thus, for example, governments, whether they are actually true to the wishes and needs of a people, will often declare that they are acting on behalf of, and in the best interests of, that people. Historically, the people have been constructed within the space of the nation and they have been thought about in political theory in terms of the role they play in the government of that nation; for example, are they ruled over by a monarchical sovereign or do they themselves, as a collective body, have sovereignty; if they have sovereignty, is it through parliament or through direct forms of participation (cf. Held, 1989; Wagner, 2001b)? For some writers, the people pre-exist the social formation of nation and state. The unities of a people – including, for example, the unities of a common language and a common culture – form the natural bedrock of any nation-state. But for others, the idea of the people is not only one that is co-extensive with the idea of the nation, but also one that is 'a product of the nation-state, and survives only within its specific ideological context' (Hardt and Negri, 2000: 102). We might expect, then, that any questioning of the boundaries and sovereignty of the nation-state will rebound on our conceptualisation of 'the people'. The correlations across people, population, nation and state are worked and reworked through the contours of history and the dynamics of modernity. In the eighteenth and nineteenth centuries, transformations in the forces and mode of production underpinned the constitution of the people as a mass industrial working class, stabilised divisions of work and gender, and differentiated national populations along the lines of competition and colonial power. In the late nineteenth and early twentieth centuries, the emergence of mass democracy led to a questioning of the accepted boundaries of citizenship, class, and social position. From the mid-twentieth and early twenty-first centuries, post-industrialisation, postmodernisation and globalisation disturb, rearticulate and re-order 'the people' and this collectivity is now dislodged further, certainly from the territory of the nation, but also from the singularity of place itself: where a people 'come from' is a question that we find increasingly difficult to answer.

It is in this context, then, that we can understand how the problematic of popular culture rests upon a problematic of the people and their sovereignty. Debates about popular culture have tended to signify struggles over sovereignty within the domain of culture: How authentic is a popular culture? Who controls a popular culture? What are the relations of representation? This said, we might expect that any questioning of how we conceptualise 'the people' to rebound, equally, on our understanding of 'popular culture'. Cultural theory has undermined any stable notion of 'the people' as an empirically solid entity and has, likewise, raised questions about some common sense understandings of popular culture. Is popular culture an everyday phenomenon? Or does it exist only in fleeting moments of crisis? Are we witnessing the death of popular culture at the moment when we see the rise of a global consumer culture? Is a popular culture (defined as it is in relation to human people) also in decline as a consequence of the growing significance of new technological innovation and of a changing environment? Is popular culture dead because there is no longer a 'people' as such? Ironically, at the moment when 'popular culture' becomes a legitimate area of academic study, its grounding in broader social and political realities begins to fall by the way. Questioning of 'the people' and 'national sovereignty' in the context of, for example, debates about globalisation, multi-ethnicity and multi-culturalism, consumer culture, and new technology, has raised a big question-mark over the appropriateness of the category of 'popular culture' for understanding collective and common forms of culture. In this chapter we look at some of these debates and at the shifting understandings of popular culture; we look at how cultural studies has investigated the problem of popular culture in the context of neo-Gramscian cultural theory; and then we look at the notion of a common culture in the context, not of 'the people', but of the related idea of the multitude.

A Culture of the People

Culture, Civilisation and Nation

A modern understanding of culture is forged within the heated struggles and mappings of the nation-state. If we trace a history of the relation between 'culture' and 'civilisation' in the French and German traditions in the nineteenth century and the development of Romanticism therein, we see an ongoing concern about the nation. A German conception of 'culture', in contrast to a French understanding of 'civilisation' as material progress, carried the connotations of a deep organic nationalism. As Norbert Elias has shown: 'the German concept of *Kultur* places special stress on national differences and the particular identity of groups; primarily by virtue of this, it has acquired in such fields as ethnological and anthropological research a significance far beyond the German linguistic area and the situation in which the concept originated' (1994: 7). Culture became a rallying call in the nineteenth century to a radical Romantic attack on industrial capitalism. But it was also presented later in the century, and early in the next, as the barricade against a decadent and foreign civilisation. An organic national culture would stand firm against the barbarous hordes amassing at the gates. Elias states that: '[i]t is clear that the function of the German concept of *Kultur* took on new life in the year 1919, and in the preceding years, partly because a war was waged against Germany in the name of "civilisation" and because the self-image of the Germans had to be defined anew in the situation created by the peace treaty'. He continues: '[b]ut it is just as clear, and it can be proved, that to a certain extent the historical situation of Germany after the war only gave a new impulse to an antithesis which had long found expression through these two concepts [of *Kultur* and civilisation], even as far back as the eighteenth century' (1994: 9). It is not surprising, then, that some commentators looked to the nation as the site of a common culture. Moreover, a common national culture was seen as a popular culture inasmuch as it was a culture of the *Volk* (people). The German philosopher and poet, Johann Gottfried Herder, who introduces the category *Kultur* into a modern context in the late eighteenth century, for example, uses this term to describe the relation between culture and nation. The *Volk* were defined as an ontological unit through their inhabitation of the bounded territorial place of the nation and its culture. A popular culture is, in this anthropological sense, defined through a common set of beliefs, traditions and language. Anthropological definitions of culture and political forms of organisation thus combine in the nation (Wagner, 2001b). A culture of the people is differentiated from other national-popular cultures and is defined against the threat of foreign civilisation.

More recent commentators have argued that there is no pre-existing common culture of the people that forms the ground upon which a nation can emerge and a state administration develop. For example, the anthropologist Ernest Gellner, writing about the development of the modern nation and nationalism, argues that in agrarian societies there is no common culture. Social meaning is highly contextualised and local. Social interaction is, by and large, face-to-face. The majority of the population, living a daily peasant existence, is not only separate from other people in other local communities, but also distanced from a higher echelon of administrators, clerics, burghers and nobility. Moreover, according to Gellner, in pre-industrial societies this motley ruling class 'has no interest in promoting lateral communication between subject communities' (1983: 10). It is only from the eighteenth century onward, with industrialisation, that we begin to see the emergence of a notion of culture in its anthropological sense as a shared atmosphere (i.e. a common language or set of languages, beliefs and customs), but, importantly, one initiated from above rather than below. Gellner talks about the development of a common national culture in industrial modernity, in terms of its origins not from ordinary folk, but from the centralised authority of the state and from the centrality of its educational apparatus:

> Culture is no longer merely the adornment, confirmation and legitimation of a social order which is also sustained by harsher and coercive constraints; culture is now the necessary shared medium, the life-blood or perhaps the minimal shared atmosphere, within which alone the members of the society can breathe and survive and produce. For a given society, it must be one in which they can *all* breathe and speak and produce; so it must be the *same* culture. Moreover, it must now be a great or high (literate, training-sustained) culture, and it can no longer be a diversified, locality-tied, illiterate little culture or tradition. (1983: 37–8)

In Gellner's sense, then, a common national culture is not a culture from below, but one formed through the development of the modern nation-state. We can see how a popular culture is not necessarily antithetical to a high culture, but rather that the latter can be seen as the condition of existence of the former: a popular culture is born out of the high, elitist culture of a modern ruling class.

Such an approach can be very clearly contrasted with that of the English cultural critic Raymond Williams and others more firmly located within the traditions of cultural studies. Williams' work can be understood in the context of a peculiarly English sensibility concerning the aesthetic and high culture. In this genealogy, it is the work of the nineteenth century critic and educationalist Matthew Arnold, the English Romantic poets and writers (such as Coleridge, Blake and Shelley), and the early to mid-twentieth century literary critics (such as F. R. and Q. D. Leavis, and T. S. Eliot) who help to shape the debate. For Williams, the problem of culture is presented, to put it crudely, in terms of the relationships between high and popular culture, and aesthetic and anthropological notions of culture. On the one hand, culture is framed within the contours of relations of class and power in the sense that a cultural division can be seen between an elite and the people. On the other hand, culture is understood either as artistic form, sensibility and ethic, divorced from social and political existence but with the power to overcome social division, or as a 'whole way of life' that defines the milieu and activity of all people. Even though, as one commentator has pointed out, Williams holds these understandings in tension, his argument, made in various places and publications, is clearly directed toward the valorisation of ordinary, and hence working class and popular, culture (cf. Couldry, 2000: 23–4). In the triumphant march of the ordinary, a Romantic aesthetic notion of culture is respected, but only as a polite gesture, as if a knowing nod to one's enemy across a crowded room. Thus, for example, Williams, writing in Cambridge, England in 1958, ticks off some of his earlier fellow travellers for failing to recognise the Romanticism in their thinking about culture: 'In many Englishmen writing as Marxists I have noticed this. A tradition basically proceeding from the Romantics, and coming down through Arnold and Morris, has been supplemented by certain phrases from Marx, while continuing to operate in the older terms' (1958: 271). For Williams, these words are addressed to artists and intellectuals in the 1930s, misguided in thinking that they had some automatic affiliation with the struggles of the working class. This was the case of an English Romantic imagination, as always, thinking ahead of itself and one firmly rooted in high cultural ideals.

And yet, despite these and other comments by Williams, his notion of culture as ordinary has equally fed too richly on the fruits of a Romantic understanding of culture. Ian Hunter, in his work on culture, government and ethics, has argued that Williams' work fails to escape the pitfalls of Romantic aesthetics and that, as a consequence, the critical practice of cultural studies more generally is equally caught up in the ethical striving for resolution to the social and political conflicts and divisions of industrial modernity, such that 'a whole way of life' comes to figure as that teleological objective: namely, as a form of that healing (cf. Hunter, 1988a, b). Hunter's genealogical reading of Williams and cultural studies strikes at the heart of any explicit political project with regard to the people and popular culture. Nevertheless, in some sense, Williams' understanding of culture as ordinary can be read more prosaically as an attempt to reduce overblown claims about the power of art and artistic practice to the everyday world of ordinary action. In one sense, ordinary culture refers to a sociological understanding of culture, such that elite and mass cultures can be seen equally as ordinary, inasmuch as both are produced through particular, situated forms of labour. For example, even high art can be seen as ordinary inasmuch as the claims of a Romantic aesthetic (regarding spirit and genius) are disavowed in favour of an understanding of it as material practice. Such a move can be seen, in different form, in the sociology of science and technology. For example, science is seen not in terms of its Enlightenment claims regarding human progress and truth, but as a series of discrete material practices whose truth claims are immanent to those practices and not transcendent (cf. Latour and

Woolgar, 1979; Lynch, 1993; Lynch and Woolgar, 1990). In this sense of 'culture as ordinary', culture levels the population inasmuch as all practice is cultural practice; all practice is ordinary.

For Williams, though, the construction of all cultural practice as ordinary cultural practice is not intended to rid ordinary cultural practice of its creativity and experimentation, but precisely to argue that creativity and experimentation are important facets of all cultural practice and not simply limited to the 'arts' and high culture. In his 1958 essay 'Culture is ordinary', he states:

> A culture has two aspects: the known meanings and directions, which its members are trained to; the new observations and meanings, which are offered and tested. These are the ordinary processes of human societies and human minds, and we see through them the nature of a culture: that it is always both traditional and creative; that it is both the most ordinary common meanings and the finest individual meanings. We use the word culture in these two senses: to mean a whole way of life - the common meanings; to mean the arts and learning - the special processes of discovery and creative effort. Some writers reserve the word for one or other of these senses; I insist on both, and on the significance of their conjunction. The questions I ask about our society are questions about deep personal meanings. Culture is ordinary, in every society and in every mind. (1997: 6)

In this sense, the claim that culture is ordinary refers to a popular culture that is framed in opposition to an ideology of the aesthetic, an ideology of the ruling class and a lens through which all culture is viewed. This sense of 'popular culture' is directed, although not unequivocally, at the bastions of 'high culture', at forms of elitism (from technical languages to the development of a literary or artistic canon) and at the spokespeople of such a cultural sensibility (such as Arnold, Coleridge, Leavis, Eliot and so on). But if the ordinariness of ordinary culture is measured with reference to the baseline of 'all the people', then this 'people' comprises a national population and is grounded in the space of the nation: namely, in the space of culture in its bounded, anthropological sense. This said, if we simply understand the relation between culture and power in the context of the very English genealogy presented by Williams, we miss out on any critique of the Romanticism engrained in the notion of culture as ordinary and as a way of life and we fail to understand how this anthropological notion of culture, as is made clear in the critique of *Bildung* and *Kultur*, dangerously cedes any notion of culture as organic to nineteenth and early twentieth century nationalism.

Mass Culture as Commercial and 'American'

The late nineteenth century and the early twentieth century saw the rise of forms of productive technologies and knowledges that facilitated the mass production of products (Aglietta, 1979). The classic apocryphal example is Henry Ford's Model-T motor car – 'any colour as long as it's black' – that was produced, not by a team of craftsmen working on the car from start to finish, but on an assembly line where each worker would contribute only to the making of a small part of the car according to their particular specialised skills. Mass production thus relied on the invention of new knowledges of production and organisation, most notably the development of scientific rationalism or Taylorism brought with it an understanding of production along the lines of time and motion studies. Mass production, though, needed mass consumers. The Model-T was made more cheaply because of increased economies of scale and hence it was more affordable to buy for larger numbers of the population. And with mass production and consumption also came mass media and advertising. The products needed to be sold in the newly formed consumer markets. The growing mass culture was a correlate of a growing mass media (film, print, radio, television), which in turn was consumed by an increasingly homogenous industrial working class (the masses). In this sense, then – in the context of a narrative of, what we can refer to as, Fordist economic, political, social and cultural organisation – we can see how concerns about mass culture stand in the face of massive social and economic change.

The longer historical context for these changes also puts into view a gendering of mass culture. Industrial modernity is noted for taking paid production out of the home and putting it in the public domain. The gendering of labour thus places men in a public realm of paid labour and women in the private realm of unpaid labour. The process of massification in the late nineteenth and early twentieth centuries constructs the home as the key site of consumption and constructs 'woman', as mother and housewife, and as the central consumer. The mass media of radio and television direct their attention to the domestic realm, to its times, spaces, and forms of conduct. In this sense, soap opera can be seen as the quintessential cultural form of Fordist industrial modernity inasmuch as, from its early days on radio to its current form on television, it combines commercialism and indefinite serial form with an address to the domestic and the woman at home (cf. Brunsden, 1981; Modleski, 1982). Thus some commentators have talked about 'mass culture as feminine', for example, in contrast to supposedly 'serious' masculine arts and passtimes (cf. Huyssen, 1986; Modleski, 1986). Of course, critics have also commented on the problem of talking in this way about mass culture as both a feminine and devalued culture inasmuch as such talk uncritically assumes certain stereotypical notions of the 'feminine' and equally stereotypical ideas about the practices of cultural consumption.

In contrast to a series of fears about the displacement of the human and the spiritual in the movement of unstoppable machinery in industrial modernity, from the early twentieth century onward we see a series of concerns and fears about the crass debasement of culture by commerce. The writing of Richard Hoggart – who was an influential figure in the shaping of British cultural policy and who, with a young Stuart Hall, set up the Centre for Contemporary Cultural Studies at Birmingham University in the 1960s and nurtured the early development of cultural studies – is symptomatic of these concerns. In his *The Uses of Literacy* (1958 [1957]), Hoggart presents a major defence of traditional masculine working-class culture in the face of massive social and cultural change. He presents a description of an authentic ordinary folk culture of the English working class embattled against mass culture and Americanisation. He makes no secret of his prejudices. For Hoggart, America takes on the mantle of the debased, materialistic edge of modern civilisation threatening the borders of an English national culture:

> The strongest argument against modern mass entertainments is not that they debase taste – debasement can be alive and active – but that they over-excite it, eventually dull it, and finally kill it ... They kill it at the nerve, and yet so bemuse and persuade their audience that the audience is almost entirely unable to look up and say, 'But in fact this cake is made of sawdust'. (1958: 197)

Hoggart conjures up crude and nostalgic images of English working-class life (such as a trip to the seaside) that are set against the 'shiny barbarism' of American mass entertainment, milk bars, popular music and fashion:

> [C]ompared even with the pub around the corner, this is all a peculiarly thin and pallid form of dissipation, a sort of spiritual dry-rot amid the odour of boiled milk. Many of the customers – their clothes, their hairstyles, their facial expressions all indicate – are living to a large extent in a myth-world compounded of a few simple elements which they take to be those of American life. (1958: 204)

Hoggart's analysis was based largely on highly subjective descriptions – albeit ones that were rich and detailed – and his understanding of industrial modernity and culture was thus powerful, but ultimately lacking validity. His understanding of popular culture was one that was split between a 'mass culture' that was degrading and anti-popular (inasmuch as it was produced outside of the home nation and sought to undermine that home nation) and a 'folk culture' that was born of the home nation, authentic in its relation to the people as ordinary folk and that was analysed in literary and nostalgic, as opposed to social scientific, terms and motifs.

From a different perspective, the work of the Frankfurt School, and Theodore Adorno and Max Horkheimer in particular, has provided a sophisticated, if somewhat maligned, analysis of the problem of massification and modernisation. In the context of their flight from Nazi Germany and their brief settlement in the US, Adorno and Horkheimer talk about 'the culture industry' in terms of an instrumental rationalisation that standardises culture and subsumes the individual within the capitalist machine (1979). Thus Adorno states:

> In all its branches, products which are tailored for consumption by masses, and which to a great extent determine the nature of that consumption, are manufactured more or less according to plan. The individual branches are similar in structure or at least fit into each other, ordering themselves into a system almost without a gap. This is made possible by contemporary technical capabilities as well as by economic and administrative concentration. The culture industry intentionally integrates its consumers from above. To the detriment of both it forces together the spheres of high and low art, separated for thousands of years. The seriousness of high art is destroyed in the speculation about its efficacy; the seriousness of the lower perishes with the civilizational constraints imposed on the rebellious resistance inherent within it as long as social control was not yet total. Thus, although the culture industry undeniably speculates on the conscious and unconscious state of millions towards which it is directed, the masses are not primary but secondary, they are an object of calculation, an appendage of the machinery. The customer is not king, as the culture industry would have us believe, not its subjects but its object. (1991: 85)

Adorno laments the destruction of high art, not in nostalgic terms, but in terms, resonant of Kant's discussion in *The Critique of Judgement* (1952), that the aesthetic provides the possibility of freedom. In contrast, the culture industry – that typified by mass culture and mass entertainment – reproduces the enslavement of a population, a people made base and vulgar (in both a spiritual and bodily sense):

> [T]he total effect of the culture industry is one of anti-enlightenment, in which, as Horkheimer and I have noted, enlightenment, that is the progressive technical domination, becomes mass deception and is turned into a means of fettering consciousness. It impedes the development of autonomous, independent individuals who judge and decide consciously for themselves ... while obstructing the emancipation for which human beings are as ripe as the productive forces of the epoch permit. (Adomo, 1991: 92)

For Adorno and Horkheimer mass culture is not only a culture imposed on individuals, but one that constructs the 'mass' as a form of standardised imprisonment and massified false consciousness. In this understanding of a common culture of the people, what is popular is only so by virtue of its capacity to address a fictionalised lowest common denominator and to imagine an audience that consumes only inasmuch as it is infantilised (cf. 1991: 91). Such a collectivity is one that is denied its sovereignty. For Adorno and Horkheimer, it is the culture industry that is king, not the people.

Popular Culture and Democracy

Herbert Gans prefaces his 1974 'sociological study of popular culture and high culture' by declaring that his is a defence of popular culture against those who see only high culture as culture and who always see popular culture as a 'dangerous mass phenomenon'. He states that he intends to study both high and popular culture from the same sociological perspective and to use the same 'conceptual apparatus':

> The apparatus itself is sociological, but it rests on two value judgements: (1) that popular culture reflects and expresses the aesthetic and other wants of many people (thus making it culture and not just commercial menace); and (2) that all people have a right to the culture they prefer, regardless of whether it is high or popular. (1974: vii)

In construing both high and popular culture as 'aesthetic' and making both equally worthy of study, Gans makes a similar move to that of the left-Leavisites (as demonstrated in Stuart Hall and Paddy Whannel's *The Popular Arts*, 1964). Popular culture is not to be discriminated against from the position of high culture; on the contrary, it is to be understood and discriminated from within. If culture is the level playing field upon which such distinctions between high and popular might be constructed, then both forms of culture may be analysed, discussed and judged using the same critical vocabulary. Furthermore, the growth of the mass media (such as print, film, television and radio) could be seen to facilitate democracy through the dissemination of works of culture from which large numbers of people have been excluded. Thus, instead of 'great works of art' being couched in the aura of untouchable genius, of something unable to be understood by the mass of ordinary people, the mass media can be seen to make such works available to all. The mass media reproduce those works in a new medium - Shakespeare on film, Mozart on the radio, Milton on television- and level their imposing authority; they become available to all and all are able to have their say and judgement as to the value of those works (cf. Benjamin, 1973).

Gans is equally concerned about the relation between cultural distinction and democracy. But for Gans, the valorisation of popular culture puts all culture on an equal footing. He claims that such an approach provides an argument for 'cultural democracy and an argument against the idea that only the cultural expert knows what is good for people and for society' (1974: vii). For Gans, as for others, popular culture is not a unitary, standardised and homogenous phenomenon. Popular culture refers, not to *the* culture of a people, but to the culture*s* of many different people. His argument, then, is not only that popular culture, as against high culture, is of value, but that culture is necessarily plural:

> [T]he strongest stimulus for more cultural pluralism will come from the users of culture. The continued existence of social and political movements among racial and ethnic minorities, women, adolescents, young adults, blue collar workers, and others and their rising interest in new roles and identities is likely to enhance both their need for new culture and their cultural creativity. In addition, the growing diversity of interests and the search for new means of self-expression among much of the rest of the population, together with the possibility of more leisure time in the future if the workday or the workweek are reduced, may also create a greater demand for more and more diverse culture. (1974: 158)

Gans articulates a popular culture – one resonant of Williams' sense of culture as witness to the 'extraordinary multiplicity' of human life – that is plural and diverse and that reflects the sociological complexity of a modern people. His argument for cultural democracy is an attempt also to reflect that complexity and to return any understanding and control of popular culture back to that people. And yet, although these people are sovereign, they are, nevertheless, tied to the long genealogy of the modern nation.

Making the Popular: Strategy and Populism

Much of this earlier discussion sets the context for debate in the 1980s that seeks not only to valorise, but to 'deconstruct the popular' (Hall, 1981). Writers such as Stuart Hall, Tony Bennett and others, sought to frame popular culture within a neo-Gramscian problematic: namely, within an intellectual context in which any determinate substance to the popular was seriously undermined at the same moment that its structural positionality was seen to be crucial to a hegemonic socialist and progressive politics. In this sense, the authenticity and veracity of a popular culture was not to be measured through an anthropology of the people. Instead, popular culture was seen to provide the cultural and ideological space within which 'a people' could be politically constructed and mobilised. This intellectual move involved: first, understanding 'the people' in constructivist, not realist, terms; secondly, disarticulating 'the people' from 'popular culture', such that the former is analysed as a consequence of the practices of the latter; and thirdly, disarticulating 'the people' from the territorial land of a nation (i.e. seeing the 'nation' and 'nation people' as ideological constructions) at the same time as construing popular culture as always a 'nation-popular' culture.

Some of the discussions of popular culture referred to in the previous section might be typified as understanding the people and culture in realist terms. Some writers talk about popular culture as if we could walk into a shop and pick out the items that could be labelled 'popular culture' and those labelled 'high culture'. Similarly, there are some writers who talk about popular culture as if it bore some correlation with 'the people', as if 'the people' were easily identifiable as a group of real individuals, with forms of collective consciousness, conduct, tastes, sensibilities, and pleasures. Moreover, some writers seek to praise popular culture on the basis that it is the authentic expression of a people and that it is formed in opposition to dominant structures of power and elitist forms of cultural expression. One of the forms that this understanding of the popular takes is as, what Jim McGuigan terms, an 'uncritical populism'. This implies, first that 'the intellectual assumption, made by some students of popular culture, that the symbolic experiences and practices of ordinary people are more important analytically and politically than Culture with a capital C' (1992: 4), and, secondly, that such a popular culture should not only be valorised, but lauded for its resistance to forms of power and commodification. An example of such an approach might be seen when Tessa Jowell, UK Minister for Culture, Media and Sport, declared in 2004 that those who were critical of moves to permit more gambling in the UK were being 'elitist' and 'snobbish'. In doing so, the minister not only posed the debate in terms of a defence of the pleasures and pastimes of 'ordinary people' (as if such people existed out there in the real world), but also connected debate to a longer history of how such entertainments have been discursively codified as 'American' (as we have seen in the work of Hoggart). Thus, a populist defence of ordinary people is also seen to be a defence against anti-American and, hence also, English nationalist sympathies.

McGuigan's argument is, in part, ranged against writers within the neo-Gramscian tradition in cultural studies, but to a large extent it is precisely these writers who have been most critical of such a populism and who have attempted to disclose 'popular culture' and 'the people' not as naturalist or realist categories, but as strategic entities defined only in the moment of politics. Of importance in this respect is the work of Ernesto Laclau on 'populism' (1977). Laclau's work is centrally important for understanding the Gramscian framing of popular culture and for understanding other writers whose work emerges out of this frame. Laclau's essay on populism is very much within political theory and hence the examples he uses are ones from the domain of formal politics. In so doing, they raise a stark contrast with many examples and cases that we might ordinarily associate with popular culture, such as those from the mass media of television, popular music and film. In Laclau's sense of the term, 'populism' might be described as that mix of traditional and modern contents which we see in the populist political movements or formations of Hitler's or Mussolini's fascism or Mao's nationalist ideological attacks against the Japanese or Thatcher's phobia about the flooding of 'English' identity or Bush Junior's mix of American imperial republicanism (as drawn from classical Roman empire) and modern military might.

Laclau maintains a strong correlation between 'class' and 'the people', not in the sense that the latter can simply be collapsed into or reduced to the former, but in the Gramscian sense that the 'national-popular' constitutes a site of prime importance for political struggle in modern industrial societies (whether capitalist or socialist or fascist). Laclau states that in political mobilisation or articulation 'each class presents itself as the authentic representative of "the people", of "the national interest"' and 'classes exist at the ideological and political level in a process of articulation and not of reduction' (1977: 161). According to Laclau, hegemonic mobilisation requires the articulation of elements that have both a class and a non-class character - namely, some elements carry the interests of the class (whether working, bourgeois or peasant class), other elements might be seen as having no particular class attachment - but also must carry sections of the dominated as well as the dominant class with it. According to Laclau, hegemony defines the attempt to iron-out potential antagonisms and contradictions through this mix.

For Laclau, then, populism is not something that is endemic to a particular class or can only be defined through a reduction of its content to a particular class; it is defined through a common appeal to 'the people', an appeal that is above class division. In this sense, to talk about a television programme as populist would not be to say that it is an expression of, for example, a bourgeois class or that the content and style of the programme are somehow middle class, but to say that the programme is addressed to and appeals to a broad community of people. For Laclau populism draws on popular traditions, but these popular elements by themselves do not carry any consistent and systematic connotations (e.g. with regard to class or, more generally, power). But these popular traditions are not arbitrary and carry some enduring, although politically indeterminable, qualities: '[t]hey are the residue of a unique and irreducible historical experience and, as such, constitute a more solid and durable structure of meanings than the social structure itself' (1977: 167).

In conditions of industrial modernity appeals to 'the people' have largely been correlated with appeals to 'the nation'. Thus, prior to its undoing, Bush Junior's appeal to the common people is also an appeal to support him as a strong leader. Bush was seen to be 'straight-talking', 'ordinary' and 'flawed'; and it was because of these ideological connotations, as a part of his populist appeal, that he was able to address both the people and the national interest. Bush was thus seen to be the man to sort out American foreign policy in the best interests of the US. But to stress this reading of Bush is precisely not to downplay the fact that it is US corporate interests that have been best served in the building of Iraq or in the proliferation of the arms trade through increased military budgets, not just in the US, but globally (friend and foe alike buying US-made weaponry and military know-how). To argue that Bush was a populist leader, who had popular appeal and who addresses the nation as a people, is not to deny, then, that these appeals carried the interests of class and capital.

Laclau argues that not all appeals to 'the people' are populist and that a discourse is only populist if it is appealing to the people, antagonistic to the dominant ideology, and 'democratic'. Populism, then, needs to be seen to contest the dominant power bloc. But, Laclau argues, it can do so in ways that may benefit the dominant classes as much as the dominated classes. Laclau refers to two senses of antagonism to the dominant power bloc: first, if the dominant bloc experiences a 'profound crisis', a new class fraction mobilises different classes across society in order to take advantage of this crisis; and secondly, if through popular struggle the dominated classes assert and win popular-democratic rights. In the first case, we might refer to Augusto Pinochet's overthrow of Salvadore Allende's Socialist Government in Chile on 11 September 1973 by mobilising popular support from the middle classes, upper working classes and the petit bourgeois classes. A crisis in the dominant power bloc allowed a right-wing party to take power. In the second case, we might refer to the growth of the Italian Communist Party after the Second World War and how, through populist appeals, it gained some democratic control. But although Laclau makes the argument that populism can take both dominant and dominated forms, it is the latter that is seen to be more consistently popular-democratic:

> If classes cannot be hegemonic without articulating 'the people', 'the people' only exist articulated to classes. The degree of 'populism', therefore, will depend on the nature of the antagonism existing between the class which is struggling for hegemony and the power bloc ... Therefore, the only social sector which can aspire to the full development of 'the people' power bloc contradiction, that is to say, *to the highest and most radical form of populism*, is that whose *class interests* lead it to the suppression of the State as an antagonistic force. *In socialism, therefore, coincide the highest form of 'populism' and the resolution of the ultimate and most radical of class conflicts*. The dialectic between 'the people' and classes finds here the final moment of its unity, there is no socialism without populism, and the highest forms of populism can only be socialist. (1977: 196-7)

Laclau's account of populism provides a significant point of contrast to and comparison with the work of other neo-Gramscian cultural theorists (such as Stuart Hall, Tony Bennett and Colin Mercer). By-and-large the neo-Gramscian moment in cultural studies in the 1980s typifies a scepticism (although by no means in any straightforward way) about claims concerning the power of the people and popular culture. Thus, in a gesture that is repeated across a number of these writers (see, for example, Fiske, 1987: 310, 1989: 24), Bennett states:

For, contrary to what appears to be its givenness and concreteness as a determinate range of cultural forms and practices, it is not possible to specify what popular culture is, or to determine what should be included within it, without first or simultaneously specifying what is *not* popular culture' (1986b: 16)

And Bennett quotes Hall:

Anybody who says 'popular culture' doesn't need to say: 'as opposed to unpopular culture, elite culture, or folk culture, traditional culture, or aristocratic culture, or whatever.' They leave that other bit absent so that it looks fuller as a term than it actually is. But unless we know what it is that it's being contrasted with, we do not get a picture of the whole field of which popular culture is, by definition, only a part ... So you have to know what it's working along with before you know what it's doing. (1986b: 16)

In a sense that certainly contrasts with Laclau's understanding of 'popular traditions', popular culture is understood in a way that foregrounds its relationality to other 'cultural' categories and thus makes visible its differential character. Popular culture is not simply defined as mass culture, folk culture or low culture and, moreover, it is not ascribed an essential form with regard to the structures of power relations. Bennett, Mercer and Woollacott argue that the neo-Gramscian turn 'would belie the assumption, dear to many forms of contemporary cultural politics, that there exists a ready-formed oppositional culture of "the people", a culture ready to burst out, a culture which would allow "the people" to assume, at last, their historically repressed identity' (1986: 3). Nevertheless, the popular and the people hold the potential – given their social, cultural and historical formation – to attract individuals and groups across demographic particularities, such as class, gender, sexuality and 'race' and ethnicity:

[P]opular culture cannot be defined in terms of some pre-given sense of 'the people' or 'the popular', for the meaning of these terms is caught up with and depends on the outcome of the struggles which comprise the sphere of popular culture ... The point is not to define 'the people' but to *make* them, to make that construction of 'the people' which unites a broad alliance of social forces in opposition to the power bloc count politically by winning for it a cultural weight and influence which prevails above others. (Bennett, 1986b: 19–20)

Thus, although disavowing any essentialist understanding of the popular, the neo-Gramscians nevertheless do pose the popular in terms of its structural relation to the dominant power bloc. The popular is defined in terms of its political potential. The popular is that structural space between dominant and dominated; it is the space of hegemony. But equally the popular is defined in terms of its oppositional capacity and inasmuch as its having no place in the dominant culture (cf. Bennett, 1986a, b; Fiske, 1989).

In the Gramscian and neo-Gramscian framework, the popular is significant inasmuch as it offers both a strategic resource (i.e. in terms of mobilising and delivering particular forces in the mechanics of power) and the basis of an ethical resolution (i.e. in the sense that through the popular we close the gap of power itself). In Gramsci this is clear, as we saw in the previous chapter, in his conception of 'common sense' and the need to carry that sense into the process of working-class hegemony. In Laclau it is clear in his argument that the highest form of socialism is populism and the highest form of populism is socialism. In Hall and Bennett, such a dialectical understanding of the popular falls into the background, but it is still there inasmuch as it establishes the strategic (not ethical) priority and potential that the popular has as an oppositional resource. We might note here that even in Bennett's later Foucauldian work, the people and the popular are conceived primarily as strategic resources. As we saw in the previous chapter, the popular is conceived as having a privileged place in the orchestrations of power and cultural government (Bennett, 1992a, b). For Bennett, the aesthetic and the popular notions of culture provide the means and mechanisms for thinking about and acting upon individuals and populations. In the Foucauldian framework, then, the people and the popular don't so much provide resources for resistance and counter hegemony, as instruments and objects of regulation. The government of culture is now an administrative and technical, not symbolic and ideological, matter.

The neo-Gramscian, but also the Foucauldian, perspective – in assuming that 'the people' and 'the popular' are not pre-existent and are only made for strategic purposes – is thus constructivist. It does not conceive of the people and the popular in realist terms. An important consequence of this is that it understands the popular not as ordinary and everyday, but as an exceptional achievement. 'The people' are not pre-given, but built through struggle, only occurring at particular social, political, and historical moments. This is clearest in the work of Laclau who talks of populism as happening at moments of hegemonic crisis (1977). In his later work with Chantal Mouffe, he argues that popular struggles are only seen to occur at 'specific conjunctures resulting from the multiplication of equivalence effects among democratic struggles' (Laclau and Mouffe, 1985: 137). In a different sense, in the Foucauldian understanding of culture developed by Bennett, the deployment of 'the people' and 'the popular' is a rarefied activity inasmuch as the production of knowledge is not seen as an activity readily available to all (cf. Foucault, 1972) and the practices of the government of culture are limited to particular expert and skilled persons. A constructivist approach – although in some ways seeming to bear a close affiliation with earlier approaches to popular culture (such as that developed by Williams) – marks a stark contrast. In many ways, it is the 'turn to Gramsci' in the 1980s that initiates this radical re-conception of 'popular culture' and paves the way for later approaches, such as that pursued by the Foucauldians. The turn to Gramsci, then, makes possible an understanding of the space of the popular as defined through a series of negative propositions: not dominant; not constant; not common; and not everyday. Popular culture, is, in this sense, extraordinary.

This said, some fellow travellers have taken to heart an understanding of the popular in terms of its structural location within relations of hegemonic power. Some, perhaps, have been more radically swayed by Laclau's claim that populism is the highest form of socialism. And some have continued to think of popular culture both as ordinary and as understood in the context of an anthropology of the people.

The confluence of these paths has led some cultural critics to proclaim the ongoing subversive power of the people and of popular culture, as if 'the people' had both political veracity and anthropological consistency. Paul Willis, for example, has argued that ordinary everyday practices are in and of themselves creative and resistant to power inasmuch as meaning is always produced not at the point of production, but at the point of consumption or reception: 'how (objective) subordination is sometimes lived (subjectively) as celebration' (1990: 156). Whatever the ideological message encoded in a cultural text at the level of production (e.g. in the editorial offices of a newspaper or the floor of a television studio), its interpretation and use at the level of consumption (e.g. by the person in the subway or in their home watching television) is only determined at that level: namely, in the context of the symbolic resources of ordinary, yet creative, people. This takes Hall's analysis of the encoding and decoding of media messages (Hall, 1980), removes the contingency of conjunctural historical and structural forces (such that there might be a structural relation between an encoded ideological message and the acceptance of that message at the level of decoding), and makes the popular and the ordinary a priori sites of creativity and resistance. But for Willis there is not simply a two-way relation between producers and consumers of culture, but multiple and different horizontal connections and circulations; messages are remade and passed on. This is seen as symptomatic of an 'inherently democratic' aspect of common culture, one that emerges now in the context of a historical narrative of 'cultural modernisation' (1990: 139). Culture is levelled in the 'extraordinary symbolic creativity of the multitude' (1990: 2).

In a similar vein, John Fiske has championed the 'progressive', not 'revolutionary', nature of popular culture (1989). In his book on *Television Culture* (1987), he makes a contrast between the moments of production and consumption and he argues that '[f]or a cultural commodity to be popular, then, it must be able to meet the various interests of the people amongst whom it is popular as well as the interests of its producers' (1987: 310). Fiske argues that 'the power of audiences-as-producers in the cultural economy is considerable' (1987: 313). But that power does not take the shape of a homogenous resistance to dominant social and political forces:

> As social power can take many forms, so too can the resistances to it. There is no singular blanket resistance, but a huge multiplicity of points and forms of resistance, a huge variety of resistances. These resistances are not just oppositions to power, but are sources of power in their own right: they are the social points at which the powers of the subordinate are most clearly expressed. (1987: 316)

A television advertisement for beer might be noted and its caricatures of masculinity slavishly adopted in order to reproduce someone's idea of the ideal man (in a kind of Duff beer and Homer Simpson scenario) or it might be turned off before it gets a chance to get to the second scene due to the invidious stereotypes that it is seen to portray or its sing-a-long tune might be 'subversively' re-written in a children's playground. For Fiske, then, the potential for interpretation and re-interpretation – or in his suggestive term 'provocation' – is indefinite. Fiske doesn't work so much with a top-down model as with a centre-periphery and a singularity-multiplicity model that he gets in part from Bakhtin:

> Resisting this [ruling ideology] is the diversity of social groups with their diversity of social interests. Their power is expressed in the resistances to homogenization, it works as a centrifugal rather than a centripetal force, it recognizes conflict of interest, it proposes multiplicity over singularity and it may be summed up as the exercise of power to be different. (1987: 317)

Resistance to power takes the form of a multiplicity as a movement away from the centre. But Fiske also draws on the work of the French anthropologist, Michel de Certeau, in his understanding of the practices of everyday life and the tactical resistances to strategic power formations. De Certeau's anthropology of the popular is framed against a Foucauldian vision of modern technologies of power. For de Certeau, everyday use, at a highly localised level, demonstrates the glorious resistances of the weak. For de Certeau, the architects may build the cities, but it is the people who walk their streets in whatever way they choose (1984). For Fiske, de Certeau offers an analytical framework for interpreting popular culture and everyday life.

Fiske's analysis is itself provocative and certainly more sophisticated than is often recognised by his critics. Nevertheless, inasmuch as it uncritically lauds the resistance of the people and the popular, it is open, in some respects, to the criticism that McGuigan makes of 'uncritical populism'. But McGuigan's response to such Fiskean populism is a *critical populism* which is seen to 'account for *both* ordinary people's everyday culture *and* its material construction by powerful forces beyond the immediate comprehension and control of ordinary people' (1992: 5). And yet, it is precisely this attempt to bring together an account of ordinary people's cultural life with a hegemonic understanding of relations of power that constitutes the kernel of Fiske's analysis and the seed of the problem. In many ways, this mix repeats in different form that earlier synthesis of Romanticism and Marxism that so troubled Williams. For Fiske, on the one hand, an anthropological conception of the people grounds the possibility of resistance to power within the ordinary and the everyday; on the other hand, the practices of the people are only understood as resistant inasmuch as a hegemonic model of power prevails. In contrast to Fiske, earlier neo-Gramscian critics, such as Hall and Bennett, downplayed any anthropological notion of the people, foregrounded a constructivist reading, and thus understood popular culture only in the context of an ongoing series of political strategies. The neo-Gramscians are far from uncritical populists. Despite the shadow of hope of a long-awaited socialism-populism, their attention to construction, mobilisation and political exigency place them emphatically in the camp of 'sceptical populism'.

Beyond Sovereignty: A Culture of the Multitude?

If 'the people' are denuded of any substantial qualities over and above a capacity to mobilise different collectivities into a hegemonic force, then its import seems to become purely rhetorical. Its capacity seems to lie only in its persuasive power. If this is so, then we might wonder how it is possible to conjure a collective body into existence unless the constituent elements lend themselves to such a construction and also question whether 'the people' is still able to deliver what it once promised. Is popular culture more than a strategic foil? And have conditions changed, such that appeals to 'the people' no longer work the magic they, perhaps, once did? A number of writers have argued that in the post-Second World War period, intensifying in the 1970s, we have seen a shift toward forms of post-Fordist economic, social, political and cultural organisation (cf. Amin, 1994; Hall and Jacques, 1989; Kumar, 1995; Murray, 1989). This shift can be seen across a broad array of sites of production, consumption, technological innovation, new forms of knowledge and social organisation. For example, the computerisation of car factories and the development of robotic technologies has meant that cars can be built at lower cost, in shorter product runs, and more highly individualised. Whereas the product life of a car (i.e. how long the car sits in the showroom before a new model or specification comes out) in the 1980s might have been measured in years, it is now measured in months. Even consumers of mass market Ford motor cars have a choice of wheels, air-conditioning, surround sound and so on. Products and services, once directed to a mass audience, are now pitched to particular lifestyles or niche markets, defined not only through the mass demographics of age, class (income and education), sex or ethnicity, but through the cultural markers of particular tastes, hobbies, and interests. Even the quintessential mass medium of television faces an identity crisis as it meets different technologies of production, distribution and exhibition; there are a plethora of channels addressed to different ideal types of consumers, scheduled by the individual consumer. And as cultural products and services become more individualised, they also become more globalised. For example, pre-school children's television programmes, such as *Teletubbies* or *Blues Clues*, make money not on any individual national market, but on a series of discriminated global markets. If a popular culture is one that is, in part, derived from the large numbers of people that consume it and if people now consume products and services at a level below and above the nation (i.e. as individual consumers and as segmented, global groups), then perhaps we are witnessing the decline of popular culture as a culture of 'the people'.

If we align popular culture with consumer culture, then we might come to the conclusion that there is no longer any authentic common popular culture. Certainly much work in cultural studies from the 1980s onward has tended, implicitly and explicitly, to understand popular culture as a consumer culture. Certainly both Fiske and Willis make such an elision and this is, in part, the point of criticism for McGuigan. And yet, this alignment is one that has not always been made. For example, if we return to Williams' discussion of 'culture as ordinary' in 1958, he talks of work, but little of consumption, or rather he talks about the latter only in the context of the ordinary practices of the former. He talks of the work of his family, of the labouring in his home valley, and of his study at university. He also points to changes in productive technologies and modes of organisation in terms of the shift from agrarian to industrial labour and of the complex relation of culture to such a shift. This is the context for Williams' understanding of 'culture as ordinary': ordinary culture is that culture – of tradition and experimentation – that is produced through labour. For us now, economic, social, political and cultural change is often seen less in terms of industrialisation, Fordism and the nation-state, than in post-industrialisation, post-Fordism and post-national realignment. In the final section of this chapter, we look at how this development provides a context for understanding a form of collectivity that Antonio Negri, Michael Hardt, and other, primarily Italian, social theorists, call 'the multitude'. For these writers, the shift from Fordism to post-Fordism, for example, is not so much a shift in cultural dominance from labour to consumption, but from the industrial to post-industrial, from 'mass' to 'social' work, or from material to immaterial labour. For these writers, the transition in typologies of work forms the basis for understanding broader social, political and cultural change. At the heart of their thinking is that these shifts in forms of labour produce new forms of collective organisation. The ideas that emerge from these writers help us to rethink the question of a common culture. It is in this sense that the figure of the multitude offers a provocation for those who have been thinking about popular culture in the present. To put it crudely, is it possible to have a common culture - or a culture of the commons - that is at once heterogeneous, global, and collective?

In an interview in 2000, Hardt discussed a now commonplace collapse of the economic and the cultural (that we discuss in more detail in chapter seven), but he refers to this collapse in terms of the notion of 'immaterial labour'. He says: '[w]e try to think of this shift under the rubric of immaterial labor, which includes not only work with images and analytical-symbolic tasks but also affective labor and caring labor. In immaterial labor, the economic and the cultural are inseparable' (2004: 171). As with many who talk about this blurring of the boundary between culture and economy, the impact of this shift is not specific to one industrial sector (i.e. the cultural industries), but to economic and social life more generally. All forms of production are now often seen to be constructed through the techniques associated with cultural and informational production and as forms of cultural production. As Paulo Virno, another theorist of the multitude, states in his book *A Grammar of the Multitude*:

> The informality of communicative behavior, the competitive interaction typical of a meeting, the abrupt diversion that can enliven a television program ..., has become now, in the post-Ford era, a typical trait of the *entire* realm of social production. This is true not only for our contemporary culture industry, but also for Fiat in Melfi. (2004: 59)

The 'era of post-Fordism' is seen to bring about the dominance of communication culture. It is argued by Hardt, Negri, Virno and others that the shift in the mode of production not only leads to a de-differentiation of culture and economy, but also that the very nature of work in the era of post-Fordism is typified by its inherently collective quality. These writers talk about the collective nature of contemporary work in terms of a notion, taken from Marx, of the 'general intellect': '[g]eneral intellect is a collective, social intelligence created by accumulated knowledges, techniques and know-how' (Hardt and Negri, 2000: 364). Immaterial labour draws on the resources of language and a fundamental commonality: '[i]mmaterial labor immediately involves social interaction and cooperation' (Hardt and Negri, 2000: 294).

This cooperation is not something that is imposed from without, rather it is 'immanent to the laboring activity itself' (Hardt and Negri, 2000: 294).

The central core of their argument, then, runs as follows: a major shift in the mode of production - from Fordism to post-Fordism, from industrial to post-industrial capitalism - brings about the conditions for the culturalisation of social and economic life, for the dominance of a form of labour that prioritises informational and affective relations, and for forms of collectivity that are predicated on a primary commonality and yet do not presuppose any reduction to a homogenising logic. These are, for the writers discussed above, the conditions for the contemporary multitude. Moreover, as we will discuss in more detail in chapter eight, the multitude, because it is seen to outgrow the logics of the people and the nation, is importantly linked to globalisation: 'Empire takes form when language and communication, or really when immaterial labor and cooperation, become the dominant force' (Hardt and Negri, 2000: 385). It is perhaps incorrect though to frame the argument in this way, as it is the multitude that brings about the dramatic shift in social, cultural and political organisation, in the sense that capitalist transnational companies, small cooperatives, niche markets, flexible working conditions, leisure time, greater sociability, the importance of an ethos of friendship at work, and so on are all seen as responses to the constituent power of creative and inventive labour.

> In the figure of the social worker [Hardt and Negri's term for the ideal-type of worker under conditions of post-Fordism] the various threads of immaterial labor-power are being woven together. A constituent power that connects mass intellectuality and self-valorization in all the areas of the flexible and nomadic productive social cooperation is the order of the day. In other words, the program of the social worker is a project of *constitution*. In today's productive matrix, the constituent power of labor can be expressed as self-valorization of the human (the equal right of citizenship for all over the entire sphere of the world market); as cooperation (the right to communicate, construct languages, and control communication networks); and as political power, or rally as the constitution of a society in which the basis of power is defined by the expression of the needs of all. This is the organization of the social worker and immaterial labor, an organization of productive and political power as a biopolitical unity managed by the multitude, organized by the multitude, directed by the multitude - absolute democracy in action. (Hardt and Negri, 2000: 409-10)

It is certainly odd, though, to hold up Fiat (as Virno does) as responsive to revolutionary social and cultural change, when, at the moment that the multitude was supposedly busy changing capital from within, Fiat sacked over 23,000 workers in Italy. Such a move, at a time just before the miners in Britain were defeated under Prime Minister Thatcher, was seen by many as marking the defeat of the workerist movement in Italy and heralding the arrival of a more insidious form of neo-liberalism and free-market globalisation (Callinicos, 2003). However, as a number of commentators have noted, the analysis that Hardt and Negri make - of the collapse of divisions between home and work, leisure and work, personal life and work, of the valorisation of flexible, horizontal, non-hierarchical, semi-autonomous working practices, and of the dominancy of symbolic labour - is one that is also presented by the spokespeople of post-industrial capitalism (such as Daniel Bell, Robert Reich, Peter Drucker, and others).

Where once social, political, and cultural theorists might have referred to such struggles, expressions and aspirations in the context of the people and the popular, Hardt and Negri see the multitude as the constituent body that sits beneath any constitution of the people. For Hardt and Negri, sovereignty, nation, and people are all part of the same problem, a problem of attempting to control from above, to speak and represent others. In their influential book *Empire*, they quote the seventeenth century philosopher Thomas Hobbes:

> It is a great hindrance to civil government, especially monarchical, that men distinguish not enough between a people and a multitude. The people is somewhat that is one, having one will, and to whom one action may be attributed; none of these can be properly said of the multitude. The people rules in all governments. For even in monarchies the people commands; for the people wills by the will of one man ... (however it seem a paradox) the king is the people. (Hobbes, *De Cive* quoted in Hardt and Negri, 2000: 102-3)

The contrast between people and multitude was one that framed a debate between Hobbes and another seventeenth century philosopher, Baruch Spinoza. Whereas cultural studies, in its attempts to understand popular culture, has tended to work through the tradition of Hobbes, Hardt and Negri (among others) have suggested that we turn to the work of Spinoza and his interpreters (such as Deleuze) in order to understand the multitude. If the people are defined by their identity, relation to sovereignty and represented homogeneity, the multitude in contrast is defined through its absolute heterogeneity and through its being a congregation of singularities. The multitude is a population in the form of a multiplicity. Thus Hardt and Negri state:

> The multitude is a multiplicity, a plane of singularities, an open set of relations, which is not homogenous or identical with itself and bears an indistinct, inconclusive relation to those outside of it. The people, in contrast, tends toward identity and homogeneity internally while posing its difference from and excluding what remains outside of it. Whereas the multitude is an inconclusive constituent relation, the people is a constituted synthesis that is prepared for sovereignty. The people provides a single will and action that is independent of and often in conflict with the various wills and actions of the multitude. Every nation must make the multitude into a people. (2000: 103)

In their book *Multitude* (2004) Hardt and Negri also distinguish the multitude from other collectivities, such as the masses, the crowd or the mob, and the working class. They argue that 'the masses' cannot be reduced to a unity or an identity, but are typified, nevertheless, by their indifference: 'all differences are submerged and drowned in the masses. All colors of the population fade to gray. These masses are able to move in unison only because they form an indistinct, uniform conglomerate' (2004: xiv). The crowd or the mob are social subjects which are 'fundamentally passive in the sense that they cannot act by themselves but rather must be led. [They] can have social effects – often horribly destructive effects – but cannot act of their own accord' (2004: 100). According to Hardt and Negri, the crowd has no common elements and is essentially incoherent. In contrast, the multitude 'designates an active social subject, which acts on the basis of what the singularities share in common' (2004: 100). But the multitude is also different from 'the working class' inasmuch as this latter collective social subject – either in its broad definition of all those who work or in its more restricted definition of industrial workers – is seen, by Hardt and Negri, as too exclusive and closed. The multitude is 'an open, inclusive concept', not limited to forms of industrial labour, but to 'all the diverse figures of social production' (2004: xiv, xv). The multitude is involved in symbolic and social production, as much as material production.

Hardt and Negri, thus, seem to offer a new and, perhaps, radical understanding of collective subjectivity. Their work is suggestive in that it provokes us to think of a common culture in the context of the multitude, as typified by biopolitical expression, a common cultural life. They argue that:

> The multitude is a diffuse set of singularities that produce a common life; it is a kind of social flesh that organizes itself into a new social body ... The common, which is at once an artificial result and constitutive basis, is what configures the mobile and flexible substance of the multitude. The constituent power of the multitude, from an ontological standpoint, is thus the expression of this complexity and the key that moves through the biopolitical common to express it ever more widely and effectively. (Hardt and Negri, 2004: 349)

Across the boundary-breakdowns of economic, cultural, social, and biological existence, the multitude is seen to give life to a new collective subjectivity. This collectivity, and the common hybrid culture that is expressed therein, is not one that is constituted from above (whether by the state, elite groups, the ruling class, or organic intellectuals) but nor is it unified and bounded as a homogenous identity (as 'the people'). The multitude forms a collective entity, but one not reducible to a single logic. It is a complex organisation, defined not by its negation (i.e. by what it is not) but only through its positivity (i.e. in terms of what it is in itself). The common culture of the multitude is heterogeneous, formed as a constituent power, levelling others, forming a global space of democratic participation. And even in its most biopolitical colouring, the multitude is still conceived as human, as a species being that lives through communication, cooperation and work.

It is in this sense that the multitude appears in its most anthropological guise - as ordinary, everyday, common, democratic, and human. Although Hardt and Negri frame their argument in terms of the ongoing battle of immanence against the forces of transcendence, there is much in common between their figuring of the multitude and accounts of ordinary, common culture, such as we saw in the work of Fiske and Willis. However much force is applied from above, culture from below - from the space of the ordinary and the commons - creatively reinterprets, reshapes and reuses. Common points of reference - such as the soap opera watched by millions or the post box that we might gather around to discuss the days events - do not rigidly fix us, rather they provide us with a means to live through our differences. Fiske, for example, in his understanding of popular culture as a multiplicity, argues that a single cultural product is 'popular', not because it provides the same meaning or gratification for all who read or use it, but because it provides each user and interpreter with novel, inventive and different forms of use and interpretation (1987, 1989).

In its formation through the common ground of language - a ground that facilitates its communication, commonality, cooperation, and collectivity - the multitude appears to founder on the problematic of the nation. It is not surprising, then, that Virno talks in this way with reference to Saussure's model of linguistics (2004: 56).The point is maybe not to attempt to understand any underlying anthropology of the multitude, to understand any commonality in terms of labour, language, and communication, but to see, for example, a group of people working together, talking with each other, and thinking collectively as an amazing contingent event, an event that is only known through its effects, not through any underlying cause. Perhaps the argument of Hardt and Negri that '[t]he multitude is an internally different, multiple social subject whose constitution and action is based not on identity or unity (or much less indifference) but on what it has in common' (2004: 100) should be turned on its head, such that the multitude is seen to be constructed *despite having nothing in common* or rather whose commonality is only by virtue of the contingent actions and coming together of its consituent elements.

And yet for Hardt and Negri, the notion of the multitude seems to hold onto that nineteenth century conception of an anthropology of the people, but unchains the people from the sovereignty of the nation, the state, and from place itself. For all the liberating of this late modern Prometheus from the shackles of national sovereignty, we can see a web of softer, less visible, more immaterial chains around the feet of this Bolshevik god. For all the desperate attempts to escape a problematic of 'the people' and 'national sovereignty', we can still see their traces.

Unlike the neo-Gramscian conception of the people, it might seem that the multitude is all substance and no form. Some critics have argued that Hardt and Negri reduce the multitude to a productive force in the same traditional sense that Marxism talks about a productive force (such as technology or knowledge) as that immanent determinant of a social, political, and cultural world (cf. Laclau, 2004; Ranciere, 2002). But we might extend this line of criticism further. The supposed current shape of the multitude - in terms of its relation to immaterial labour and the general intellect - is defined by Hardt and Negri through a shift in the mode of production from Fordism to post-Fordism. Any agency or constituent power the multitude might seem to display is very much tied to the conditions of possibility of a post-Fordist mode of production. Thus, over and above the supposed primacy of the multitude in the shaping of this story, we might want to question why such a constituent power follows such a well-trodden narrative path and why its expression is not more inventive and creative (cf. Fitzpatrick, 2004). Why does the multitude sing from the same song sheet? And why does it sing to the hymn of contemporary global capitalism and its chorus of management gurus?

This is certainly puzzling if we also consider the multitude in the context of political agency. For Hardt and Negri, singularities within a multitude are not agents able to mobilise other agents; the relation between singularities is such that any element cannot be 'represented' by any other. A positive reading of the multitude would suggest that we need to radically rethink our conception of politics and the political; a more critical reading, such as that made by Laclau, would suggest that Hardt and Negri's concept of the multitude offers the antithesis of politics; the multitude is an agency that doesn't articulate, represent or strategise (2004). This may be no bad thing, but given the 'triumphalist vision' of the multitude that Hardt and Negri narrate and the rather paltry list of demands (whether of the multitude or of Hardt and Negri as its spokespeople) that they list at the end of their weighty tome, we should be circumspect as to both the veracity and authenticity of this new political anthropology.

In the context of attempts to understand some basic questions of how we are formed and how we live together with others or how we do so differently from others in conditions of social transformation, the puzzle of popular culture has dominated the thinking of many people for over two centuries. Is a popular culture supportive or antithetical to authentic community and to democracy? Is popular culture a mechanism of power or resistance? Many of the central discussions of the nineteenth and twentieth centuries have attempted to think through and resolve questions about culture in the context of the nation, the state, modernisation, the decline of traditional authorities and communities, mass democracy and industrial and post-industrial development. It is with the neo-Gramscian turn that we see a more reflexive understanding of the popular, such that it is not seen to signify in any realist sense, as if constituted within real social and historical conditions, but seen to resolve particular structural inequalities and to provide a space for a counter-hegemonic commons. Recent thinking has pushed this quest for a politicised resistant common culture to a new post-national dimension with the figure of the multitude. What is not clear though is the extent to which this figure of the multitude simply repeats old patterns with regard to culture and power, the common and the elite, and the low and the high. In many ways, it might be better not to institute the multitude as a new political subject of resistance – as if akin to the working class as the revolutionary subject and motor of history – but to think about culture in the first instance as inventive and as a multiplicity. In that sense, we shouldn't expect to see divisions of power simply repeated onto divisions between high and popular culture, for example, or expect that 'the people' will always offer the possibility of political mobilisation. We should always look to patterns that we find through empirical research and be equally surprised by their difference as by their repetition.

Chapter Summary

- Popular culture is a defining object of cultural studies.
- Any definition needs to locate popular culture in relation to what might be understood as 'the people'.
- The history of thought on culture discloses culture in the context of a concern with the nation and the people and within a Romantic critique of industrial modernity. The historical debates about culture and civilisation are a feature of these concerns.
- Cultural studies has attempted to valorise popular culture in its anthropological sense as the culture of the people in contrast to limited definitions of culture as high or elite culture. In this sense, all social action becomes conceived as cultural, as forms of ordinary cultural practices. Any divisions and distinctions are not essential, but the result of cultural practice.
- But such an understanding of popular culture is problematic precisely because of the historical relation between people, culture and nation. Thus early work in cultural studies reproduces an English national culture embattled against an 'American' industrial modernity.
- Work on 'mass culture', such as that by Adorno and Horkheimer, is problematic because mass culture is seen as passive and de-individualising, but significant because it allows us to understand culture in the context of broader productive forces and changes (i.e. concerning organisation, knowledge, technology and so on).
- In this sense, given recent 'post-Fordist' shifts (e.g. in terms of mass to niche consumer markets), we might question not only whether there is a mass audience, but also whether there is a popular culture. Moreover, if there is no meaningful designation to the category 'people'

other than one that confines the people to the ethnos of a nation and hence carries deep nationalistic sentiments, we might wonder whether there is any value to foregrounding the 'popular' as against other forms of culture?

- A significant strand of cultural studies though has understood popular culture not in terms of its relation to a realist sense of 'the people', but in relation to the constructive project of building a people.
- Neo-Gramscian (including Laclau, Hall and early Bennett) and post-Foucauldian analyses (such as late Bennett) look at the construction of the popular in a strategic, rather than realist, sense.
- Nevertheless, there is still the problem of the people/nation/culture relation and work that contrasts the 'people' with the 'multitude' has been productive in looking to understanding 'common cultures' across and beyond the national.

FIVE Identity: Between Subject and Object

When I got up this morning, I went downstairs, staggered into the bathroom, turned on the light and took a good look at myself in the mirror. Through my sleep-filled eyes I could see myself looking back, just as intently; this was me! It seems like we've all had these moments of recognition. The mirror seems to hold a privileged place in the problem of selfhood, precisely because it poses the self as an identity; the image in the mirror is the same as, or identical to, the person looking in front of it. The mirror seems to offer an unmediated access to one's self. And yet the signs 'in' the mirror are peculiar kinds of signs. They appear as absolute icons or rather doubles of the signs standing in front of the mirror. My slightly stubbly chin, my hair that is in desperate need of a cut and my nasal hairs that need trimming; these intimate bodily signs are doubled in the mirror (Eco, 1984). But whereas signs ordinarily allow that which is represented to be absent from the sign that represents, my face in the mirror disappears as soon as I move. It does not stay to be seen and examined by another. In that sense, these signs are indexical in a highly motivated way. But what is peculiar is that although the face that looks out at me looks like me and is me, in some kind of way, it is also not me. When I look in the mirror and cough, my reflection is silent. My image is not me; it is the inverse of me. If I hold some writing in front of the mirror (da Vinci like), the writing is the inverse of its original form. This uncanniness of the mirror-image – that which seems like me, but isn't exactly me – is the staple diet of psychological horror. Evil always lurks in the mirror-image. When I wipe the steam from the reflective surface, I see, not myself, but an other.

In this chapter, I want to consider some of these questions about recognition and misrecognition, about the relations between selfhood and semiotics, but also to move beyond these issues and to move beyond the mirror as a privileged metaphor for self-identity. When I look in the mirror on most mornings, I do not think about who I am or about what the mirror-image means to me. These are largely philosophical issues that have a lot more to do with the place of 'recognition' in the history of philosophical questions about self-identity than they do about day-to-day cultural practice. Robert Lowell, writing about his time in a psychiatric institution in the US, pins the mirror to an unbearable reflection that in many ways says less about mental illness than it does about our imagining of it in our obsessions about mirrored identity:

> After a hearty New England breakfast,
> I weigh two hundred pounds
> this morning. Cock of the walk,
> I strut in my turtle-necked French sailor's jersey
> before the metal shaving mirrors,
> and see the shaky future grow familiar
> in the pinched, indigenous faces
> of these thoroughbred mental cases, twice my age and half my weight.
> We are all old-timers,
> each of us holds a locked razor. (Lowell, 1974: 68–9)

Ordinarily, when I look in the mirror, I am holding a brush, brushing my hair and making sure I look reasonably tidy. Or I will be holding a razor, not waiting to execute the evil fiend that hides behind my face or reflecting on the sanity of my self-being, but shaving the stubble off my chin. The mirror does no more than the weighing scale; it does its job and allows me to do mine. In this sense, we would do well not to overestimate the place of the mirror and questions about recognition in discussions of cultural 'identity'. The mirror, even as a metaphor, is no more a reflective surface than a computer screen, a glass of water, a classical concert or a popular film nor can it be seen as the model for all forms and experiences of selfhood. The mirror can no more offer a solution to theories of cultural identity than it can a resolution to the interminable problem of difference. In the course of this chapter, we look first at the relation between self, other and language in modern European philosophy and particularly in the context of structuralism and post-structuralism; then we look at the work of three major cultural theorists of identity – Stuart Hall, Homi Bhabha and Judith Butler – who shift from questions of identity to identification and to an understanding of the subject as always in process; and in the final section we move away from the problem of self and the symbolic to an understanding of the self as singularity, as becoming, and as translated through material semiosis.

Recognition and Language

Much contemporary discussion of cultural identity, at least that which goes by the name of structuralism and post-structuralism, implicitly or explicitly draws on a Hegelian dialectic of self and other and a post-Saussurian understanding of language as a system of differences. Whatever the name and whatever the complexities that are assumed by certain writers, the basic terms of the debate are relatively straightforward. The traditional starting point for this debate is with the seventeenth century French philosopher Rene Descartes and with his conception of certainty and the modern soul: namely, if there is one thing that I can be certain of in this world it is that I can think; therefore, all knowledge of the world must be predicated on this one certainty of self-consciousness, of '*cogito ergo sum*' (I think therefore I am) (Descartes, 1968). This is the Cartesian subject, the indivisible thinking being in a world of divisible matter and machines. The world is known, as it is known to me, through the representations I receive. Without going into the way in which God lends a hand in verifying this world and consciousness, we can see how Descartes' idea of self-identity feeds into solipsistic, atomistic ideas of the individual.

But, instead of thinking that the world is made up of individuals, conscious of the world around them, perceiving people and things in the world and understanding this world of not-'I' only in terms of the representations that 'I' receives, we might think of the arena within which these representations circulate as one typified by struggle, such that the relation between the self-identity of consciousness and the identity of its other is typified as a relation of struggle. We might, following the nineteenth century German philosopher G. W. F. Hegel, refer to this field of struggle in terms of the notion of *negativity*: namely, the relation between self-identity ('I') and its other is understood in terms of the desire of the one to negate, or destroy, the other (Hegel, 1977). In this sense, the relation between self and other is understood in terms of *mastery*. The relation of mastery is read as a relation between master and slave. The slave is seen as a warrior defeated in the fight for recognition, but if the other is destroyed by the master then nothing would be gained. The slave needs to be kept a slave in order that he can provide the master with a sense of his own identity and sense of his mastery. How can we say that a battle has been won without the spoils of war to demonstrate the victory? The slave provides the master with this recognition; the identity of the master as master is thus dependent on the slave representing to the master that image of self. Moreover, the desire of the master, as a desire for recognition, is dependent on the slave. Negativity is not simply the negation of a given, but the negation of another's consciousness and self-identity;

it is the negation of negation. In this Hegelian dialectic of desire and recognition, the identity of self is dependent on the desire of the other in such a way that the identity of self is alienated from itself. The identity of self is not within the self, but in the desire of the other. I am only master inasmuch as the other recognises me as such. I only know myself and the world inasmuch as it is facilitated by the desire of the other. It is only with the end of the dialectic of negativity, with the end of history, that knowledge, as absolute knowledge, is fully achieved. At this point, this *telos*, or ending, self and other, subject and object are no longer divided; the struggle for mastery is over (cf. Descombes, 1980; Kojeve, 1980; Soper, 1986).

Hegelian thought helped to shape modern philosophy and an understanding of the modern self. Those who read him championed his works in different ways and in different fields of knowledge. Alexandre Kojeve's reading of Hegel, in terms of the humanisation of nothingness, and his popular seminars, attended by Raymond Aaron, Georges Bataille, Pierre Klossowski, Jacques Lacan and Maurice Merleau-Ponty, set the stage for the growth of French existentialism (e.g. in the work of Jean-Paul Sartre) and the development of a psychoanalytic conception of the desiring subject (e.g. in the work of Lacan). For contemporary cultural theory, Hegelian thought provides an important context for understanding an otherness, or alterity, at the heart of the subject, but also for recognising, albeit in a highly philosophical form, as Gilroy notes, 'the intimate association of modernity and slavery' (1993a: 53). And yet, it is also the reaction against Hegel, inasmuch as the dialectic of desire and recognition is predicated on an intersubjectivity, that begins a ground shift in thinking about the self and that gives language, as a symbolic system, a central role in the construction of subjectivity. It is in the context of questions about language and the symbolic that cultural studies has investigated theoretical issues of alterity and mastery. The problem of language and the constitution of the subject is found notably in the psychoanalytic works of Lacan (1977, 1980) and of Kristeva (1982, 1984a), also in the linguistics of Emile Benveniste (1971), in the philosophy of Derrida (1976, 1987), and the literary theory and semiology of Roland Barthes (1974, 1977). In the remainder of this section instead of providing a reading of the work of any one of these writers, I will provide a largely schematic account of the relation between language and subjectivity.

Let's start with some music. David Freeman's song 'No more "I love you's"', written and originally sung by The Lover Speaks in 1986, but made popular in the performance by Annie Lennox, takes on the ideas of the French semiologist Barthes, particularly from his work *The Lover's Discourse* (1990). Freeman talks of the desire and despair of romantic love and the way in which it has been transformed in contemporary popular culture into recurrent motifs, such as the singing of 'buttonhole tunes' when one is in love or the endless waiting for the lover to come back. In the chorus, he writes:

> No more 'I love you's'
> A language is leaving me.
> No more 'I love you's'
> A language is leaving me exiled.
> No more 'I love you's'
> Changes are shifting me outside the words.
> (*No more "I love you's"*, A&M Records, 1986)

The lover who speaks these words is clearly distinct from the words themselves. The sentence 'I love you' has been spoken so many times in so many different contexts. As we saw in our discussion of Bakhtin, to think that the words simply express an inner feeling would be naive. The words are assembled into an utterance that is addressed to another. The 'I' of the sentence – or *the subject of the enounced* or the spoken subject – is apparently the same 'I' that is speaking the sentence – or *the subject of the enunciation* or the speaking subject. Thus Benveniste, in his discussion of subjectivity in language, recognises that such personal pronouns as 'I' are unique in that they refer neither to a concept (that might have universal reference) nor to any particular individual (as if 'I' functioned like the name of an individual such as 'Maria del Carmen') (1971: 226). There is not some thing in the world called 'I' that 'I' names and that pre-exists its naming. These pronouns refer to anyone that takes up the position of 'I', but equally the 'I' that is uttered does not refer to a concept that incorporates all the 'I''s that have ever been uttered (e.g. Maria del Carmen as well as Julius Caesar as well as Napoleon). The 'I's that any one subject utters would have no necessary relation to the 'I's uttered by another subject. The 'I' is, in that sense, unlike the signifiers 'cat' and 'table' that act as concepts that refer to all possible cats and tables throughout history, and such that all particular cats and tables bear some resemblance to the concepts of 'cat' and 'table':

> It is in and through language that man constitutes himself as a *subject*, because language alone establishes the concept of 'ego' [or 'I'] in reality, in *its* reality which is that of the being. The 'subjectivity' we are discussing here is the capacity of the speaker to posit himself as 'subject'. It is defined not by the feeling which everyone experiences of being himself ... but as the psychic unity that transcends the totality of the actual experiences it assembles and that makes the permanence of the consciousness. Now we hold that 'subjectivity'... is only the emergence in the being of a fundamental property of language. 'Ego' is he who *says* 'ego'. That is where we see the foundation of 'subjectivity', which is determined by the linguistic status of the person. (Benveniste, 1971: 224)

But the fact that the utterance 'I love you' can be spoken by anyone also means that, although I can occupy the space of that 'I' and hence constitute myself as a subject, the 'I' of the enunciation is radically divided from the 'I' of the enounced; the subject who speaks is divided from the subject who is spoken. In different types of discourse, or speech genres, we are constructed differently. When I speak to my mum on the telephone my tone of voice, the things that I might say, the way the verbal exchange flows is very different from when I'm in a bar with my friends which is equally different from when I speak in a lecture theatre giving a lecture. There is no single 'I' or subject that is defined or positioned in any one of these or other discourses. There are numerous discourses and hence numerous discursively constructed subject positions. In that sense, the subject is fragmented across language, across the different discourses within different social and cultural settings.

We might assume, then, that although the spoken subject is different according to the way that it is positioned in discourse, the speaking subject is consistent across all the different discursive sites. This idea would assume that the subject has a unity, an identity, over and above its discursive construction. But as we have seen, the subject is only that space that is designated as such in language. Moreover, when we speak, when our language leaves us, we are no longer – as if we ever were – in possession of the meaning of the words that we speak. Language appears as if a mirror to us, as if to provide a point of recognition: 'Here this is who you are!' But this mirror is imaginary, a trick; instead language – that which seems most able to provide us with a means of understanding and recognising who we are – only divides us from ourselves. It is language that both constitutes us as subjects and divides us at the same time. We are then forever searching through language for this final resting place. As with Odysseus' bed, it is this *telos* that we search for, that final meaning that will still our dreams, adventures and desire. Language is not the means for us to find meaning; it is the cause of our exile. It is in language that we are alienated from ourselves. As with Hegel, and as we will see in the following section, the tropes of empire and diasporisation are evident; a model of the subject is predicated on the condition of displacement of peoples, of exile, and of 'not being at home' in a culture.

This understanding of desire in language and of the mirror as that which provides the place of imaginary wholeness is one offered by Lacan in his psychoanalytic account of subjectivity (1977, 1980). Lacan talks of how the infant (a being literally without speech) has a primary relation with the mother and part of the separation of the infant from mother involves the child's recognition of itself as a separate being. The infant recognises itself in both literal and figurative mirrors. The mirror is thus both an important stage in the individualisation of the child and something that is caught up in the imaginary and maternal desire. Suffice to say, Lacan construes the formation of the subject in language in terms of the Freudian oedipal scenario. The imaginary dyadic relation between mother and child is broken up with the interrupting phallic power of the father; the child, now subject, constantly wants to return to that imaginary oneness they had with their mother. What Lacan does is read Freud in terms of a structural analysis of language. The tripartite structure of the oedipal scenario is translated to the tripartite structure of the imaginary, the symbolic and the real. The symbolic order takes up the position of the castrating authority of the father (that which disrupts the imaginary relation between mother and child and feigns a relation to the real only as an impossibility) and brings about the constitution of the subject as a subject that speaks and a subject with consciousness and unconsciousness. This is the division of the subject that takes place in the psychoanalytic account. This is the foundational moment of alterity. For Lacan, this is the structural origin of all subjects; subjects are only subjects inasmuch as they pass through this version of the oedipal scenario, namely only inasmuch as they are constituted in language. But once within the symbolic order of language, the subject only understands the world and their history through the interplay of desire and the symbolic, namely through fantasy. In this sense, this originary moment before language and the symbolic, before the formation of the subject, can only be known as a fantasy, a fantasy of origins (Laplanche and Pontalis, 1982).

Lacan, thus, understands how the subject does not exist in one place, but is necessarily distributed across language: I speak from where I am not (Lacan, 1980). The subject is not centred as in the Cartesian subject, but decentred in the symbolic order of language. Moreover, unlike the Cartesian subject, the Lacanian subject is not simply a consciousness, an identity that thinks consciously. The Lacanian subject is both conscious and unconscious. The symbolic order, although an order of positions and differences, is infused with the unconscious to the extent that it is the unconscious itself that is structured like a language (Lacan, 1980). Lacan's understanding of language is post-Saussurian. He believes that the symbolic order is linguistic and that it is structured as a system of differences and that its primary mechanisms are those of association and combination (although Lacan reads these mechanisms through the work of linguist Roman Jakobson (Jakobson and Halle, 2002). The law of the father is the law of language as a system, the law that structures the unconscious. When we dream, our dreams tell a story through the associations (metaphors and condensations) and combinations (metonymies and displacements) that govern the law of the symbolic order. If we can know the unconscious, we can know it only through its language.

The Lacanian subject – divided in language between the subject of the enunciation and the subject of the enounced and between the conscious and unconscious – is one that continually tries to heal this originary wound. It searches through language for an ending to its troubles. Each object that it finds may seem to offer some hope, but because language is a system of differences the meaning that the object offers is carried off into the system again. Just as the meanings of words in the dictionary only lead to other meanings and words, so the desire of the subject only leads to other signifiers never to the final signified. The Lacanian subject is a subject structured by this desire, a desire for completion, fullness and wholeness; but it is a desire that is always forlorn. The image in the mirror (but it could equally be a film, a book, an advertisement, a fireman walking across the street) that I so easily recognise, that holds my desire, is always a mis-recognition; it is a point of identification, but such that the identification never completely matches with who I am. Desire is structured as a lack, as a wanting; it is one that rests on needs and bodily drives (that psychoanalysis construes in terms of certain basic bodily functions, such as sucking at the breast, eating, shitting, fucking), but it is ultimately structured in the field of language. This desire is directed toward the other (as that which can provide wholeness and satiate the lack) and is figured in the field of the Other (i.e. language as the field of the unconscious). The Hegelian subject – predicated on the dialectic of desire and recognition – is now fully transposed onto a post-Saussurian semiology. This is the basic foundation of many structuralist and post-structuralist ideas about subjectivity and language.

Diaspora, Hybridity and Performativity

The formulations of subjectivity presented above seem overly philosophical and much work in cultural studies has grounded, criticised, and developed these ideas in relation to the lived experiences of subjects, most notably in relation to the lived experiences of gender, sexuality, 'race' and ethnicity and particularly in the context of late-modern cultural life.

Diaspora and Articulation

In the opening paragraph of an article 'Minimal Selves', Stuart Hall makes the following comments:

> Thinking about my own sense of identity, I realise that it has always depended on the fact of being a *migrant*, on the *difference* from the rest of you. So one of the fascinating things about this discussion is to find myself centred at last. Now that, in the postmodern age, you all feel so dispersed, I become centred. What I've thought of as dispersed and fragmented comes, paradoxically, to be *the* representative modern experience! This is 'coming home' with a vengeance! Most of it I much enjoy – welcome to migranthood. (1987: 44)

Hall reflects on his own experiences of migration. He talks about himself coming from a lower-middle-class family in Jamaica and about the aspirations of this family to be an upper-middle-class, English Victorian family. And he talks of his desires to move to England, to take up a place studying at Oxford, in terms of his desire to escape from his mother and family life. Migration, then, for Hall is about displacement, but not simply the displacement of peoples in foreign territory. For Hall migration is also about displacement in a very subjective sense: '[t]he problem, one discovers, is that since one's family is always already "in here", there is no way in which you can actually leave them' (1987: 44). The 'home' that one tries to leave is always 'locked up' in one's head. Equally, the place in which one settles is never really 'home'. One is always, in this sense, alienated from the culture in which one finds oneself:

> Identity is formed at the unstable point where the 'unspeakable' stories of subjectivity meet the narratives of history, of a culture. And since he/she is positioned in relation to cultured narratives which have been profoundly expropriated the colonized subject is always 'somewhere else': doubly marginalized, displaced always *other* than where he or she is, or able to speak from. (1987: 44)

For Hall, this passage of alienation is a 'one way trip'. There is no longer any 'real' home to go back to, to return and become re-settled. But the fact of migration does not simply imply that one has cut oneself off from what one has left, that one is now disconnected from one's roots. On the contrary, the condition of migration is tied to the condition of diasporisation. The term *diaspora* originally refers to the exile of the Jewish people after the destruction of the second temple by the Romans, their dispersal across different territories and their desire for 'home'. The term was taken up in the US by African-Americans, influenced by Biblical narratives, to describe the condition of slavery and enforced exile. In cultural studies, especially in the works of writers such as Hall and Gilroy, diasporisation refers to the geographical dispersion of peoples across the globe and the forms of connection to family, friends and others (Hall 1990). Hence the notion of a 'black diaspora' refers to the forming of community, whether real or imagined, across distance. Clearly, in late modernity, media communications technologies, such as video, satellite television and the internet, play a central role in facilitating these 'communities'. The logic of diasporisation works above and below the level of the nation. But it also disturbs the framing of the 'nation' and throws up territorial, cultural and social spaces that are multi-ethnic. Hall has discussed this phenomenon in terms of the notion of 'new ethnicities' (1988b). This clearly has an impact on thinking about both the politics of 'race' and multiculturalism. In this context, then, racist questions addressed to the migrant in their new found lands – 'why are you here?' and 'when are you going back?' – are necessarily unanswerable. For Hall, these experiences and questions speak not only to the subjective experiences of those who are physically displaced from their 'homelands', they also point to, and help elucidate, '*the* representative modern experience' (1987: 44). The conditions of 'homelessness', 'alienation', 'fragmentation', and 'displacement', so often discussed in the context of philosophies of the subject, sociologies of industrial modernity and social theories of postmodernity, are now 'racialised' and overcoded in the context of European empire and servitude.

Other writers, such as Rosi Braidotti, have talked about these experiences in terms of *nomadism*. Braidotti has talked about 'how nomadic consciousness is an epistemological and political imperative for critical thought at the end of the millennium' (1994: 12). For Hall, though, the 'mobility' of, and in, the subject is not to be understood as a feature of postmodern discourse. Rather there is a recognition that emerges from a postmodern discourse of identity that identity has always been problematic and that we all, more and more, feel 'recently migrated'. In this sense, the fact of migration as a condition of modern subjectivity is something with which we all increasingly have to live. It is not a form of 'critical consciousness' (cf. Braidotti, 1994: 5). Moreover, far from rejoicing in the 'total dissolution of the notion of a center' (Braidotti, 1994: 5) Hall's analysis demonstrates that one's positionality vis-à-vis the centre and margins is, and has been, historically important. It is an important political move to place what were once marginal experiences and identities at the centre, to show that this reversal matters. However, it is problematic to suggest that if the *form* of migrant subjectivity now defines modern subjectivity *per se*, then the *experiences* of migration, homelessness, alienation in a foreign land are also those of the settled native communities. As a white middle-class English-Welsh academic living in London, my experiences in this respect are far from those who have faced enforced exile due to victimisation, economic hardship or war. Nevertheless, the ethical and political weight or value given to particular experiences over others contributes to, but does not provide a criticism of, our understanding of the conditions of marginality and migration as centred and as central to understanding late-modern cultural identity.

For Hall, the claim that the subject is necessarily unstable and in process is not a postmodern claim that we are now all in the same position. He states:

> The trouble is that the instant one learns to be 'an immigrant', one recognizes one can't be an immigrant any longer: it isn't a tenable place to be. I, then, went through the long important, political education of discovering that I am 'black'. (1987: 45)

This, though, is not a claim to have discovered the 'real me'. 'Blackness' (as with 'whiteness' and other racialised categories) is itself an unstable identity category, itself in process, negotiated, contested, always open to change. Hall's recognition of his 'blackness' then is not a claim to an essential, fixed identity. It is a recognition that the movement of the subject is always contingent. If the subject is in process, in movement, it is a movement predicated on a particular positionality, a movement from Jamaica to England, from family to university, from 'immigrant' to 'black' and so on. In this sense, the migration or movement of the subject is always specific and particular. This helps to explain why Hall and other significant cultural studies scholars (such as Ali, 2003; Gilroy, 1993b, hooks, 1991, 1992) translate some of the central terms of post-structuralist theories of subjectivity into ones that immediately carry the connotations of particular forms of lived experience. Lived experience provides the context for theoretical understanding and development. Thus to claim that there is no absolute closure to identity and to stress that there is 'no necessary or essential correspondence of anything with anything' is not to assert a postmodern politics of 'anything goes', a 'free-for-all'. It is rather to point to the fact that if there are partial closures or contingent correspondences, then this is because identities are always *articulated*. We are necessarily connected to others (people, ideas, material contexts and so on) and we always speak from a particular position (however unstable that position might be). Hall reminds us that articulation refers to both speaking and connection: we articulate words and sentences, but we also refer to lorries driving down a highway as articulated (i.e. in terms of the link between the freight container and the cab).The movement of the subject implies its articulation, disarticulation and rearticulation as a potentially constant process.

In this sense, Hall talks about identity as a problematic that concerns the relation of the subject to the social, but he does so in a way that constitutes the problem not simply as one concerning identity-categories ('black', 'woman' and so on), but also concerning *identification*: '[i]t seems to be in the attempt to rearticulate the relationship between subjects and discursive practices that the question of identity recurs – or rather, if one prefers to stress the process of subjectification to discursive practices, and the politics of exclusion which all such subjectification appears to entail, the question of *identification*' (1996: 2). The problem of identity, for Hall then, concerns the articulation of the social and the subject. Hall's argument leads to the notion that identification constitutes the primary (perhaps only) mechanism of this articulation. But what is identification? Hall states:

> In common sense language, identification is constructed on the back of a recognition of some common origin or shared characteristics with another person or group, or with an ideal, and with the natural closure of solidarity and allegiance established on this foundation. In contrast with the 'naturalism' of this definition, the discursive approach sees identification as a construction, a process never completed – always 'in process'. It is not determined in the sense that it can always be 'won'

> or 'lost', sustained or abandoned. Though not without its determinate conditions of existence, including the material and symbolic resources required to sustain it, identification is in the end conditional, lodged in contingency. (1996: 2–3)

Psychoanalysis, for Hall as for Butler and Bhabha (as we will see later in this chapter), provides a major resource for thinking about identification. In a similar move to Bhabha and Butler, Hall discusses how the subject-in-process (cf. Kristeva, 1984) always exceeds the identity-categories with which the subject partially identifies. Post-Lacanian psychoanalysis provides Hall with the technical language to talk about identification in terms of a subject necessarily split between conscious and unconscious. Identification constitutes a form of investment that is ambivalent in the sense that the object of investment, attachment and fantasy can be both an object of love and hate. Psychoanalytic theory is useful to Hall because it provides an account – admittedly problematic in its exclusive focus on sexual difference and the rigid form of the oedipal scenario – that talks about the originary moments of the subject (Who am I? Where am I from? Why do I exist?) as points of fantasy (Laplanche and Pontalis, 1982) and about the formation of the subject in terms of the necessary exclusion and repression of its other. As Hall says 'identities can function as points of identification and attachment only *because* of their capacity to exclude, to leave out, to render "outside", abjected' (1996: 5). Although Hall's account gives empirical texture to some of the more philosophical discussions of subjectivity, we might want to question the reliance on psychoanalysis (and the limitations therein in terms of its a-historicism and universalism) and the limited focus on identification as the primary (or only) mechanism through which we might understand the articulation or suturing of the subject with cultural practice. But this is a more general problem that we will notice in the following discussion of Bhabha and Butler.

Hybridity and Translation

The notion of hybridity originally carries a series of biological and organic connotations (i.e. that plants and livestock can be inter-bred in order to produce pedigree entities). When this is translated onto the breeding of racial phenotypes, a more sinister set of issues arise. In contrast, cultural studies proposes an anti-essentialist notion of hybridity, one that emerges through an understanding of empire, post-coloniality and diasporisation. In cultural studies, hybridity emerges as a concept that raises the question of cultural authority (i.e. as one that construes colonial cultural authority as deeply ambivalent) and one that helps to explain the condition of migration as a major feature of late-modern cultural life. The work of Homi Bhabha has been central to our understanding of hybridity in cultural theory: '[i]n the poignancy and poetry of these partial identifications, this culture of relocation and migration, these hybrid cultural moments, I feel that there was a great theme for the late-modern age' (1994). In Bhabha's early writings, the notion of hybridity is discussed in relation to colonial discourse. Bhabha is sympathetic to, but also critical of, Edward Said's work on orientalism. Said, the Palestinian critic and American professor of comparative literatures, had argued that the 'Oriental' as a space of power and knowledge was a construction of the West and constituted a form of colonial authority (Said, 1979). Images of 'eastern exoticism', harems, belly dancers, the fanaticism of Islamic fundamentalism, the despotism of Arab rulers and the inability to govern democratically can easily be seen as orientalist constructions that serve to stereotype the East and to construct it as foreign, other and the site of colonial imagination. As Said does in his later work (1985, 1993), Bhabha warns against simplifying the direction of power from West to East. He writes:

> There is always, in Said, the suggestion that colonial power and discourse is possessed entirely by the coloniser, which is a historical and theoretical simplification. The terms in which Said's Orientalism is unified - the intentionality and unidirectionality of colonial power - also unify the subject of colonial enunciation. (1983: 25)

Bhabha is not simply interested in how a particular colonial discursive formation constructs the Orient as exotic and other, but in how colonial discourse constitutes both coloniser and colonised in relations of both knowledge and power *and* desire and fantasy. Bhabha draws on a Foucauldian account of modern power, but also on psychoanalytic understandings of subjectivity, from Frantz Fanon's analysis of the doubling of the colonial subject and Freud's account of representation and the unconscious.

In an essay 'Signs taken for wonders' (1985), Bhabha discusses the place of the Bible and the English Book in nineteenth century India. The use of the Bible in the civilising mission of English imperialism could be seen simply as the imposition a colonial order. But Bhabha shows how the authority of the Book is always in question:

> The discovery of the Book installs the sign of appropriate representation: the word of God, Truth, Art creates the conditions for a beginning, a practice of history and narrative. But the institution of the Word in the wilds is also an *Entstellung*, a process of displacement, distortion, dislocation, repetition - the dazzling light of Literature sheds only areas of darkness. (1985: 91)

The placing of the English Book in nineteenth century India is seen to draw on a wider series of ideological forms, such as 'empiricism, idealism, mimeticism, monoculturalism' in order to sustain 'a tradition of English "national" authority' (Bhabha, 1985: 92). In the passage to India, the imaginary and originary presence of English cultural authority is intended to be repeated across different sites of reception and interpretation, as if each reading of the Book simply reaffirmed the colonial presence and brought the native to heel through the stamp of imperial order. But for Bhabha, the Book is not this imaginary, pure text, rather the colonial text is precisely defined as that which is repeated. In this context the colonial text is paradoxical: it signifies a *difference* (between England and India, coloniser and colonised) only within its conditions of *repetition* (i.e. within this particular context). There is no colonial text until it has travelled in the lands of the colonised. Its meaning as a colonial text (and thus as a sign of colonial power) is constituted in relation to both coloniser and colonised:

> Consequently, the colonial presence is always ambivalent, split between its appearance as original and authoritative and its articulation as repetition and difference. It is this ambivalence that makes the boundaries of colonial positionality - the division of self/other - and the question of colonial power - the differentiation of coloniser/colonised - different from both the Hegelian master-slave dialectic or the phenomenological projection of 'otherness'. It is a *differance* produced within the act of enunciation as a specifically colonial articulation of those two disproportionate sites of colonial discourse and power: the colonial scene as the intervention of historicity, mastery, mimesis or as the 'other scene' of *Entstellung*, displacement, phantasy, psychic defence and an 'open' textuality. (1985: 93-4)

The colonial text is thus always contested and negotiated; its mode of authority is agonistic because it is always the effect of a *double inscription*. The colonial text both institutes the authorised differences of colonial rule (the 'stereotypes' of colonial difference - 'the *inscrutability* of the Chinese, the *unspeakable* rites of the Indians, the *indescribable* habits of the Hottentots') and brings about their disruption. For Bhabha this double inscription cannot be accounted for within a Foucauldian analysis of power/knowledge alone, but only with the assistance of a psychoanalytic understanding of the unconscious, as that which introduces desire, fantasy and transgression into the picture: '[f]or domination is achieved through a process of disavowal that denies the *differance* of colonial power - the chaos of its intervention as *Entstellung*, its dislocatory presence - in order to preserve the authority of its identity in the universalist narrative of nineteenth century historical and political evolutionism' (1985: 96). The subject is not simply the coloniser engaged in a power struggle with its other, the colonised. Instead, colonial discourse is constitutive of both coloniser and colonised as a form of doubled or split subjectivity. The Other is not external to oneself, one's subjectivity; it is internal; it is that which constitutes oneself as a colonial subject. In this sense, Bhabha's focus on the doubling of colonial subjectivity draws on the work of Fanon (1967, 1986), but also bears some resemblance to W. E. du Bois' notion of 'double consciousness' (1989) and to Gilroy's development of this notion in his analysis of the 'black Atlantic' (1993a). For Bhabha the doubling effect of colonial power is a form of hybridity:

> Hybridity is the sign of the productivity of colonial power, its shifting forces and fixities; it is the name for the strategic reversal of the process of domination through disavowal (i.e. the production of discriminatory identities that secure the 'pure' and original identity of authority). Hybridity is the revaluation of the assumption of colonial identity through the repetition of identity-effects. It displays the necessary deformation and displacement of all sites of discrimination and domination. It unsettles the mimetic or narcissistic demands of colonial power, but re-implicates its identifications in strategies of subversion that turn the gaze of the discriminated back upon the eye of power. For the colonial hybrid is the articulation of the ambivalent space where the rite of power is enacted on the site of desire, making its objects at once disciplinary and disseminatory; or in my mixed metaphor, a negative transparency. (1985: 97)

He continues:

> If the effect of colonial power is seen to be the *production* of hybridisation rather than the hegemonic command of colonialist authority or the silent repression of native traditions, then an important change of perspective occurs. It reveals the ambivalence at the source of traditional discourses on authority and enables a form of subversion, founded on that uncertainty, that turns the discursive conditions of dominance into the grounds of intervention. (1985: 97)

Furthermore, Bhabha states that: '[h]ybridity is a *problematic* of colonial representation and individuation that reverses the effects of the colonialist disavowal, so that other "denied" knowledges enter upon the dominant discourse and estrange the basis of its authority – its rules of recognition' (1985: 98). Thus Bhabha argues that colonial *mimicry* (the adoption of the signs of colonialism) does not entail Fanon's imperative 'turn white or disappear', but something more ambivalent. Bhabha turns to Lacan's explication of mimicry: 't]he effect of mimicry is camouflage in the strictly technical sense. It is not a question of harmonising with the background but against a mottled background of being mottled – exactly like the technique of camouflage practised in human warfare' (quoted in 1985: 103).

For Bhabha, as with Gilroy and others, the colonial moment defines the central trope in the institution of modernity (1988: 17) and it is in this framework that hybridity needs to be understood. But for those drawing on Bhabha's work the notion of hybridity is discussed generally in relation to conditions of migration and, in Bhabha's later writings, although the focus is centrally on (post)coloniality, the notion of hybridity is used more generally to define the question of cultural authority and subjectivity. Hybridity defines a particular logic of ambivalence and negotiation that can be seen across a range of different political sites and struggles. It is a logic that is at once predicated on political struggle, but not reducible to a logic of opposition. Bhabha seeks to open up: 'a space of "translation": a place of hybridity, figuratively speaking, where the construction of a political object that is new, *neither the one nor the Other*, properly alienates our political expectations, and changes, as it must, the very form of our recognition of the "moment" of politics' (1988: 10–11). The logic of hybridity is seen to open up a 'third space', a space of negotiation that might be set against a more traditional sense of identity politics. This hybrid space is contrasted with a sense of identity defined through a community of experience or biological giveness. It is contrasted with an understanding of identity, such that the political interests of women are seen to be different from those of working-class people or people of colour. In this traditional form of analysis one set of interests is often prioritised (e.g. in terms of a Marxist understanding of capitalism or a feminist understanding of patriarchy) to the exclusion or marginalisation of other political interests. In this sense, for example, one can only be a woman first, and working class secondarily. In contrast, Bhabha's notion of hybridity opens up the possibility of translation across these interests, such that these interests are performed and in process (i.e. always and constantly negotiated) in the moment of translation:

> [T]he transformational value of change lies in the rearticulation, or translation, of elements that are *neither the One* (unitary working class) *nor the Other* (the politics of gender) *but something else besides* which contests the terms and territories of both. This does not necessarily involve the formation of a new synthesis, but a negotiation between them *in media res*, in the profound experience or knowledge of the displaced, diversionary, differentiated boundaries in which the limits and limitations of social power are encountered in an agonistic relation. (1988: 13)

In his later writings Bhabha ties his work on hybridity to Bakhtin's work on the *dialogic* (Bhabha 1990a, b). Bakhtin's notion of the dialogic, as we have seen, refers to the way in which meaning is constructed through utterances, not statements, as a constant process. For Bakhtin the dialogic is democratic, destabilising all authority because it suggests that meaning is always constituted through a relation to, and with, others (namely through relations of addressivity). The space of the utterance (enunciation and address) is hybrid, a space of doubling and negotiation (1988: 58). Bhabha's work on hybridity thus points equally to a democratic space, a space within which cultural authority and cultural identity are always questioned.

Performativity and Materialisation

In feminist and sociological studies, the distinction between sex (male and female) and gender (masculine and feminine) has been used in order to distinguish between the biological (or natural) and the social (or cultural) and to foreground the role of society in the construction of gendered characteristics and features that might ordinarily be seen as rooted in biology. However, although the distinction between sex and gender helps to contest the essentialist 'truths' of nature, it still presupposes an individual that is a biological, bodily and sexed entity and one that pre-exists that subject's social construction as gendered. This is problematic because it can be seen to present heterosexual relations and heterosexual reproduction as 'normal' and 'natural'. Thus, men have a penis and testicles; women have a vagina and ovaries; put the two together and they make babies! Sexed identity is seen as, at root, about reproduction (i.e. heterosexual sexuality). Some feminist writers, then, have argued that it is important to engage with the way in which material biological bodies are sexed and not to see this as simply about social roles, but to think about the way in which both sex and sexuality are performed materially. The cultural theorist and philosopher, Judith Butler has provided the most sustained and influential critique of theories that leave unquestioned the sexed body and that construe the cultural as purely symbolic. Butler's argument draws on the work of Foucault (for an understanding of the constitutive and regulatory effect of the discursive), J. L. Austin, the Oxford philosopher of language (for a concept of the effectivity of language as speech act) and Derrida (for a sense of how reiteration both works toward closure and instability) in order to deconstruct the heterosexual matrix and the way that this matrix regulates a dominant version of sex and gender relations. For Butler the relation between man and woman is defined through a normative understanding of sexual reproduction (i.e. sex is about the reproduction of children, in the particular, and the species, in the universal). In this sense, relations of gender ride on the back of relations of sexual reproduction. Central to her argument is the notion that the sexed body is something performed; it is the result of performative actions.

What, then, does Butler mean by performativity? Butler reads Austin in order to understand not simply how language works but how the relation between language and materiality is processual. Austin, in his book *How to Do Things with Words* (1962), distinguishes between kinds of *utterances*, or speech acts, that *do* things and *statements* that pertain to the *description* of things: namely the difference between saying 'Throw me the ball' and 'A house is a building with walls and windows and a roof'. The first type of speech act is one that does not attempt to describe the world or a state of mind, rather it pertains to a request to act in a certain kind of way. The second type of statement describes a state of affairs in the world and can be judged as true or false with reference either to the meaning of the word 'house' (i.e. the predicate provides a definition of the subject) or to empirical reality (e.g. to the house sitting in front of me): namely, its truth or falsity is either a priori or a posteriori, analytic or synthetic. The first type of speech act that pertains to action is referred to as a performative and for Austin it can be subdivided into different kinds. But we won't go into that here, as Butler is interested less in Austin's theory of language than in the import of his understanding of utterances as things that do things to the world. For Austin a performative speech act concerns a subject bringing into being that which they name. Austin describes performative speech acts in the example of a man and woman getting married. After each has sworn their respect and dedication to each other, the priest says 'I now pronounce you husband and wife'. The saying of these words (this speech act) performs the ceremony of marriage. These words do what they say they do. The union between man and woman is sealed by these words. The words produce the effect that they describe. There are other examples of performatives, such as betting, promising and so on. Obviously, context is important. In Christian marriage, the priest needs to be an ordained priest. The ceremony needs to take place on consecrated ground. Without these contextual factors, the words of the priest have no authority.

But for Butler no individual or institutional authority pre-exists the performative act. For example, the authority to confer marital union resides in the performance of the marriage itself, not in some entity that exists outside that performance. Butler understands a performative in terms of the 'reiterative power of discourse to produce the phenomena that it regulates and constrains' (1993: 12). For her, the authority is contained in the repetition of the acts themselves and it is through their repetition that marriages are 'materialised'. Priests come and go (frocked and defrocked); marriage is not simply conferred by the Christian church, but by other churches and by the state. There is no identity that stands behind the performative, that uses the performative to express authority and power: '[t]here is no power that acts, but only a reiterated acting that is power in its persistence and instability' (1993: 9). There is no marital union without the words 'I pronounce ...', but equally if the acts of priesthood cannot be repeated regularly and daily, there can be no priests: '[p]erformativity is thus not a singular "act", for it is always a reiteration of a norm or set of norms, and to the extent that it acquires an act-like status in the present, it conceals or dissimulates the conventions of which it is a repetition' (1993: 12). The repetition and reiteration of performative acts confers subjectivity to the subjects it constitutes (i.e. no 'husbands' and 'wives' without 'I pronounce ...'). These subjectivities are produced as identifications, but also disidentifications (i.e. as points of refusal, resistance and disavowal). But reiteration also produces subjectivities as material entities 'as *a process of materialization that stabilizes over time to produce the effect of boundary, fixity, and surface we call matter*' (1993: 9).

Thus, in relation to the distinction between sex and gender, Butler provides us with the means for understanding not simply the constructedness of 'gender', but also the constructedness of 'sex', of the body and of the material. She continues:

> That matter is always materialized has, I think, to be thought in relation to the productive and, indeed, materializing effects of regulatory power in the Foucaultian sense. Thus, the question is no longer, How is gender constituted as and through a certain interpretation of sex? (a question that leaves the 'matter' of sex untheorized), but rather, Through what regulatory norms is sex itself materialized? And how is it that treating the materiality of sex as a given presupposes and consolidates its own emergence? (1993: 10)

To repeat, then, power and materialisation are dependent on a prior field of performatives in the sense that what can be said is dependent on what has been said before. When I release a bottle of champagne onto the hull of a ship and declare that it is called the 'Queen Cleopatra', my words and actions have meaning and have an effect only in as much as they accord with a prior genre of how to name and launch a ship. Any utterance is a citation from that prior field of utterances. The authority of the utterance is thus not dependent on any force that exists as a discreet identity prior to the utterance; it is only so as a consequence of the iteration of the utterance itself: '[i]f a performative utterance provisionally succeeds (and I will suggest that "success" is always and only provisional), then it is not because an intention successfully governs the action of speech, but only because that action echoes prior actions, and *accumulates the force of authority through the repetition or citation of a prior, authoritative set of practices*' (1993: 227). Equally though, if all performances are repetitions (or reiterations or citations), then each repetition opens a space for contestation and negotiation. For example, the authority of marriage as heterosexual is dependent on its repetition as such. If priests started to confer marital union to lesbian and gay couples, then the performance of 'marriage' as a heterosexual institution would be questioned and made unstable. If two men can get married in Amsterdam, then this 'fact' seriously destabilises the notion that marriage is only, and universally, a heterosexual union: namely, that the definition of marriage as a heterosexual union is an a priori truth.

We've been talking here about speech acts, but we could equally include other forms of semiotic enunciation (e.g. gestural and kinesic) in our discussion of performativity. In this sense the fashioning or styling of oneself can be seen as performative. Butler has commented on, and been used to comment on, 'drag' as a gender-bending form of self-fashioning (Butler, 1990, 1991). A man wearing 'women's clothes' is not simply a man *pretending* to be a woman. It is not that the copy (i.e. the man in women's clothes) does not match up to the original (i.e. woman), but that the copy deconstructs (or questions) the originality and the primacy of the original (i.e. that women's clothes are for women and that there are such things as 'women's clothes' that are not the reiteration of semiotic conventions). The signs of gender (e.g. the dress) do not necessarily assign, or command, a gender (i.e. femininity). Moreover, if sexual difference is only visible through the signs that are repeatedly performed and mark one's body, then the sex of a body is understood as the accumulation of those performances inasmuch as they are materialised on the body or more accurately as a body.

Butler's theory is persuasive but we should consider some questions. First, Butler argues that performatives are productive and specifically productive of matter. Performatives bring about materialisation. She conceives of performatives through a linguistic model. But is she then saying that the *form* that materialisation takes always and necessarily accords with this linguistic model? Secondly, Butler talks about how the stability or instability of authority is a consequence of the repetition and reiteration of a performative. And yet, within any single performance, there seems to be an assumption that a performative is able to perform (i.e. to be productive of matter) on that occasion. The performative is like a magical incantation that conjures things into existence. And yet if this is so, then any single performative act has an absolute power (i.e. in terms of producing matter) and there is no instability. However, if Butler is arguing that the capacity to produce matter is not within the time and space of a single performance, but across the time and space of a number of performances, then the matter that is produced in a performance must itself be dependent on matter *pre-formed*, albeit partially, from prior performances. Thus if we are wary of reducing that prior matter to a linguistic form, then matter matters. If we take the example of a man wearing women's clothes, then the performative works with and works on existing materials (e.g. clothes, bodies, gestures, and so on). In that sense, the matter *worked on* matters as much as the matter *worked into*.

Technologies of the Self

Although this is undoubtedly a simplification of the problem, we can see particular common strands that connect the arguments made by Hall, Bhabha and Butler: namely, an understanding of the subject within a field of performatives, such that identity is always unstable and subjectivity is always in process. Moreover, although the materiality of the subject is a significant point of discussion, it is secondary to the performativity of the utterance. The body that matters, whether that be the ethnic, 'racialised', sexed or gendered body, is one that is the consequence of reiterative performative practices; matter is never itself constitutive in the process of performance. Hence the model of the performative is, despite itself, always linguistic and symbolic, always a repetition across linguistic difference; whereas for difference to be different and for it to make a difference it has to be across different kinds of things (cf. Deleuze, 1994). How then might we begin to construe the subject in a world, not just of language, but also of objects?

Karin Knorr-Cetina in her recent work has adapted a Lacanian account of subjectivity to look at how the subject is distributed not only through a symbolic universe, but also through an object world (2001). Her starting point is to think of social relationships as involving humans not just with other humans, but with objects and non-human entities as well. She reworks Lacan's account of the constitution of the subject in the symbolic order in terms of an understanding of the self in post-industrial society. She talks about how the mirror has been exteriorised in contemporary social formations and how it reveals 'the subject to him/herself as a piece of unfinished business composed of ever new lacks'. In the new proliferating network of mirrors and means of self-reflection – from shopping malls to magazines to cinemas – the subject is dispersed through new post-industrial channels: '[t]o a considerable extent, the lack-wanting dynamic has changed hands altogether and appears to be articulated by complicated and dispersed machineries of professional image production – of industries that produce movie stars and fashion models, TV programmes and films, shopping catalogues and advertisements' (Knorr-Cetina and Bruegger, 2002: 173). Although some might contest Knorr-Cetina's reading of the Lacanian mirror, her analysis begins to take us away from the oedipal scenario that fixates psychoanalytic understandings of subjectivity and enables us to project the subject into the cultural and social life of late-modern society, not just in terms of the articulation of a pre-existent psyche and the social, but in terms of the very being of the soul. Late-modern life is predicated on lack and wanting that will supposedly be fulfilled in the consumption of ever more goods and services, but is never satiated. For Knorr-Cetina such an understanding necessitates the inclusion of objects and material entities in this world of desire and lack:

> [T]he subject has agency in relation to objects – when object relations are possible – and when objects are the kind described, that is when they are unfolding structures of absences ... [T]hey provide an organized context for giving 'lack' a precise institutional and personal meaning that directs unspecific wants toward clear goals. (Knorr-Centina and Bruegger, 2002: 174)

We, as subjects, are distributed, or decentred, in relation to a world of both language and objects and, although Knorr-Cetina doesn't address this, the dynamics of that relationality will be one tempered not simply by the rules of language, but also by the materiality of the objects to hand. Our relation to an object world, Knorr-Cetina argues, is grounded in institutional settings (i.e. in particular forms of organisation and ways of organising): '[t]he institutional translation we have given of lacks and wantings is sociologically important: it sustains a view of contemporary society as one in which particular models of self become institutionally articulated and in which major transitions in relational engagements are taking place' (Knorr-Cetina and Bruegger, 2002: 181). For Knorr-Cetina, these major transitions refer not only to major sociological shifts from industrial to post-industrial forms of organisation, but also to the relative importance of post-social over social relations as traditionally conceived. In this sense, traditional notions of social solidarity give way to ones predicated on the relation between humans and non-humans.

Nevertheless, despite beginning to take account of post-social relationality, Knorr-Cetina is still wedded to a Lacanian account and one that presupposes the determinacy of the law, a structural law and a law of structure that is transhistorical and transsocial. Although in Lacan's account, the law of the symbolic could be understood with reference to a post-Saussurian account of the linguistic order (such that the law of language is the law that governs the subject), a post-social analysis that takes into account the role of objects has no simple recourse to such a law. The dynamics of objects do not accord with the dynamics of language. Does a cup falling on the floor accord with the law of gravity or linguistic association? Obviously in a book or a film, a falling cup takes on a poetic significance, but if we are to account for objects as objects then, even if we don't want to have recourse to 'scientific' accounts, we still need to accept the different types of materialities that objects have and of their difference from linguistic entities. We will deal with some of these problems in the next chapter, but for the moment let us deal with the problem of a structural law that institutes the subject as a subject.

In chapter two we looked at Wittgensteinian and Foucauldian understandings of language and social organisation and at how these accounts don't have recourse to a universal law that constitutes experience, but to a notion of the building up of piecemeal actions, capacities and forms of conduct. The literary critic Ian Hunter is again useful for pursuing these issues:

> [W]e can form a picture of human beings, as bearers of a dispersed array of practical capacities. These are built up through piecemeal mastery of a patchwork of social technologies ('language games'). They possess no general form or conditions of possibility, save those found in actual forms of social organisation ('forms of living'). (1984: 420)

Although the reference to 'language games' is problematic in its prioritisation of the linguistic over more distributed forms of organisation or technology. This type of argument is one that is pursued by a number of social and cultural theorists such as Michel Foucault, Nikolas Rose and Tony Bennett. Hunter argues that there is 'no general level of experience' (1984: 421) but rather a number of specific methods or techniques through which people have a relation to things, other people and the world. As we saw in chapter two, colour is not experienced with reference to a linguistic system, but with reference to particular techniques such as colour charts, rainbows and so on. We have a relation to colours within particular institutional and discursive contexts, such as schools, scientific laboratories and so on: '[s]ocial agency has no general form (subjectivity) whose structure can be read-off from a theoretical analysis of meaning or the subject positions made available by a linguistic system' (1984: 423). Subjectivities emerge in particular social and historical contexts in response to quite specific problems. Thus, Nikolas Rose invites us to ask the questions: '[w]here, how and by whom are aspects of the human being rendered problematic, according to what systems of judgement and in relation to what concerns?' (1996: 131).

In this sense, there is no 'theory of the subject' only a genealogy of its problematisation (i.e. a history of the present that considers how questions about the self have been made significant in particular social settings at particular historical times and in relation to particular problems) (cf. Rose, 1989, 1992a, 1996). Particular subjectivities emerge in relation to particular forms of schooling, particular forms of psychiatric care, particular forms of television viewing, particular forms of shopping and so on. This form of analysis invites us to become much more empirical in our declarations about subjectivity. This is the argument that Foucault makes in his *History of Sexuality, Vol. 2* and *Vol. 3* (1986, 1988): namely, that our relationship to ourselves as desiring subjects is one that is historically formed in the context of particular practices, discourses and institutions in ancient Greece and Rome and early Christian Europe. Moreover, that subject of desire is not unified across history. Rather it changes dramatically as the institutions, practices and discourses that support and construct it themselves change. Thus the subject of ancient Greece is different from that of the one of early Christianity. We should stress that this difference is in terms of the techniques of the self that Foucault considers and talks about, rather than the whole of array techniques that undoubtedly circulated at the time in contrast and in contestation with those concerned with ethics and existence: namely, ones associated with women and slaves that Foucault fails to consider adequately and for which he has been criticised strongly.

Such an understanding of the subject is predicated not only on a shift away from a post-Saussurian notion of linguistic system (as the basis for a structural law), but also away from a Hegelian dialectic of desire and recognition. Deleuze has been instrumental in this shift (1983, 1994). He rereads the late nineteenth century philosopher Frederick Nietzsche (primarily his

Genealogy of Morals, 1998 [1887]) in order to move away from the master/slave dialectic as framed by Hegel. In the Nietzschean genealogy, the master is seen in terms of the affirmation of their happiness and goodness without need of reference to an other for recognition. In contrast, it is the slave that is caught up in the play of recognition. The slave has an image of the master as bad and thus, in opposition to that image, posits themselves as good. The slave's identity is posited not in relation to a primary affirmation, but in relation to a primary negation; they are not the master. Thus, what for Hegel appears as a dialectic of opposites, for Nietzsche is no such thing at all. For Nietzsche, master and slave are constituted according to two different logics that run past each other, but are different. To elaborate further, Nietzsche tells the tale of a bird of prey that devours a lamb not in order to negate the not-I, but because it is in its nature to do so. This is how the master acts. But the slave is like the lamb who sees the bird of prey as an enemy and as bad; the lamb construes itself as meek and thus wants the bird of prey to be as it is: the badness of the bird of prey is the negation of the goodness of the lamb. Whereas, for Nietzsche, the bird of prey is 'active', the lamb is 'reactive' (Nietzsche, 1998). The subjectivity of the master is active, affirmative and based on the will to power; the subjectivity of the slave is reactive, oppositional and predicated on recognition and negation. The slave only sees opposition; the master only sees difference (cf. Descombes, 1980). The Lacanian subject, inasmuch as it rests on the Hegelian dialectic of desire and recognition, constitutes the subject as always wanting and always lacking. Its desire for recognition is akin to that of the slave; it is in a position of submission and subjection. Moreover, although the post-Saussurian notion of language as a system of differences foregrounds difference, it is a difference that is always caught in the specular trap of recognition, identity and negation. It too is predicated on the binary 'A is not B' meaning that 'A is the opposite of B': namely, man is not woman because woman is not man. Whereas in Deleuze's reading of Nietzsche, difference as affirmation implies a logic of singularity, such that 'A is not B' does not mean that A's being is B's non-being, but rather that A is something other than B (Deleuze, 1983; cf. Descombes, 1980: 163). Thus man and woman are not defined by a logic of binary opposition, but by a non-oppositional difference.

One of the oppositions that has troubled theories of subjectivity for a long time has been one between the inside and the outside: namely, there is a notion that subjectivity is about what is inside someone and the social is what is outside. For example, in traditional accounts of socialisation, that go back to the ideas of the eighteenth century philosopher John Locke, the subject is seen as an individual that is a blank slate that is made social and gradually transformed into a 'social being' through various mechanisms of education, enforcement and so on. In contrast, socio-biological and cognitive-psychological accounts construe the individual not as a blank slate, but as a pre-wired being that interacts with the social world and through each interaction the individual develops into a social being. For example, in the Piagetian understanding of child psychology, the normal child is pre-disposed to cognitively develop according to a particular linear model of development. Different from both these accounts is the Lacanian model of the subject that is initially nothing but a mess of drives without identity. Lacan playfully referred to this pre-linguistic being as an 'hommelette' - a mix of the French for a little man and an omelette. Once the subject is constituted through the linguistic order, it has no substance as such. For Lacan, the subject is always a lack; it is always an absence. When we try to fill that lack (i.e. when we try to give it substance and definition), the subject simply unfolds along the signifying chain. The Lacanian subject, as we have seen, is formed through a structural law and it is formed with certain structural features (i.e. its structure of desire, recognition, and so on). Thus, although in the Lacanian model the inside and the outside are more ambivalent - as what is inside is what was once outside - the boundary is structurally held in place; there is an inside to the subject, albeit one defined as a fundamental emptiness or lack.

In contrast to these earlier models, that implicitly or explicitly construct the relation between subject and social as a relation between inside and outside, some social and cultural theorists have picked up on Deleuze's notion of the subject as a folding (1988, 1993). For example, Rose has argued that:

> The concept of the fold or the pleat suggests a way in which we might think of human being without postulating any essential interiority, and thus without binding ourselves to a particular version of the law of this interiority whose history we are seeking to disturb and diagnose. The fold indicates a relation without an essential interior, one in which what is 'inside' is merely an infolding of an exterior ... Folds incorporate without totalizing, internalize without unifying, collect together discontinuously in the form of pleats making surfaces, spaces, flows and relations. (1996: 142)

Rose argues that such thinking about the folding of the self is in many ways common sensical. For example, we quite happily talk about bodily organs, such as the digestive tract and the lungs, as no more than invaginations or infoldings of the outside inside our bodies. Deleuze talks about the fold being shaped by force relations and what is inside the fold (i.e. A) is only separated from what is outside (i.e. B and C) on the basis of these force relations. Inside and outside are not structured a priori. Nevertheless, the diagram of the fold marks out different spaces between inside and outside the loop (i.e. the difference between A on the one hand and B and C on the other) and between one side of the line and on the other (i.e. the difference between B on the one hand and A and C on the other).

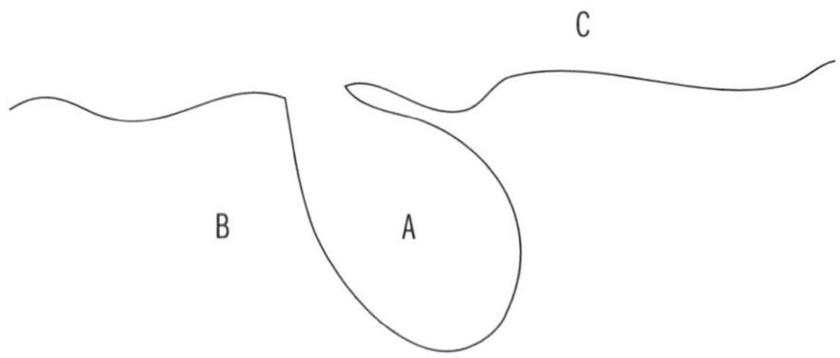

We might wonder then whether the self is that which is inside the fold or whether it includes the boundary of the fold itself or even whether it extends to that which is external to the fold? The notion that the self is folded seems never properly to escape a logic of inside/outside and of negation: A is not-B inasmuch as A is the non-B of B. However, if we are to try to construe a notion of subjectivity that is constituted through difference – as A is not-B inasmuch as A's being is different and not the opposition or negation of B's being – then the relations between the subject and its outside or even the relations 'within' the subject (whatever that might be) must be construed in terms of a translation across material difference, in terms of a logic of singularity: namely, a logic of multiplicity, such that the outside of a particular subject cannot be measured against the inside of that subject, a difference of kind, but also translation. Thus, for example, if I stub my toe on a doorstep and I feel the pain, we cannot say that the action of my foot on the doorstep is equivalent to the pain I feel. The pain I feel is a translation of that action. The outside (i.e. the action of foot to doorstep) is not equivalent or measurable in terms of my feelings inside. Similarly, if I watch a horror film and get scared, my fear is not equivalent to the 'horror' represented on the film; it is only my reaction to that horror. This understanding of the subject moves radically away from one predicated on recognition, identity and identification.

More in keeping with this understanding of the subject in terms of a logic of singularity and translation is a notion of the subject as a site of becomings. If the subject is a space that makes possible certain translations – from quotidian ones such as stubbing one's toe to more dramatic ones such as having plastic surgery – these translations constitute either momentary or longer lasting changes. These changes can be seen as becomings and can be seen in terms of the kinds of connections that we make in our daily lives. Deleuze and Guattari talk about becoming in terms of changing territorial boundaries: deterritorialisation and reterritorialisation. They give the example of a wasp that flies up to an orchid, takes the pollen, and then flies on to another orchid. The wasp, flying from one plant to another, helps with the reproductive system of the orchid. The orchid needs the wasp to take the pollen from one plant to another:

> The orchid is deterritorialised by forming an image, an exact tracing of the wasp; but the wasp reterritorialises itself in this image. The wasp is deterritorialised, however, by becoming part of the orchid's reproductive apparatus, but it reterritorialises the orchid by transporting its pollen. The wasp and the orchid thus make a rhizome, insofar as they are heterogeneous. (Deleuze and Guattari, 1983a: 19)

This relationality is constituted in such a way that it is not based on identity or resemblance, but on translation and becoming. Becoming 'wasp' or 'orchid' is not imitation or resemblance, but 'an explosion of two heterogeneous series in a line of flight consisting of a common rhizome that can no longer be attributed nor made subject to any signifier at all' (1983a: 20). Both wasp and orchid need each other to become, but their becoming does not mean that each is equivalent or replicated by the other. It is a becoming as 'a-parallel evolution' (1983a: 21). This is a rhizomatic relationship: '[*b*]*etween* things does not designate a localisable relation going from one to the other and reciprocally, but a perpendicular direction, a transversal movement carrying away the one *and* the other, a stream without beginning or end, gnawing away at its two banks and picking up speed in the middle' (1983a: 58).

In the philosophy of the subject, the shift in nomenclature from 'individual' to 'person' to 'self' to 'consciousness' to 'subject' and 'subjectivity' is complex, but indicative of the shifts in thinking about cultural identity. Nevertheless, what is absolutely clear is that what we thought of as the 'individual' can be seen as nothing more than a fiction. As the notion of the individual refers, from its roots in European Christian theology, to an entity that cannot be divided, modern thought – since Descartes' claim that the thinking soul was indivisible – has investigated just how divisible it is (whether in terms of different faculties, states of knowing and unknowing or across different linguistic fields). We have come a long way from Descartes' notion of the soul as a thinking thing. Structural and post-structural theories of the subject (such as those of Lacan, Bhabha, Butler and Hall) have showed how the subject is always outside itself, necessarily distributed, plural, mixed, and always in process. The subject is always constructed through action and hence any settling (as to what or who it is) is always provisional. But the subject does not only come into being through the mechanism of recognition and identification; it does not only unfold within the realm of language and the symbolic; it comes into being through a range of different media, mechanisms and technologies; and it is distributed through different materialities. The subject is made up of different things and it has a relation to different things. Things don't always act as mirrors (although they do sometimes, for example, when I have a shave) nor are they always points of recognition (unless constructed as such). The things that get assembled in the making of subjectivities (be they words, blood, organs, feelings, thoughts, and so on) do not have a meaning once and for all time. They change according to the connections that are made. When I type a letter to a friend on the computer, the keyboard and the screen constitute a distribution of myself across these objects: I am somewhere between these things. Without the computer I don't have the thoughts on the page. When I then pick up a glass of wine, I am a drinking being: the glass and the wine are integral to the particular drinking being that I am then at that moment. My becomings as a subject enfold in different ways and I am far from one thing.

Chapter Summary

- Philosophies of the subject, since Descartes' statements about an indivisible thinking being, have been concerned with divisions in the subject. Hegel's understanding of the self and other in a relation of negativity is central to this discussion. Moreover, it is central for cultural theory inasmuch as it constructs the significance of alterity and servitude for a modern understanding of subjectivity.
- Cultural theory has been influenced by work on the construction of the subject in language in terms of divisions between speaking and spoken subject and between the conscious and unconscious.
- The work of Stuart Hall, Homi Bhabha and Judith Butler is taken as exemplary with respect to locating philosophical ideas about subjectivity within the context of political, lived experiences of race, ethnicity, sex and gender.
- Hall, Bhabha and Butler offer different responses to a common problematic that can be typified in the following manner:
  - subjectivity is put under the sign of identity and difference and is caught in the dialectic of recognition and desire;
  - cultural authority is always in question and identity-categories (points of recognition) are always provisional and problematic;
  - subjectivity is disclosed as a problem of the relation between the psyche and the social.
- Work on understandings of the self in terms of its co-relationality with objects, as well as language, throws up a significant array of problems concerning the folding of the subject, its constitution through affirmation rather than negation, and its singularity as a series of becomings.

SIX Body: Between Nature and Techonology

Much contemporary thinking on identity talks about the situated and embodied nature of the self. In this chapter I want to consider the question of the body not only in relation to the human body, but more broadly in the context of recent work within social and cultural theory, cultural anthropology, science and technology studies and sociology that investigates the body somewhere between nature and technology. Cultural studies, as with other disciplines, has favoured an understanding of culture as the leading critical edge against the conservatism of essentialist notions of nature, technology and the body. Thus, for example, to talk about people or things as having 'natural' qualities or features has often been thought of in terms of those qualities or features as being fixed and essential. This is clearly problematic when the relation of representation is also seen as a relation of power. If an Afro-Caribbean man is defined as having certain 'natural' features, then we might want to question how these features are ascribed to that person and the how the term 'natural' is being used in this ascription. Typically, then, 'nature' in this sense has been used to fix particular qualities to a person or thing. The response to this has been to argue that all ascriptions of qualities to persons or things are conducted within linguistic, semiotic or cultural systems. It is not that a person has 'natural' qualities, but that particular cultural or signifying practices encode that person with those qualities and that the naming of some thing or person as 'natural' has an ideological function. Hence, in focusing on the way that people and things are constructed allows us also to focus on the more sociological aspects of relations of power (i.e. who is doing the speaking or representing, from what institutional and discursive location, and who is being spoken for or represented). As Stuart Hall has noted, with respect to the construction of 'blackness':

> Typical of this racialized regime of representation was the practice of reducing the cultures of black people to Nature, or *naturalizing* 'difference'. The logic behind **naturalization** is simple. If the

> differences between black and white people are 'cultural', then they are open to modification and change. But if they are 'natural' – as the slave-holders believed – then they are beyond history, permanent and fixed. 'Naturalization' is therefore a representational strategy designed to *fix* 'difference', and thus *secure it forever*. It is an attempt to halt the inevitable 'slide' of meaning, to secure discursive or ideological 'closure'. (1997b: 245 bold in orginal)

One of the problems with this type of argument is that it seems to lock us into a series of a priori assumptions: that fluidity is politically valued over fixity; that nature is politically reactionary and culture is progressive; that the disciplines that anchor these categories (i.e. most starkly, nature is rooted in biology and culture in the human sciences) have de facto politics; and that those who speak for culture, as thus defined (e.g. cultural studies researchers, some cultural anthropologists, some sociologists and so on), are more progressive than those who speak for nature (e.g. biologists, geneticists and so on). This leads us into rather odd situations whereby we might be forced into thinking that statements made by contemporary geneticists – for example, that there is no scientific genetic grounding to racial theories of population differentiation – should be questioned and discredited as naturalising discourses. We could, on the contrary, argue that 'culture' is way behind in terms of its representation of 'race' and nature, whereas genetics is more progressive; moreover, it would also seem that culture provides the ground for a new racism which essentialises racial identity with cultural boundaries and belonging (cf. Ahmed, 1999; Balibar and Wallerstein, 1991; Gilroy 1993b, 1995).

The central issue here then is not to get fixated on 'nature' or 'culture' as having any a priori political value, but that any political value is constructed, as Hall states above, strategically. Thus, although we might notice that the nineteenth century and much of the twentieth century was dominated by a notion that nature was a fixed unchanging thing that by and large supported conservative values concerning sexuality, 'race', ethnicity and gender, we could not assume that this was necessarily the case for all practices and events within this period nor could we assume that it was the case now. Moreover, as a consequence of the rapid changes in computer and biotechnologies and the recovery of earlier Classical, pre-modern and Enlightenment understandings of the relation between nature, culture and technology, we might be more open to the fluid opportunities that cross over these supposedly traditional boundaries. It is with this in mind that we will look to the work of Donna Haraway and Deleuze and Guattari on organisms and machines, to Bruno Latour and his colleagues on what has been called 'actor-network theory', and to the question of 'bio-power', or the power over life, as understood through the lens of Foucault and the French historian of science Georges Canguilhem. Of importance to the work of these writers is not only the impact of a changing world – and of the centrality of science and technology in these changes - but also the extent to which it is valid to think of judgement or knowledge (whether political or ethical, social scientific or human scientific) outside of the dynamic and energy of the mixed relations of organism, machine and matter. In the field of cultural politics, we could put this crudely in terms of the extent to which it is possible to have a politics that stands outside of - as if like Descartes, mind thinking separately from the mechanical world - life itself.

Cyborgs

The term *cyborg* (short for 'cybernetic organism') appears in a paper titled 'Cyborgs and Space', by an engineer and psychiatrist, Manfred Clynes and Nathan Kline, in 1960. The paper describes an 'augmented man' designed to survive and to be able to manipulate a strange and hostile environment. The body of an astronaut would be controlled through intravenous injections of drugs to enhance the function of their body and to enable them to maintain a state of alertness. But this is just one of many forms of organic and machine hybrid. In the post-war period cyborgs have proliferated and become highly popularised figures, from the Six Million Dollar Man to Robocop to Russian monkeys in space called HAM to artists, such as Stelarc, attaching machine-parts to themselves across computer networks.

In cultural studies a key figure responsible for drawing our attention to the complex relations between and across organism, technology and matter is the once biologist, now cultural theorist Donna Haraway. Although the figure of the cyborg stretches across much of her work, one article in particular is responsible for much of the excitement about human and non-human figurations. In 'A cyborg manifesto: science, technology, and socialist-feminism in the late twentieth century' (1991a [1985]), she makes the case for three 'boundary breakdowns' between: human and animal, organism and machine, and physical and non-physical. First, in relation to the breakdown between animal and human, we could think of how primatologists have discovered the complex social systems of apes and of their capacity for linguistic acquisition, so culture and language cannot be seen as a unique human achievement. We might also cite how animal rights activists have countered claims about human uniqueness and have argued that animals not only have a capacity for feeling pain, but because of this they have a natural right to well-being. For example, the calls by animal rights activists for the closure of scientific animal experimentation factories have been made on the basis of the animals' rights to full and happy lives according to their species-being. The political comparison is made between oppressed peoples and exploited animals. As Haraway declares in a slightly different context: '[f]ar from signalling a walling off of people from other living beings, cyborgs signal disturbingly and pleasurably tight coupling' (1991a: 152). Secondly, in relation to the breakdown between organism and machine, we might look to the way in which machines are integral to modern forms of human life: seeing with the aid of contact lenses or living with a pacemaker or breathing with a respirator. Is it possible to think today without the aid of a writing instrument and recording surface (pen and paper or computer word-processor) to help organise our thoughts? Can we go shopping without a list? And thirdly, in relation to the breakdown between physical and non-physical, we might think of the rise in importance of 'cultural' matters, of the way in which modern economies are weighted toward 'soft' goods and services (media, computer, lifestyle and so on) and of the centrality of computers in the miniaturisation of machines so that they appear 'post-industrial' due to their apparent disappearance.

In this early article, these boundary breakdowns are firmly located, through description and example, in late twentieth century US political and scientific culture. They rest upon broad shifts in the biosciences and biotechnology, in engineering, and in computer science and technology, and upon the role these sciences and technologies play in contemporary culture and economic organisation. Haraway states:

> I argue for a politics rooted in claims about fundamental changes in the nature of class, race, and gender in an emerging system of world order analogous in its novelty and scope to that created by industrial capitalism; we are living through a movement from an organic, industrial society to a polymorphous, information system – from all work to all play ... Simultaneously material and ideological... from the comfortable old hierarchical dominations to the scary new networks I have called the informatics of domination. (1991a: 161)

But the questions remain as to whether and to what extent the ordering that Haraway observes is one that emerges in a particular narrative of progress and out of a particular place. Is the cyborg the latest manifestation of progress and civilisation? Is the US at the forefront of this post-industrial modernity? Moreover, is this ordering unevenly figured across the globe? If so, what are the conditions that give rise to greater 'development' in one region and lesser 'development' in another? And if we see these boundary breakdowns across human and animal, organism and machine, and physical and non-physical, for example, in post-Ba'athist Iraq should we look for the lines of power that run back to a US military and transnational capital central command?

It is legitimate to ask these questions because in many ways the figuring of the cyborg by Haraway is more than just an issue of the breakdowns that she poses. In many ways the boundaries between animal and human, organism and machine and physical and non-physical have been the central issues in philosophical enquiry from, and before, Plato and Aristotle to Descartes and La Mettrie to Heidegger and onward. Moreover, the fictional figuring of cyborg-like monsters is abundant, for example, in classical mythology (chimera and gorgons), in Jewish folk stories (the golem) and in English literature (Frankenstein's monster). In the late eighteenth century a mechanical chess player was built by a European by the name of Wolfgang von Kempelen (cf. Wood, 2002). The chess player had remarkable skills and took on and beat the great chess players and royalty across Europe. It was only later that the automaton was discovered to house a man within the machine (despite earlier attempts to reveal such a truth). Is the chess player a cyborg? Or is the emergence of the cyborg specifically tied to a particular epochal shift (i.e. computers and bioscience make the world different or are symptomatic of a different world)?

For Haraway, the cyborg becomes a way of foregrounding the relations between the organic and machine, body and sign, and technology and meaning. For her materiality and semiosis are always figured simultaneously as the 'material-semiotic' (1997, 2000). Commenting on this aspect of the figuring of the material-semiotic in Haraway's writing, Claudia Castañeda states that:

> A figure ... is the simultaneous material and semiotic effect of specific practices. Understood as figures, furthermore, particular categories of existence can also be considered in terms of their uses - what they 'body forth' in turn. Figuration is thus understood here to incorporate a double force: constitutive effect and generative circulation. (2002: 3)

But if the material-semiotic is figured or shaped, it is not on the basis that either the material or the semiotic is active and the other is passive. For Haraway, matter is not passive and inert; it is active, mobilising and meaning-generating. Although Haraway is not clear about this - and offers no real elaboration - it could be said that either matter is made up of actors with equal weight to, and always tied to, semiotic actors or rather material agency of necessity always has semiotic agency, such that the material and the semiotic are only formally and not substantially distinct. Whatever the case, Haraway, in her analyses of the cultural studies of science and technology, doesn't construe scientific knowledge as active and constructive and matter as that which is constituted within the cultural practices of science. For Haraway, the object of knowledge is also an actor. Haraway moves away from a logic of representation. Witnessing is never naked, always materially constructed, situated and articulated. Haraway deconstructs and situates the modest witness (as discussed for example by Steven Shapin, 1994) as a masculine figure:

> This self-invisibility [of the witness] is the specifically modern, European, masculine, scientific form of the virtue of modesty. This is the form of modesty that pays off its practitioners in the coin of epistemological and social power. This kind of modesty is one of the founding virtues of what we call modernity. This is virtue that guarantees that the modest witness is the legitimate and authorized ventriloquist for the object world, adding nothing from his mere opinions, from his biasing embodiment. And so he is endowed with the remarkable power to establish facts. He bears witness: he is objective; he guarantees the clarity and purity of objects. His subjectivity is his objectivity. (Haraway, 1997: 23–4)

The notion of the material-semiotic thus presents a problem with regard to some traditional understandings of epistemology (theories of knowledge or ways of knowing) and ontology (theories of being or forms of existence). Instead of assuming that the subject of knowledge is an active subject and the object of knowledge is a passive entity waiting to be known, Haraway – in making matter an active matter – does not allow matter to just sit there under the microscope, as it were. In Haraway's account the microbe, the cell structure, the metal and so on, jump back and catch the observer within a more complex kind of 'cat's cradle' (to use one of Haraway's metaphors). In this sense, epistemology and ontology are intimately related and often blur. And this is nowhere more apparent than in relation to the kind of organic-technological hybrids that Haraway investigates. Cyborg biotechnological fusions deliver entities that make us question our often taken-for-granted categories and divisions between the human and non-human or the organic and machine. In typically hyperbolic rhetoric, Haraway declares:

> Biological narratives, theories, and technologies seem relevant to practically every aspect of human experience at the end of the twentieth century. The biological body – and its mirror twin, the informational body – is the wormhole through which explorers will be hurtled into unexplored territories in the New World Order ... Fueled by important social concerns, large infusions of capital, epistemological confidence, international relevance, and the sheer excitement and fascination of the subject, every area of biology is expanding ... Never has there been a time when engaging the heterogeneous practices of constructing biological knowledge has been more important. (1997: 117)

Biology – as the cutting edge of contemporary technoscience – is, as cyberfeminist Sarah Kember has argued, '*the* hegemonic discourse of the late twentieth and early twenty-first centuries' (2003: 178). As another commentator on Haraway's work has stated: '[b]iology, woven in and through information technologies and systems, along with information technology, is one of the great "representing machines" of the late twentieth century' (Goodeve, 2000: 26). In this sense, 'new media technologies' refer to the way in which new genetic technoscience construes the body as 'coded' and 'codeable'. Not film nor television nor literature, but 'life itself' is the leading-edge representing machine of contemporary society. What was the 'content' of earlier representing machines, such as film, print and television, has now become a *medium* itself. Biology now represents and carries representations. Biology is understood, not just as knowledge, but as code and codeable bodies: DNA is seen as the quintessential late modern medium of communication. Haraway says: '[t]he genome is a historically specific collective construct, built by and from humans and nonhumans. To be "made" is not to be "made up" ... The reality and materiality of the genome is simultaneously semiotic, institutional, machinic, organic, and biotechnical' (1997: 99).

In this respect, Haraway's work connects with, although is somewhat different to, other *constructivist* (but not *social* constructivist) thinking. For example, Deleuze and Guattari argue that there is no opposition between human and nature or between industry and nature; on the contrary, everything is seen in terms of production (1983b: 2). For Deleuze and Guattari the issue is not to examine pre-existing fixed entities such as 'human' and 'nature', but to look instead at how productive processes, or machines, are productive of particular connections. They state: '[a]n organ-machine is plugged into an energy-source machine: the one produces a flow that the other interrupts' (1983b: 1). Thus, eating a cheese and pickle sandwich is about the connection between a flow of food (the sandwich) that is dissected by a cutting machine (the teeth) and that gets reproduced by an organ-machine (the digestive system) into energy and so it goes on. Things get connected to things, but in doing so, they necessarily disconnect those things from the things to which they were originally attached. Assemblages are formed through connections and breaks. Machines produce flows of connections and breaks; but, in turn, every machine is itself but a series of connections and breaks. In order to construe these machines with motivation, Deleuze and Guattari talk about machines as 'desiring-machines'. But the desire is not external to the machine; it is only composed within the machine and through its ability to cut, shape and organise. Machines that slice bread originally came from iron ore turned into steel and shaped into machine parts: breaks and flows making different flows and breaks:

> [E]very machine functions as a break in the flow in relation to the machine to which it is connected, but at the same time is also a flow itself, or the production of a flow, in relation to the machine connected to it. This is the law of the production of production. (1983b: 36)

If material cultural life is composed of machines that connect and disconnect, then some assemblages are formed rather than others: '[d]esiring-machines make us an organism; but ... within the very production of this production, the body suffers from being organised in this way, from not having some sort of organisation, or no organisation at all' (1983b: 8). In Deleuze and Guattari's thinking, bodies are not organic entities (as we might ordinarily understand the term), rather they refer to entities that have organs attached (i.e. a human body has a respiratory system, a digestive system, a reproductive system, plus arms and legs, eyes, hearing, tasting and smelling functions). But unlike classical Aristotelian thinking that argues that the organism is the form, or the collective organisation, of those organs, Deleuze and Guattari argue that the organs are detachable and have no necessary relation or interpretation with regard to a specific body-form.

In this sense, Deleuze and Guattari talk about bodies without organs as entities that exist and that need organs attached to them in order to exist. Thus, as a short-sighted person, I need glasses or contact lenses to see far away. The glasses are organs. Or a disabled woman who is unable to walk unassisted needs a wheelchair in order to move. The organ of the wheelchair is not peripheral to her existence; it helps to define her existence (e.g. in terms of her exclusion from certain forms of transport such as escalators, small cars or buses and so on) and her connectivity to other machines (e.g. wide check-out aisles in supermarkets). Just as the desiring-machine acts as a writing machine, the body upon which the organs are attached – the body without organs – acts as a recording surface. But the recording surface – in order for it to be written on – must eradicate any signs of possible interpretation: it must be a clean piece of paper. The recording surface allows signs or machines or organs to be connected on itself such that when these machines are connected the recording surface slips from view. Thus the recording surface – the body without organs – makes possible the connectivity of machines, but as such it cannot be a machine itself. Moreover, before the machines are connected, the recording surface must be unseen, unadorned and unknown:

> The body without organs, the unproductive, the unconsumable, serves as a surface for the recording of the entire process of production of desire, so that desiring-machines seem to emanate from it in the apparent objective movement that establishes a relationship between machines and the body without organs ... Machines attach themselves to the body without organs as so many points of disjunction, between which an entire network of new syntheses is now woven, marking the surface off into co-ordinates, like a grid. (Deleuze and Guattari 1983b: 11–2)

If the connection of desiring-machines marks the body without organs as a grid or a network, then the form of the network is a multiplicity: '[i]t is only the category of the multiplicity, used as substantive and going beyond both the One and the many, beyond the predicative relation of the One and the many, that can account for desiring-production: desiring-production is pure multiplicity, that is to say, an affirmation that is irreducible to any sort of unity' (1983b: 42). Thus the recording surface (the body without organs) – or what Deleuze and Guattari also refer to as a 'plane of consistency' (1988) – allows machines to become connected, but does not shape their connection: '[t]he plane of consistency is the organless body of all axiomatic systems; it is not the total being of the machinism, but the impossibility of concluding or totalising machinic expression' (Guattari, 1984: 125).

Unlike Deleuze and Guattari's multiplicitous or rhizomatic understanding of cyborg relations, Haraway's cyborg is figured within the terms of hegemonic struggle. In her early essay (as in much of her writing) a quick-witted and joyful turn of phrase places the cyborg as a political myth of our times. It becomes a figure through which we can think and imagine our complex relation not just to others (beings and things), but to political change: '[t]he cyborg is our ontology; it gives us our politics' (1991a: 150). The epistemology and political subjectivity of the cyborg is enframed within the logic of cybernetics (information and feedback, command and control) and information theory (message, code, sender/receiver). The cyborg is caught in a feedback loop. It is at once produced within the conditions of late modernity and also the agent of change. Haraway's cyborg manifesto is an attempt to formulate a form of 'critique' that: deconstructs the traditional boundaries of Western modernity; de-autonomises, de-centralises and de-subjectifies power; constructs a politics of articulation (i.e. the building of alliances through the construction of elective affinities, situated knowledge and the shift away from standpoint politics and epistemology); and is not critique, but *diffraction* (i.e. not about revealing truth, but intervening and creating new patterns) (cf. Haraway, 1991b). The cyborg, then, is in keeping with a particular critical political theory at that time (i.e. one developed through the resources of anti-humanist, post-structuralist and neo-Gramscian cultural theory). But Haraway's cyborg (or cyberfeminist) politics marks a difference in terms of a radical deconstruction of, and proper engagement with, the relations across and between nature and culture. Biology is no longer held at arms length. Moreover, Haraway's favoured critical engagement is not critique (which she typifies in terms of its negativity), but the positivity of 'diffraction'. Diffraction literally refers to the splitting of light into different bands or coloured spectra. For Haraway, diffraction – unlike Voloshinov's 'refraction' which concerns the deflection of light or the accenting of signs (1973) – is about critical political change predicated upon production, connection and creation:

> My invented category of semantics, *diffractions*, takes advantage of the optical metaphors and instruments that are so common in Western philosophy and science. Reflexivity has been much recommended as a critical practice, but my suspicion is that reflexivity, like reflection, only displaces the same elsewhere, setting up the worries about copy and original and the search for the authentic and really real. Reflexivity is a bad trope for escaping the false choice between realism and relativism in thinking about strong objectivity and situated knowledges in technoscientific knowledge. What we

> need is to make a difference in material-semiotic apparatuses, to diffract the rays of technoscience so that we get more promising interference patterns on the recording films of our lives and bodies. Diffraction is an optical metaphor for the effort to make a difference in the world. (Haraway, 1997: 16)

In that sense, Haraway's is a critical practice shaped within, as I said above, a neo-Gramscian framework of counter-hegemonic alliances and politics. Diffraction is about 'articulation', the connection between things (cf. Campbell, 2004). It also bears some relation to the ideas of Deleuze and Guattari's inasmuch as change is only ever construed as production and creation. It draws on, as discussed in the previous chapter, a Nietzschean affirmation and activity (as against the *ressentiment* of a reactive politics of negativity). But equally, diffraction, according to Haraway, is not concerned with the light rays as they are divided on the screen (i.e. in terms of their separate identities), 'it's about registering process on the recording screen' (2000: 104). Thus, for example, primate politics cannot simply be fixated on the construction of apes in scientific knowledge and it cannot simply say over and over again, 'You've got it wrong'; it has to connect to that scientific knowledge and resituate it within ecological change, environmental politics, rain forest and jungle de-forestation and so on. The gorilla or the proboscis monkey provide the recording screen that allow articulations to be made and processes to be registered in connection to each other. Unlike an earlier form of cultural theory that based its politics on an anti-realism, Haraway's politics and critical practice (as with Deleuze and Guattari's) is a form of realism; the point is not to reveal the mythic status of the supposed 'nature', but to (re)construct new connections as real durable connections.

For some readers of Haraway the politics of the cyborg raises significant problems. Baukje Prins, the Dutch feminist philosopher, argues that Haraway figures an ethics of antihumanism and of solidanty (1995). Twisting the argument slightly, we can see how the cyborg is caught within a contradictory ethics both Nietzschean and anti-Nietzschean at the same time. On the one hand, the account of boundary breakdowns (between human/animal, organism/machine and physical/non-physical) takes the form of Nietzsche's genealogical deconstruction of binaries (i.e. between two identities). The cyborg is neither organism nor machine, but both and neither. Equally the deconstruction of these boundaries is premised on an anti-humanism: namely, the 'human' as an a priori subject does not exist. People exist within extended kinship systems (including both animals and machines). On the other hand though, the figure of the cyborg is rooted in a Judeo-Christian ethics of care and solidarity (or at least it's re-articulation in the context of nineteenth century industrial society in terms of the rising-up of the oppressed, the hero(ine) taking on the sins of the world and the 'human' (as saviour) figured against an encroaching de-humanising machine). Haraway's cyborg is figured within a narrative of redemption, a version of a Hegelian and Marxist master-slave narrative. The epochal themes in Haraway's cyborg manifesto provide evidence for such a reading. Some writers, such as Mike Michael (2000), in his reading of Haraway, sees no problem with aligning these two ethics. However, without the theoretical labour to make these ethics happily coexistent, we have to wonder *contra* Prins if they are not only antagonistic but contradictory. The question then is: is an ethics of cyborg life always prone to this contradiction?

Actors and Networks

Although Haraway is insistent that the cyborg is not humanoid, inevitably the striking figures in her work take on this form. HAM, the cyborg, FemaleMan©, and Oncomouse™ all have anthropomorphic features. Moreover, her characters come to life within broad and 'imaginary' historical periodisations (or 'narratives'), such as the 'Second Christian Millennium', and socio-political spaces, such as the 'New World Order inc.' (1997: 2). These times and spaces figure as canvasses or forms of *mise-en-scene*. They provide a setting for the characters; they are not shown to be constructed by the characters themselves. In contrast, the work of the French and British sociologists of science and technology Michel Callon, Bruno Latour and John Law – whose work is often collectively referred to as 'actor network theory' or 'ANT' – have sought to understand how things get made from scratch. The starting point of actor-network theory – or, as it is also called, the sociology of translation and association – is supposedly to start at the beginning and to presume no pre-existing concepts or contexts. Even in the rare cases, such as Latour's *We Have Never Been Modern* (1993), when the broad sweep of Eurocentric history is considered from the pre-modern to modern to post-modern, it is done so in order to problematise such grand understandings of time and space and to pursue a more localised, micro-sociological sensibility with regard to the mixedness, or hybridity, of culture and nature. In many ways, then, the sociology of translation is a method or way of understanding, pure and simple; it is not a theory as such.

The sociology of translation began in the 1980s with the work of Callon, Latour and Law within the context of debates within the sociology of (scientific) knowledge (SSK) and to a certain extent within the sociology of technology. But whereas SSK foregrounded and privileged 'social' understandings and explanations, ANT tried to understand the problem from, as it were, both, or all, sides. Thus, if ANT is a method, it is one that is posed against the pitfalls of the traditional social and natural sciences that construe 'society' (and its adjective the 'social'), 'nature' (and the 'natural') and 'technology' (and the 'technological') as a priori starting points or privileged means of explanation. The intention, then, was not simply to deconstruct these categories or the divisions of knowledge (i.e. as between biology and sociology or mechanics and anthropology) upon which such categories are entrenched, but to treat all agency as unmarked and symmetrical: namely, not to presume, for example, that a door spring is an inert object that does not have intentionality or autonomous agency. In order to mark this symmetry, ANT refers to these agents as actors or actants and it presumes that each actor carries no necessary or pre-existent qualities other than those that are constructed within a network within which it necessarily finds itself. Moreover, ANT is explicitly concerned with mapping the semiotic movement and consolidation of material entities, hence the focus on things technological and scientific. We will discuss this in more detail later, but for the moment let us look at an example.

In 1986 Callon wrote an article about the decline of the scallop (a mollusc-like sea creature that clings to rocks) population in St. Brieuc Bay in north-western France, about three marine biologists brought in to develop a conservation strategy for the scallops, and about the fishermen who want a healthy scallop population to fish and thus make a living. For Callon these different characters constitute different actors within a scientific, social, economic and natural event and, instead of assuming that the actors come to the event with ready-made characteristics, Callon suggests that all must be treated symmetrically. Thus, no single group of actors has a priori power over other actors. We cannot assume from the start – and with regard to this particular event – who has power and who does not. Moreover, we cannot assume, Callon argues, that each actor has certain essential capacities rather than others: namely, that it is only the humans who have agency and the scallops not, or that one set of actors lives on the side of culture and society and are governed by those rules and laws and that another set of actors are governed by the laws and rules of nature. Callon, then, approaches these actors in an idiosyncratic fashion and talks about the scallops, for example, as having intentionality, motivation and interests, just as the fishermen and the scientists. He talks about the scallops not obliging the scientists in their experiments and wilfully not clinging to the rocks. This is what is meant by symmetry: treat all actors – whether they be humans, tools, animals, plants, or matter – the same.

In this particular article, Callon is interested in how scientific knowledge is constructed and so much of his discussion looks at the issue of the declining scallop population in terms of the way in which the scientists are able to make their knowledge indispensable to the other actors. The scientists need to construct an approach to the problem that makes them indispensable to both the scallops and fishermen and in doing so they need to make their research indispensable to a wider scientific community. The scientists construct interesting and valid scientific knowledge, but they also construct knowledge that is able to travel outside of the particular locale of St. Brieuc. The knowledge they produce must have some consistency across time and space; the knowledge must be encoded, in Callon and Latour's phrase, through particular 'immutable mobiles'. For example, a scientific paper is able to travel from the scientific laboratory to the conference hall and then to an academic journal. While the contexts change around the paper, the paper remains constant. Moreover, the knowledge must not simply be valid in a positivist sense of representing the world in a truthful way, but it must be persuasive: namely, it must persuade others, not only the scientific community, but also the fishermen and the scallops. Callon talks about how the scallops and fishermen must become enrolled in the scientists' account of the decline of the scallops. The scallops must wilfully agree to the way in which the scientists represent their behaviour; they must, in this sense, not act up, but act in accordance with the will of the scientists. The scientists, then, are mobilised as spokespersons for the other actors; they represent, or rather translate, the interests of the other actors. In speaking for the other actors, the scientists attempt to establish themselves as gatekeepers, or to use Callon and Latour's phrase, 'obligatory passage points'. All other actors must 'pass through' the scientists in order to meet their objectives. All accounts must be refracted through the account of the scientists in order to pass muster.

Instead of understanding bodies of knowledge, bodies of material, and agentic bodies as enclosed and sealed, ANT seeks to make visible the mechanisms, mobilisations, and translations that go into producing closure. In a similar fashion to those analysing the process of essentialisation or naturalisation of a discourse or social relation, ANT looks at how socio-technical-natural relations are 'black-boxed': namely, how a technology is made to appear as if it worked on its own without the help of a series of networks that facilitate its invention and use, or how certain scientific 'facts' are 'black-boxed' inasmuch as they are made to appear truthful, impenetrable, fixed and unchangeable.

The language of ANT is that of politics and strategy and it is in many ways similar to that of Gramsci and the neo-Gramscians. Alliances must be formed, actors mobilised, interests represented, and, although they never use this term, hegemonies constructed. Moreover, any hegemonic consensus serves the interests of the dominant spokesperson, but their interests are never served pure and are always a negotiated settlement with the others. This is the nature of consent. As with Gramsci, both Callon and Latour have a particular affinity to Machiavelli's sixteenth century analysis of the political figuring of the 'Prince' (cf. Latour, 1988; Machiavelli, 2003). But for ANT, the prince is of machines as well as humans. Or rather, the very divisions between 'nature', 'technology', 'society' and 'culture' are seen as the outcomes of mobilisation, not the qualities of the actors or networks themselves. That said, we should be wary of assuming that all mobilisations are successful or of looking at actor-networks only from the perspective of their successful outcome. We should be wary of framing actor-networks within a 'mock-heroic history' (cf. Barnes, 2001: 344) and we should be aware that networks are cut as well as assembled (cf. Strathern, 1996).

Just as Callon, in his analysis of the happenings of St. Brieuc Bay, presumes that intentionality and calculation are not only facets of the human, but also of the scallop, we can approach historical and institutional divisions as outcomes of localised action, association, and mobilisation. Consider for example the case of the television industry and contemporary media analysis. Instead of assuming that television audiences sit on one side of the fence and television producers sit on the other (that is, audiences interpret, use and are affected by television programmes, whereas television producers make programmes, control people making the programmes, control budgets and sell or pass on their programmes to the distributors) we might want to look at the slow building of that division of labour between audience interpretation and television production. These activities are not qualitatively different kinds of activity (production and interpretation). These activities are only ascribed these qualities – 'meaning-based' or 'labour-based' – within particular forms of practice (i.e. academic media studies). Instead of assuming that there is an essential difference between these activities, we might want to consider how that distribution of competencies, dispositions, and actions is itself constructed and mobilised within academic and industrial practice (cf. Oswell, 2002). Equally though, we should be wary of presuming pre-existing networks. We should be wary of assuming, for example, the pre-existence of a technological network such as 'the internet' and then framing 'human' activity around such networks. Such an analysis would a priori assume a divide between technology and human and would tend toward a sort of technological determinism. In contrast, ANT invites us to consider the building-up of a network and allows us to investigate the heterogeneous engineering of complex networks in such a way that doesn't prioritise the nature or the determinant of the network. This is a methodological gesture that can be found elsewhere in the human sciences, for example, in ethnomethodology and in Foucauldian genealogy.

Unsurprisingly the core ontological units of ANT are 'actors', who, through their association, form 'networks'. In their early writings, Latour and

Callon suggest that it is correct to refer to the agents that get mobilised within networks as 'actants', rather than as actors. It should be noted that although they say this, they rarely keep to using the term 'actant' themselves. Nevertheless, one of the reasons that they give is that - unlike the notion of 'actor' which might be seen only to refer to human agents - the notion of 'actant' refers to both human and non-human entities. The term itself comes from Algirdas Greimas' work on structural semiotics and particularly his re-reading of Vladimir Propp's formalist analysis of folk tales (Greimas, 1984, 1987). Propp divided folk tales into their different narrative functions, of which he discovered 30 or so, including the villain, the hero and so on (1968). For Propp every folk tale could be reduced to a set of relations between these narrative functions. Greimas reduces the number of narrative functions even further and talks not of functions or characters, but of actants (cf. Barthes, 1977). Greimas analyses actants grammatically and he translates Propp's narrative functions into a series of oppositions between subject/object, donor/receiver and helper/opponent. For example, in *The Wizard of Oz*, Dorothy is the subject of the narrative in search of a way home to Kansas (i.e. her object). Her opponents are the wicked witches and her helpers, the lion, scarecrow and tin man. But actants are not equivalent to characters and we can see that a single actantial function can structure the actions of a range of different characters. Thus, the lion, scarecrow and tin man collectively have the same actantial function. Moreover, the actions of any one character can be structured by more than one actantial function. Thus, Dorothy is the subject of the narrative, but she is also the receiver of a gift (namely, the red shoes as her means of getting home) given to her by the Good Fairy (i.e. the donor). Actants are not characters, are not defined by intrinsic personality, and can include many different actors. Moreover, actantial functions in one particular narrative have a formal equivalence to similar functions in other narratives.

For Greimas, then, the actant can be understood only within the logic of structural analysis. Actants are structural types. But, in contrast, ANT insists on the actant as having a necessary relation, not to structure, but to particular networks. Although the methodological imperative of symmetry implies that all actants must have a formal equivalence prior to their association and mobilisation, actants, for ANT, are not defined as structural types nor are their actions typified with reference to a structural logic. For ANT, actants are particular actors; they can only be defined by their particularity because to do otherwise would be to suggest that they have a prior definition: namely, one constructed outside of the network within which they are positioned. In this sense, then, it may be better to refer to actors as 'actors', rather than as 'actants'. ANT provides a strategic model of socio-technical-natural relations, not a structural model. The term 'network' is deployed for precisely that reason, to emphasise the instability and contingency of any network. Again Greimas provides a useful point of contrast. Greimas reduces narrative actions to a limited set of actantial functions and this defines narrative structure in terms of a limited set of axiomatic relations (i.e. between subject/object, helper/opponent and donor/receiver). Any particular story might involve a different permutation of the structural elements; but that particular story would, nevertheless, be a model or representation of a narrative structure. Thus, for example, although the story of *Shrek 2* is very different in many ways from *The Wizard of Oz*, it nevertheless contains the same structural relations. Shrek, the subject of the narrative, must recover his relationship with Fiona (the object of his quest). He is helped by Donkey and Puss in Boots, plus other minor characters, such as Pinocchio and the Gingerbread Man, and he is hindered by the Fairy Godmother and Prince Charming. Both Shrek and Fiona are transformed into beautiful humanoid figures by a magic potion given by (or stolen from) the wicked Fairy Godmother. As Dorothy's love of home is truly revealed to her at the end of *The Wizard of Oz*, so too do Shrek and Fiona truly recognise that love is not tied to beauty or human form. In both quest stories, although there is a movement from equilibrium to disequilibrium to equilibrium, the narrative movement results in a transformation. Both *The Wizard of Oz* and *Shrek 2* contain the same actants and represent the same narrative structure.

In contrast, then, to forms of analysis that foreground the structural sameness, or isomorphism, between two or more groups of elements or actors, ANT holds that any particular actor-network is the result of a particular series of associations and mobilisations. In the actor-network model there is movement, contingency and instability at the levels of both actor and network. In this sense, the hyphen between actor and network indicates that the instability of the former is dependent on the flux in the latter and vice versa (cf. Callon, 1992). Networks are defined by their mutability. They change, but in changing, the 'identity' of the actors also change. One of the reasons why they change is that, at the outset, any series of associations cannot be defined prior to their mobilisation and, in that sense, any network is, *in potentia*, open. Any closure that may occur is only the result, a posteriori, of the boundary formations of the actor-network (cf. Star and Griesemer, 1989). If a new actor enters the chain, the other actors change accordingly. In this sense, networks, unlike systems of differences (as in Saussure) are strategically flexible and are more akin to Deleuze and Guattari's 'rhizome': 'the rhizome is made only of lines: lines of segmentation and stratification as dimensions, but also lines of flight or of deterritorialisation as the maximal dimension according to which, by following it, the multiplicity changes its nature and metamorphoses' (Deleuze and Guattari, 1983a: 48). In these and other ways, some writers working out of the tradition of ANT have used more explicitly the work of Deleuze and Guattari (cf. Law and Hassard, 1999).

As we have already seen, any relations between actors are seen to be predicated on no prior asymmetry. We cannot presume, for example, that any actor has prior definition or substance or unequal access to resources. And yet, we must presume at the outset that actors are capable of willed action, of some sorts, and that they have the capacity to form associations, and that they seek to mobilise others. We must also presume that if actor-networks are to be formed, then the mobilisation of certain actors over and against others is dependent on, at least, a presumed asymmetry in terms of the substantive resources that those actors, rather than others, have, or are imagined to have, to hand. Thus, for example, in Callon's story of St. Brieuc Bay, we might imagine that the fishermen call upon the scientists to help with the problem of the declining scallop population only because the scientists are perceived to have certain capacities, resources, talents, and authority that would be different from that of a group of bankers, lawyers, or schoolteachers. With the proviso that the identity of the actors are themselves shaped through the network, different actors are construed, not as being formally equivalent, but as having strategically defined greater or lesser resources and authority than others.

In many ways though, the particularity of the actor-network needs to be defined with reference to the differences perceived by the actors, but also to actual substantial differences. In order to get a sense of how this adds to our understanding of actor-networks and how this is different from a naive realism, we need to look at how the relation between actors is a relation of translation, not representation. Callon in his paper on St. Brieuc Bay talks about ANT as a sociology of translation. The problem though is that across the body of work within ANT different understandings of the notion of 'translation' circulate. One reading of translation construes it in a quite conventional political and aesthetic sense of 'representation'. The actor at the end of the mobilisation, as it were, is able to bring closure (albeit partially) and represent or become spokesperson for the actors hereto assembled below them (cf. Pels, 2000; Star and Griesemer, 1989). Translation is seen to equal hierarchical representation. The representation necessarily represses that which is represented. For example, Callon and Latour argue that:

> By translation we understand all the negotiations, intrigues, calculations, acts of persuasion and violence, thanks to which an actor or force takes, or causes to be conferred on itself, authority to speak or act on behalf of another actor or force ... Whenever an actor speaks of 'us', s/he is translating other actors into a single will, of which s/he becomes spirit and spokesman. S/he begins to act for several, no longer for one alone. S/he becomes stronger. S/he grows. (1981: 280)

In this sense, ANT is understood within the classic model of will and representation as understood, for example, in the work of Jean-Jacques Rousseau: namely, the general will stands in for that which is being represented. There is an absolute equivalence. The spokesperson stands in for that which is spoken for; in doing so, that which is spoken for is reduced to a cipher. But in the same article there is also a more radical sense of translation as that which carries the force, even the materiality, of that which is spoken for, such that what is spoken is never pure, but always hybrid. In this sense, translation does not involve substituting one actor for another, or one voice for another, rather it involves assembling actors together as allies, such that one actor speaks with the support of others.

> An actor ... becomes stronger to the extent that he or she can firmly associate a large number of elements - and, of course, dissociate as speedily as possible elements enrolled by other actors. Strength thus resides in the power to break off and to bind together. (Callon and Latour, 1981: 287)

Strength cannot be seen as a purely formal endeavour; it is built up through numbers of units or through gathering heavier, weightier, stronger units or through being more tactical and sensing that fleet-of-foot is required over stability and weight. Whatever the case, this is not a question of formal equivalence, but of the substantive nature of translation whereby the spokesperson cannot speak for the others without the weight of the others. In this more materialist sense, an actor only changes its identity, if and only if the chain of actors within which it is a part has sufficient weight or power to make that change possible. Changes do not occur just because a new element is added or one of the actors in the network has been changed.

In this latter sense of translation the spokesperson does not repress the other; rather it carries the other with it, but in doing so, the other - and the otherness of the other - is central to the work of translation. This is a notion of translation that is more akin - albeit in a more material way - to Bhabha's notion of translation and hybridity. This is a notion of translation as irreduction (cf. Stengers, 2000). That which translates the other does not repress it (or represent it). Of necessity, that which is translated is irreducible to that which translates. Both are held in tension. The feeling of pain when I tread on a nail does not repress the cut, the wound caused by the nail; both cut and feeling of pain are irreducible and necessarily present. Translation is semiotic and material, formal and substantial. In the terms of Michel Serres, whose work has provided some of the more philosophical inspiration for the ideas of Callon, Latour, and Law (cf. Brown, 2002; Law, 1997; Serres, 1982, 1990), communication is only possible because there is noise and interference. Translation is never representation, as such a pure transference or communication from sender to receiver would imply that no difference (from outside) has entered the passage from A to B:

> The channel carries the flow, but it cannot disappear as a channel, and it brakes (breaks) the flow, more or less ... perfect, successful communication no longer includes any mediation. And the canal disappears into immediacy ... There are channels, and thus there must be noise. No canal without noise ... The best relation would be no relation. (Serres, 1982: 79)

In this sense then the translation across actors is never a purely formal endeavour; it must be also material. Moreover, it must be substantial in the sense that actors become tied to the network that were not intended to belong to the network and actors always carry traces (substances) that are formed outside of the network under consideration. No analysis of the formation of an actor-network can hope to replay the story of creation as if from the beginning. Thus, paradoxically, over and above the principle of symmetry and the fantasy of originary equality, the fact of association and mobilisation relies on a wealth of historically sedimented genealogical resources that help to shape the substantial differences between actors and that helps to figure the particularity of each actor-network.

Thinking within 'Life Itself'

If Haraway makes us aware of the hybridisation of modern bodies constructed simultaneously in nature and culture, matter and semiosis and across the diverse regimes of power and capital, then Latour and Callon show us how 'Nature' and 'Culture' are not sufficient to explain the assemblages of relations across bodies, natures, cultures and technologies and how 'bodies' are always complex assemblages, distributed across different and contingent actors, and entangled and mangled through complex heterogeneous engineering. In many ways though, although ANT is correct in its deconstruction of the shibboleths of 'Culture' and 'Nature' (as demonstrated in Latour's *We Have Never Been Modern,* 1993) and the associated sciences and forms of reasoning, a certain paranoia begins to see these abstract universals everywhere, the response to which is the reduction of social, historical, and natural differentiations to a single plateau, the plane of symmetry upon which everything is built. Despite its many talents, ANT is neither a good historian of science nor a good philosopher of history and so before rushing headlong into the folly of a hybrid primordial swamp, we should maybe tread with some caution, understand the specificity of ANT's and Haraway's accounts and offer a more attenuated account of the relations between nature, culture, technology and the body.

There is no better way to start than with the question of 'life itself'. In *The Order of Things: An Archaeology of the Human Sciences* (1970), Michel Foucault presents a now familiar argument that has changed our understanding of the history of the sciences of life. He argues that before the nineteenth century there was no conception of 'life', only a distinction between 'living' and 'non-living' matter. Although Foucault takes no account of earlier ancient Greek philosophical discussions of life (most notably in Aristotle's *De Anima* and *De Generatione Animalum*) or medieval and early modern theological debates concerning the soul, he argues that 'life' properly emerges as an object of the emerging biology in the nineteenth century. In the classical age (a period that Foucault understands as referring to the time between the seventeenth and mid-eighteenth centuries) an earlier natural historical knowledge divided up living and non-living things into animal, vegetable and mineral kingdoms. At this time, natural history, but also other forms of knowledge, including general grammar and the analysis of wealth, were based on a form of epistemic understanding or logic of representation that ordered the world according to the table. Things were differentiated from other things in a tabular form. For example, the natural historical museum takes this form in its organisation of animals and plants into taxonomic series, classifications sitting side-by-side. In contrast, the nineteenth century brought into being a form of understanding and organisation based, not on the table, but on the notion of function and norm: living beings were seen, not only according to their differentiation by species and genus across a table, but also according to their internal development over time.

In *The Order of Things*, as in his other archaeological works (methodologically laid bare in *The Archaeology of Knowledge*, 1972), Foucault focuses on the discursive organisation of rare and discrete forms of discourse (i.e. scientific knowledge) and he understands the emergence of 'life' only in the context of the emergence of a new biological knowledge. Foucault's analysis, in this book, is not the object itself, but its constitution through organisation (i.e. its visibility through organisation). Foucault provides an account of biological knowledge over and above one made up of 'great men' as authors and inventors or one located in social and economic context. His account of the emergence of 'life' and its relation to 'human being' comes out of the French tradition of historical epistemology, namely that history and philosophy of science associated with the work of Gaston Bachelard and Georges Canguilhem.

For Canguilhem historical epistemology is concerned not with the object of science, but with its history:

> [T]he history of science is the history of an object – discourse – that *is* a history and *has* a history, whereas science is the science of an object that is *not* a history, that has *no* history ... The object of the history of science has nothing in common with the object of science. (2000: 26)

For Canguilhem, the scientific object is constituted by 'methodical discourse' and is secondary, although not derived from the initial natural object (the 'pre-text'). The history of science considers the secondary non-natural cultural objects (i.e. the sciences), but equally is not derived from them: '[t]he object of historical discourse is, in effect, the historicity of scientific discourse. By "historicity of scientific discourse" I mean the progress of the discursive project as measured against its own internal norm' (Canguilhem, 2000: 26). There is a certain affinity of these statements about the nature of historical epistemology and Foucault's analysis in his archaeology of the human sciences. But, in contrast to *The Order of Things* and other works of this period, Foucault's later work on genealogy, power and knowledge take a different turn.

In his later work on power and knowledge, Foucault extends the significance of the modern focus on 'life' to the extent that it provides the basis for a new form of power, 'bio-power'. This argument is clearly visible in the *History of Sexuality, Vol. I* (1979) and in surrounding lectures, interviews and articles. We have already reviewed much of the ideas of Foucault on power and governmentality and so my comments here will rest upon that earlier discussion. In *History of Sexuality, Vol. I* Foucault describes two poles of the development of bio-power:

> One of these poles ... centred on the body as a machine: its disciplining, the optimisation of its capabilities, the extortion of its forces, the parallel increase of its usefulness and its docility, its integration into systems of efficient and economic controls, all this was ensured by the procedures of power that characterised the *disciplines*: an *anatomo-politics of the human body*. The second, formed somewhat later, focussed on the species-body, the body imbued with the mechanics of life and serving as the basis of the biological processes: propagation, births and mortality, the level of health, life expectancy and longevity, with all the conditions that can cause these to vary. Their supervision was effected through an entire series of interventions and *regulatory controls: a biopolitics of the population.* (1979: 139)

These poles are construed within his work, broadly conceived, on governmentality concerning the government of individuals and populations and have been understood by-and-large in terms of the emergence of concerns about the welfare and well-being of individuals and populations: namely, in terms of the social and political administration of population growth, sexual disease, medical health, social insurance, psychological well-being, education and so on. One understanding of this new bio-power interprets the individual body and the collective body of the population as entities that could be controlled from the outside, as it were. Bodies could be constructed as particular kinds of bodies, as particular kinds of problems and they could be orchestrated, disciplined, diagnosed, manipulated, and so on, but they could not be radically altered as bodies. Bodies could be constructed in scientific discourse or through photographic imagery. Bodies could be moved around in space and time, in the school, the factory, and the home. And people could perceive their own bodies and relate to their bodies through forms of therapy and medical knowledge. But in this general understanding the unity of the physical body is not contested. These socio-political forms of power and knowledge are seen in terms of their construction *of* the body, not their organisation *with* or *through* the body. Such an understanding, though, misses Foucault's major innovation in our thinking: namely, his reconceptualisation of how we can think of the relations between power, knowledge and bodies, such that power and knowledge work on both the inside and the outside of bodies. Twentieth century dentistry, for example, uses discourse, image and other tools, but it acts directly on the teeth and the mouth. It adds fillings, reshapes jaw lines, as well as advising us to brush our teeth and not eat sweets (Nettleton, 1992).

The problem of bio-power in the writing of Foucault is posed most eloquently and interestingly by Pierre Macherey in his essay 'Towards a natural history of norms' (1992). His essay holds *The Order of Things* against *History of Sexuality, Vol. I* in order to think about what we mean by the exercise of power and, following both Canguilhem's and Foucault's interest, by 'normalisation' in particular. He asks on the opening page: 'how can one move from a negative conception of the norm and the way it acts, founded on the model of juridical exclusion and related to that which is permitted and forbidden, to a positive conception, which on the contrary insists on its biological function of inclusion and regulation, in the sense not of a systematic regulation but a regularisation, with reference to the distinction, confirmed by the so-called human sciences, between the normal and the pathological' (Macherey, 1992: 176). Whereas juridical norms are seen to be concerned with constraint, biological norms are seen as productive. Bio-power is the power over, and through, life (not death). Bio-power is not about the socio-political regulation of the body (one way of reading Foucault) where the discursive, or governmentality, stands-in for the socio-political; it is about the movement of, and through, bodies (action on action). For Foucault, the productivity of bio-power is such that it does not reproduce the division between inside and outside. Bio-power is not external to the 'life' upon which it acts; it is productive of the inside; it works through the inside, but only in the sense that the 'inside' is thoroughly visible to power. As Foucault says: 'the purpose of the present study is in fact to show how deployments of power are directly connected to the body – to bodies, functions, physiological processes, sensations, and pleasures; far from the body having to be effaced, what is needed is to make it visible through an analysis in which the biological and the historical are not consecutive to one another, as in the evolutionism of the first sociologists, but are bound together in an increasingly complex fashion in accordance with the development of the modern technologies of power that take life as their objective' (1979: 152). The object of *History of Sexuality, Vol. I* is not sexuality as an ideology, but sex as real, as ontology. Bodies don't have a fixed identity either within or outside of discourse. Bio-power is concerned, not with identity, but with problematisation (cf. Foucault, 1984). Moreover, bodies are co-related within events. Events are sites of power/knowledge, not because things are closed down, reduced to identity, but because they are opened up, disclosed to the multiplicity of connections.

We should be clear that such an encounter with the real, with the body, with life, does not mean that there is an indiscriminate blurring of the boundaries between culture and nature and between, for example, the disciplines of biology and cultural history. There is not a general or universal breakdown of the boundaries; we are not all cyborgs. For example, even in the limited and discrete field of transsexual intervention, the relations of power and knowledge constitute the object of knowledge and intervention through a series of particular and uneven fields. Whereas for some people, psychotherapeutics might constitute a resolution to the unease with one's body, for others surgical operation might offer a solution. Different objects, different knowledges and different forms of action. In this sense it is important to add a note of caution to accounts that point to the emergence of new genetic knowledge and new biotechnologies and to claims that we are witnessing a general 'penetration' of the body by technology. Equally, the language of genetics has adopted a terminology originally deployed in information science, but we should be wary of argument that suggests that we are witnessing a general collapse of the relations between culture and nature and that the body is now cultural in and of itself, as if all is artificial and artifice. Even more sanguine accounts, such as that of Paul Rabinow who states that '[n]ature will be known and remade through technique and will finally become artificial, just as culture becomes natural' (1992: 242) and Sarah Franklin who argues that 'culture becomes the model for nature' (2000: 194) have a tendency to proclaim a new age of understanding and forms of life.

It is without doubt, though, that the discovery of DNA by James D. Watson and Francis Crick has had a profound impact on our understanding of the biosciences and their relation to contemporary culture. As Canguilhem noted some time ago of biology in 1966:

> It has dropped the vocabulary and concepts of classical mechanics, physics and chemistry, all more or less directly based on geometrical models, in favor of the vocabulary of linguistics and communications theory. Messages, information, programs, codes, instructions, decoding: these are the new concepts of the life sciences. (2000: 316)

The body, once understood as a machine that worked like clockwork or as mix of physiological and chemical reactions, is now understood in the context of the code. And as Canguilhem also notes, the communication of coded information across generations has more than a striking resemblance to an Aristotelian notion of a *logos* inscribing the being of life, as its very form. But to make such a statement is not to believe in the perfection of genetic translation. On the contrary, Canguilhem argues that error is central to this process:

> If life is the production, transmission and reception of information, then clearly the history of life involves both conservation and innovation. How is evolution to be explained in terms of genetics? The answer, of course, involves the mechanism of mutations ... Thus, if life has meaning, we must accept the possibility of a loss of that meaning, of distortion, of misconstruction. (2000: 318)

For Canguilhem, human being – both living and producing knowledge – is to be 'dissatisfied with the meaning one finds ready to hand' (2000: 319).

If we are to understand, then, the relations across culture, nature, technology and body, we must understand them in the context of a history of errors and distortions within life itself. Thus, for example, if we understand medicine as an art of living, we must also, according to Canguilhem, understand it in the context of life itself and not simply as a distinct and intervening force outside of life:

> We do not ascribe a human content to vital norms but we do ask ourselves how normativity essential to human consciousness would be explained if it did not in some way exist in embryo in life. We ask ourselves how a human need for therapeutics would have engendered a medicine which is increasingly clairvoyant with regard to the conditions of disease if life's struggle against the innumerable dangers threatening it were not a permanent and essential vital need. (2000: 339)

Canguilhem poses a notion of scientific knowledge as that which is produced within the context of human being and its environment. Medical knowledge, in this sense, is necessarily the action upon and reaction to that environment:

> The expressions 'natural selection' and 'natural medicinal activity' have one drawback in that they seem to set vital techniques within the framework of human techniques when it is the opposite that seems true. All human technique, including that of life, is set within life, that is, within an activity of information and assimilation of material. It is not because human technique is normative that vital technique is judged such by comparison. Because life is activity of information and assimilation, it is the root of all technical activity. (2000: 342–3)

Providing the caveat noted above, regarding caution about the particularity of knowledge, technology and field of application, there is no reason to assume that such an understanding of knowledge, technology and the body could not be applied to more 'cultural' contexts. The work of Lisa Cartwright, for example, has shown how cinema constitutes a form of bio-power in its relation to medical science and in its visualisation of the body (1995). Franklin has similarly looked at the role of popular culture in the bio-politics of reproductive technology (1991), cloning technology (2003a, b) and genetic knowledge (2000). Such 'cultural' technologies do not have a lesser and more distanced relation to life, only a different one to that of the medical or genetic sciences. Haraway frames this reflexive relation in terms of biology:

> There are two aspects to emphasize when discussing biology. The first is: *We live intimately "as" and "in" a biological world* ... And the second aspect, which represents a major gestalt switch from the previous point, is: *Biology is a discourse and not the world itself.* (2000: 25)

But Foucault, in an essay on Canguilhem from 1985, frames it more broadly about 'knowledge about life':

> Canguilhem wishes to discover, by means of the elucidation of knowledge about life and concepts which articulate this knowledge, the nature of the concept in life, that is to say of the concept as one of the modes of the information which living beings draw from their milieu. The fact that man lives in a milieu which has a conceptual architecture does not prove that he has turned away from life through some process of forgetting, or that a historical drama has separated him from it; but only that he sees things in a certain way ... Forming concepts is a way of living, not a way of killing life. (quoted in Macherey, 1992: 180; see also Foucault, 1989: 20–1)

Knowledge of 'life' is part of life itself. It is not the death of the body, of soma (as in some versions of semiotics, cf. Kristeva, 1984a). Equally though, 'life' is not the epistemological preserve of biology, but of the bio-knowledges and bio-cultures more broadly defined. Such a broad definition would include biographical literature as much as medical diagnosis, filmic representations of modern life as much as codings of DNA, the practices of diary writing as much as anatomical dissection. Moreover, it is harder to make any simplistic divide between different media, not only of cultural expression, but of bio-cultural expression. Haraway's argument about the bio-sciences and genetic media are certainly suggestive, as are ANT's on the heterogeneous engineering of relations of and between bodies. The implications of this are far reaching and as suggested earlier, we should be wary of assuming any generalised collapse of boundaries between either nature and culture or the bio-sciences and cultural sciences. Nevertheless, if we take these ideas seriously – and I think that we need to see them as significant or, at least, as symptomatic of epistemological, if not necessarily ontological, change – then we need to begin to rethink some long-held assumptions about culture and about its relation to nature and technology. A questioning of the ontology of the body has become a major provocation in this regard. Haraway, Deleuze and Guattari and ANT all want to unpack the black box of essentialised relations. Their work, in different ways, questions simple divides between nature and society, human and non-human, machine and organism. Changing conceptions of culture are central to this work and to understanding relations within and between bodies, but an important lesson is that culture is intimately entangled within life itself.

Chapter Summary

- In contrast to forms of criticism that seek to expose 'naturalisation' as a cultural practice, much work on cultural studies of the body, nature and technology has sought to understand the body as between nature, culture and technology.
- Donna Haraway's work on cyborgs is pivotal to understanding the relation between body, nature, culture and technology in cultural studies. New developments in the biosciences and computer technology have led to a hybridised production of the cyborg body. For Haraway the cyborg stands as an icon to these epochal shifts, but also figures as a trope for understanding the complex relations across the material-semiotic and for thinking about contemporary politics and critical practice. Haraway talks not of critique but of 'diffraction'.
- Gilles Deleuze and Felix Guattari also provide an analysis of the hybrid production of organic matter and machine. They talk about this in terms of the connections between desiring-machines.
- The work of Michel Callon, John Law and Bruno Latour is significant in allowing us to think of actor-networks, namely the way in which bodies or agents are mobilised and assembled. For these writers, forms of organisation cannot be reduced to either the technological or the organic or the cultural, but need to be seen across these categories.
- The organisation of bodies in terms of power relations has been analysed by Michel Foucault. His work is significant inasmuch as it allows us to think of power through bodies rather than power over or controlling of bodies. Important in this respect is the production of knowledge. Rather than seeing knowledge as separate and distinct from life, Foucault, following the work of Georges Canguilhem, argues that knowledge is very much part of life.

SEVEN Economy: Between Structure and Network

Things economic have long been of interest to those working within cultural studies. Many in the discipline have held the economic separate from the cultural and yet others have argued that such a division is no longer tenable, whether because things economic are really cultural or because things cultural are really coded only through the economics of exchange. Whatever the case, it is generally agreed that the term 'economic' is most readily understood with reference to a system of relations between firms, consumers and markets, in that markets follow particular logics according to factors such as price, rates of interest, demand, supply, investment and savings. Far from being an essential and natural domain, ideas about the economic can be seen to have distinct moments and conditions of historical emergence. Thus, as we have seen previously, Foucault notes how the economic as a distinct domain of government emerges in the eighteenth century alongside the emergence of the population. No longer contained through a discipline tied to the domestic management of noble estates (i.e. *oeconomy* in its classical and premodern sense), the economy emerges as an entity with its own laws (e.g. cycles of growth and decline, rates of trade, and so on) and tied to the regularities of a population (as in Malthusian economy). This emergent object is understood and governed through the newly formed social sciences and statistical knowledges, through measuring the peaks and troughs, and through understanding relations across the micro- and macro-levels and between firms and nations. Such a conception of this domain has been readily, although not uncritically, accepted in the analysis of culture. Either we see, as in Marcuse (1968) and much of Western Marxism, the economic is placed on the side of civilisation (as material production) and culture on the side of the 'spiritual world' of ideology (as ideational reproduction) or as in Weber (1930), culture provides the means of distinguishing between different forms of economic system (e.g. between different forms of capitalism). In understandings of the economic, things cultural are often seen as altogether more qualitative and messy than quantitative and statistically ordered reality. This said, it should not be forgotten that untidy cultural things, such as aesthetic objects, bodies, desires and identities are themselves readily discussed in terms of their economies. The Romantics, the Freudians and others, have all talked of economy, albeit in ways both similar and different from the economy proper.

In this chapter we look at the division between the economic and the ideological in Western Marxism, paying particular attention to Althusser's model of structural causality; we then look at the refocusing of debate in the 1970s onward with regard to consumer culture and the framing of some of this debate in terms of an understanding of the cultural through a model of economy; and in the final sections we look at how the economic is itself seen as a cultural phenomenon, one that is configured through networks, regulatory regimes and the life of commodities.

Economic Structure and Culture

In a sense, the traces of that earlier, pre-modern understanding of economy (as *oeconomy*) on the model of the domestic household can be seen in Karl Marx and Frederick Engels' metaphor of the 'real foundation', such that they take the architecture of the house, limit the economic to that of the foundation or base structure, at the same time as they extend or stretch the architecture of the household to include the whole of society. In this understanding it is not the landed nobles or the new capitalist class who manage the economy, but they are themselves organised by the regularities of the economic. In Marxism, the economic base-structure refers to the forces (i.e. the technology and scientific knowledge) and relations (i.e. in capitalism, the relation between capital and labour) of production. The forces and relations of production are organised in certain ways according to the historical epoch in which they find themselves. Thus Marxism talks about the movement of history in terms of the structural shifts from one mode of production to another (i.e. from feudalism to capitalism). As Marx poetically states, 'The handmill gives you society with the feudal lord; the steam-mill, a society with the industrial capitalist' (1971: 109). In contrast to, but determined by, the economic material base is the superstructure. Superstructure refers to the particular structural forms, such as the family, politics, and law, that help to support the relations of production. In a capitalist mode of production, we would expect to see laws that supported the ownership and inheritance of private property and capital, to see political structures that helped to keep in place the embedded power of the bourgeois class that owns capital and to see family forms that allowed the socialisation of offspring into particular classes and forms of labour. These superstructural forms are held together through particular ideas or ideologies, but, as Marx and Engels originally argue in 1845, these ideas are determined by the economic base:

> The class which has the means of material production at its disposal has control at the same time over the means of mental production, so that thereby, generally speaking, the ideas of those who lack the means of mental production are subject to it ... In so far, therefore, as they rule as a class and determine the extent and compass of an epoch, it is self-evident that they ... among other things ... regulate the production and distribution of the ideas of their age: thus their ideas are the ruling ideas of the epoch. (1970: 64)

This formulation can be used to understand how the ruling families of the nineteenth century in England owned the means of distributing daily news. Working-class newspapers and pamphlets were beaten down either through physical and violent means or through the force of the market place (cf. Curran, 1977). Thus the ideas that were most widely distributed across the population were those of the ruling class.

A less instrumental understanding of the relation between base and superstructural forms can be found in the following quotation from Marx:

> In the social production of their existence, men enter into definite, necessary relations, which are independent of their will, namely, relations of production corresponding to a determinate stage of development of their material forces of production. The totality of these relations of production constitutes the economic structure of society, the real foundation on which there arises a legal and political superstructure and to which there correspond definite forms of social consciousness. The mode of production of material life conditions the social, political and intellectual life-process in general. It is not the consciousness of men that determines their being, but on the contrary it is their social being that determines their consciousness. (1976: 3)

The turning of Hegel on his head (as Marx said referring to the way that historical materialism prioritised the historical movement not of ideas, spirit or consciousness, but of material forces in all their brutality and hope) presented more starkly the problem of determination.

Much of Marxist cultural thought in the twentieth century, up until the 1980s, has been taken up with this question of determination. Thus, for example, the structural Marxist Louis Althusser, writing in the late 1960s, makes the distinction between three forms of causal relation between base structure and superstructure (Althusser and Balibar, 1979). First, Althusser refers to a *linear causality* that he describes as 'transitive' and 'mechanical' and that he sees as originating in the writings of Descartes. This form of causality is defined in terms of simple relation between cause and effect or stimulus and response. If I roll a striped pool ball (A) at a plain pool ball (B), the second ball (B) moves away from the first with roughly equal speed to that of the first ball (A). If the second ball (B) hits a third ball (C) that goes into the pocket, then we are able to see clearly that there is a line of determination or causality from A to C and from my rolling the first ball to the third ball rolling in the pocket. Althusser calls this form of causality 'transitive', because it concerns the relation between an action on a definite object (as with transitive verbs) and mechanical, because it rests on a simple notion of mechanical laws of force and motion that were thought to govern the universe. One of the many objections to this notion of linear causality is that it suggests that the material relations governing a cultural form are simply deterministic in the sense of the pool ball example. Thus, if you have steam-mills, you have industrial capitalism. If you have bourgeois capitalists running the television media, then you have derogatory ideologies of working-class rights. This model is often seen as too 'deterministic' in a negative sense of the term.

Secondly, Althusser refers to a form of causality that he terms *expressive causality*. He sees this form as deriving from the ideas of the German philosophers Leibniz and Hegel. This form of causality concerns not simply the relation between two elements (or a linear series of elements, i.e. A, B, C, etc.) but the relation between the whole and its elements. In this model, the elements are seen to be expressions of the whole; they are phenomena that contain the essence of the whole. This model, then, presumes that the whole has a single inner essence and that each element simply expresses or represents that inner essence. Thus, if we take a stereotypical representation of a girl with pink ribbons in her hair, a pink dress, pink shoes, and carrying a doll, we might (if we were not students of culture!) assume that these items of dress represented an inner essence of 'girlhood femininity'. We might look at each item in turn (the dress, the shoes, and so on) and say that each item contained that inner essence of girlhood femininity. This model of causality allows us to consider the whole, but only inasmuch as that totality is seen to have a singular essence and thus removed of any sense of complex structure. The model is able to provide an understanding of the relation between the totality and the individual elements, but not an understanding of how that totality as structured.

Thirdly, then, Althusser presents a notion of *structural causality*. Althusser turns to Marx's concept of *Darstellung* (or representation) and his theatrical metaphor to understand structural causality. The two previous models can be thought of in the following way. In the case of linear causality, the theatre director shapes the set design and the acting of the actors. In the case of expressive causality, the set design and the acting are expressions of the inner will or ideas of the director. However, in structural causality, the set design and the acting are shaped, but not by any underlying directorial intention. The play is not understood in terms of the intentions of the author. On the contrary, the acting and set design are understood in terms of their structural relation to each other such that the structure determining them is not external to them (i.e. behind the stage), rather it is only present in the effects produced on stage. Althusser refers to this in terms of 'the existence of the structure in its effects' (Althusser and Balibar, 1979: 188): 'the effects are not outside the structure, are not a pre-existing object, element or space in which the structure arrives to *imprint its mark*: on the contrary, it implies that the structure is immanent in its effects, a cause immanent in its effects ..., that *the whole existence of the structure consists of its effects*, in short that the structure, which is merely a specific combination of its peculiar elements, is nothing outside its effects' (1979: 189).

For Althusser, there is not simply one structure, the economic, and its epiphenomenal expression as superstructure, but a number of structurally interrelated structures, including the economic, the political-legal, the scientific and the ideological. Each historical mode of production, or each social formation, has a structure that is dominant. It has a structure that *overdetermines* the social relations within that formation. To put it crudely, in feudalism, religious ideology took precedence and determined how, for example, to understand the relation between serf and master. In capitalist social formations the dominant structure is the economic. The dominant factors shaping our lives and others are economic ones, to do with, for example, economic globalisation, commodification, poverty and so on. In each social formation, then, the economic, political-legal and ideological structures that constitute the social totality overdetermine each other, but only one resides as the *structure in dominance*. Nevertheless, although the economic is not always the dominant structure in any given social formation, it does always determine 'in the last instance', in the sense that it determines which structure (economic, political-legal or ideological) will be actually dominant in any given social formation. However, for Althusser, the last instance is a theoretical abstraction that never comes.

Althusser's analysis of 'determination' is complex and moves beyond any simple model of causality. It is, though, clearly beset with problems especially concerning the 'in the last instance' clause that seems to revert the complex structural analysis, at one moment at least, to a simple linear model. Despite, or perhaps because of, the sophistication of Althusser's model, his analysis only remained popular at the intellectual margins of cultural studies, leaving the field open for the more adaptable ideas of the English cultural critic Raymond Williams. Williams, as with Althusser, conceived of culture as deeply material and not as some ethereal, spiritual or intellectual form.

Culture is seen as a type of practice that involves work, as with all forms of production, and as such is embedded as a material practice. One of the ways in which Williams considers the relations between different forms of material practice and in which he opens up the debate about the relation between base and superstructure is to look to the language originally used by Marx and Engels. For Williams, the German term *bestimmen*, that is translated as 'determine' in English translations of Marx, is linguistically complex (Williams: 1977: 83–8; cf. Williams, 1980). The sense of determination by a compelling external force that leaves us (the compelled) helpless and passive is only one meaning of the term. Another sense, and one that Williams and others in cultural studies have favoured, concerns the setting of limits. In this sense, for example, computer networked communications, such as the internet, set limits to the kinds of material that might be distributed or the forms of production and consumption. The making of a webpage, displaying that page on the internet and receiving two million hits on that page is far less costly than making a television programme and broadcasting it to similar numbers of people. The economic and technological structure determines the cultural form, but only in the sense that it sets limits to how each form of communication is organised. It does not specify what that form might be.

The question of determination between base and superstructure is one that helped shape the contours of a field of cultural analysis known as the political economy of culture. But in many ways the political economy of culture has settled for an understanding of the relation between base and superstructure, less in terms of a rigidly analytical understanding of 'determination' and more in terms of a disciplinary emphasis: namely, that economic organisation, at micro- and macro-sociological levels, is an important and central point of focus. Thus two important figures from the field of the political economy of culture, Peter Golding and Graham Murdock, talk about the 'traceable consequences' between the economic and the symbolic:

> [T]he political economy perspective ... [is distinguished by] its focus on the interplay between the symbolic and economic dimensions of public communications. It sets out to show how different ways of financing and organizing cultural production have traceable consequences for the range of discourses and representations in the public domain and for audiences' access to them. (1991: 15)

They rightly stress that the study of culture should take a broad micro- and macro-sociological route: '[f]our historical processes are particularly central to a critical political economy of culture; the growth of the media; the extension of corporate reach; commodification; and the changing role of state and government intervention' (1991: 19). But, equally though, it can be argued that these sociological factors are discussed and commented on within a number of theoretical perspectives, not simply Marxist or neo-Marxist.

Analytical frameworks that account for the inter-relations between the economic, social and political and that suggest that we consider symbolic forms and practices within such complex inter-relations are now not restricted to Marxist political economy (although they clearly owe their debt to the incredible work of Marx in the nineteenth century).

For us though, the significant issue here is not simply the relations of determination, but also the way in which a series of lengthy discussions over the course of the nineteenth and twentieth centuries have worked to make a distinction between 'culture' and the 'economic', such that the latter is very clearly inscribed as the base and also, at times, the model for culture. Although early critics understood culture as ideological and as determined by the economic, later writers, such as Althusser, Williams and others, understood culture as material practice, as work: either culture is determined by work or is itself conceived as a form of labour. The theoretical resources used to make sense of culture in relation to, or as, material always refer back to, in these discussions at least, the economic. But what if we turned tables and begin to conceive of the economic as cultural, to think about economic organisation through the metaphors and interpretative resources of culture? We will return to this question in the final sections of this chapter, but in the next section we will consider how culture was understood through a model of economy in the context of debate about consumer culture.

Consumer Culture

As the economic and cultural sociologist, Don Slater has argued:

> Consumption is always and everywhere a cultural process, but 'consumer culture' - a culture *of* consumption - is unique and specific: it is the dominant mode of cultural reproduction developed in the west over the course of modernity. Consumer culture is in important respects *the* culture of the modern west. (1997: 8)

Slater argues that consumer culture is typified by the construction of freedom of choice and individualism in terms of market relations, by the presentation of this as a universal system, and by the necessity of the system not only to reproduce itself, but also to constantly innovate in order to meet the unlimited and insatiable needs of consumers. The emergence and growth of consumer culture in conditions of modernity has meant that consumer culture has become a privileged site in the exercise of modern power to the extent that it has also become the privileged medium for negotiating identity in post-traditional society (Lury, 1996; Slater, 1997). Important for Slater, as for others, is the notion that: 'consumer culture denotes a social arrangement in which the relation between lived culture and social resources, between meaningful ways of life and the symbolic and material resources on which they depend, is mediated through markets' (1997: 8). It is thus in the context of debate about consumer culture – its emergence and its significance for contemporary cultural, economic and social life – that we see most clearly, within the field of cultural studies at least, an understanding of culture as itself economic. Most important in this respect are the writings of the French sociologists, Jean Baudrillard and Pierre Bourdieu.

In many ways, the early work of Baudrillard can be framed less in terms of a 'culturalisation of the economic', than in terms of making visible an economic model at the very heart of culture. But we should add the proviso that the economic is not seen as a model of determination, but as the very structure of culture as a system of exchange (Baudrillard, 1975, 1981). In his early essay 'Toward a critique of the political economy of the sign' (1981), he makes the argument that the logic of the commodity (as analysed and described by Marx and Engels) is equivalent to the logic of the sign (as understood in the ideas of Saussure):

> [T]he logic of the commodity and of political economy is the very heart of the sign ... [S]igns can function as exchange value and as use value ... [T]he structure of the sign is at the very heart of the commodity form ... [T]he commodity form can take on, immediately, the effect of signification. (1981: 146)

Just as signs only have meaning through their differentiation from other signs, so too are commodities only meaningful and individuated as a consequence of their differentiation from other commodities. But for Baudrillard the implications of this move are far reaching. He goes on to say:

> The referent in question here is no more external to the sign than is the Signified: indeed it is governed by the sign. It is carved out and projected as its function; its only reality is of that which is ornamentally inscribed on the sign itself. (1981: 151)

As we saw in our discussion of Saussure, our understanding of a referent (i.e. the 'real' object) is contained within the sign itself, as a concept or signified. For Baudrillard, this breakthrough has implications for our understanding of the commodity. A chair, for Marx, might be defined in terms of its use value, that is in terms of its use or function (e.g. as an object upon which one can sit). In capitalism, a chair is made, but also sold in market conditions. In these conditions, it has an exchange value (i.e. its value in market conditions). For Baudrillard, the commodity, as with the sign, is only differentiated in conditions of exchange, not in terms of its use: a beautifully designed Eames chair or one from the furniture chain IKEA can both be sat upon, but their exchange value would be very different. Thus commodities, as with signs, only have a value or meaning within the system of differentiation and exchange and not in terms of any intrinsic, functional value or meaning or in terms of any value constructed through production. Labour (as the quintessential synecdoche of production in industrial modernity) no longer provides the model for culture, but culture, defined as economic, provides the constitutive force. These arguments have wide-ranging implications regarding our understanding of the relations between economy, culture and materiality, not least in the sense that consumption, rather than production becomes the primary motor of commodity signification.

By and large, Baudrillard has been understood in terms of how the economic has become aestheticised and dematerialised; the economic is understood in terms of how it has become subsumed within the logic of the symbolic and the image (cf. Featherstone, 1991; Lash and Urry, 1994). In many ways though, Baudrillard offers an understanding of how materiality, in this sense of economic materiality, is not the site of fixity, solidity and that which can determine from its foundational base, but rather the unstable texture of elasticity and fluidity. This understanding becomes more clear in his later writings on simulation and hyperreality:

> The very definition of the real becomes: that of which it is possible to give an equivalent reproduction ... At the limit of this process of reproducibility, the real is not only what can be reproduced, but that which is always already reproduced ... The hyperreal transcends representation ... only because it is entirely in simulation. (1983a: 146–7)

In this sense, then, it is not that the real has become fake or has become reduced to the symbolic, rather it is that the real itself is now opened to the possibilities that were once conceived only in relation to the symbolic:

> The hyperreal represents a much more advanced phase, in the sense that even this contradiction between the real and the imaginary is effaced. The unreal is no longer that of dream or fantasy, of a beyond or a within, it is that of a hallucinatory resemblance of the real with itself. (1983a: 143)

Culture, in and of itself, takes on economic value. Moreover, in a social formation that is predicated on the economic value of the cultural differentiation of commodities and forms of life and on the circulation of information about commodities and forms of life, then we see the potential of an overproduction of information, a surfeit of information that leads to a complete dissolution of fixed meaning. Baudrillard argues that:

> We are in a universe where there is more and more information, and less and less meaning ... Thus information dissolves meaning and the social into a sort of nebulous state leading not at all to a surfeit of innovation but to the very contrary, to total entropy. (1983b: 95, 100)

Baudrillard's argument, then, has major philosophical as well as sociological implications regarding the dominance of the economy of the sign and the flattening of 'reality' (and our ability to know and understand 'reality') therein.

In contrast to Baudrillard's flattening of the economy of culture, Bourdieu argues that such an economy is typified not simply by differentiation and equivalences, but by distinction. To talk of a cultural world in terms of the economy of the symbolic, for Bourdieu, is not to disavow questions of inequality. On the contrary, it is to lodge the question of inequality at the heart of the logic of the cultural. At stake in the cultural world in which we live is the question of the distribution, not simply of symbolic goods, but of the capacities and dispositions to accumulate such goods and services – namely, the cultural capital at the disposal of some people rather than others – but also the capacities and dispositions to produce further distinction and differentiation on the basis of that accumulation (Bourdieu, 1984). Bourdieu, for example, talks about the way in which taste is a social, and not aesthetic, practice and about how such taste is constitutive of class differentiation (i.e. on the basis of the unequal distribution of cultural capital, as against economic capital or educational capital). For Bourdieu, class is not defined with reference to a reified structure of stratification. It is not defined through certain fixed properties, such as gender, sexuality, 'race', ethnicity, age, educational level or income. It is not defined by the fixity of a class in relation to the relations of production (i.e. between capital and labour). For Bourdieu, class is defined in terms of a dynamic model of structural relations: 'the structure of relations between all the pertinent properties which gives its specific value to each of them and to the effects they exert on practice' (1984: 106). The value given to the accumulation of these properties, as defined through their dynamic structural relation, is called 'capital' and Bourdieu talks of different types of capital, such as economic, educational, social, symbolic and cultural. Forms of capital do not have a universal value, good for all times and place, good for all conditions. For Bourdieu, capital has value according to the field in which it is put to practice. He states:

> To understand why the same system of properties (which determines and is determined by the position occupied in the field of class struggles) always has the greatest explanatory power, whatever the area in question – eating habits, use of credit, fertility, political opinion, religion etc. – and why, simultaneously, the relative weight of the factors which constitute it varies from one field to another – educational capital being most important in one area, economic capital in another, and so on – one only has to see that, because capital is a social relation, i.e. an energy which only exists and only produces its effects in the field in which it is produced and reproduced, each of the properties attached to class is given its value and efficacy by the specific laws of each field. (1984: 113)

In particular fields of practice only certain forms of capital are used, as certain forms of capital have greater value or currency. Bourdieu's analysis can be applied to the production and distribution of a television programme or to the career trajectory of a city banker or to the choice of clothes when going out with a group of friends to a restaurant. In the latter case, we might choose either smart or casual clothes, sexy or plain, to be scented or unscented, according to factors such as whether someone we fancy is going to be present, the status of the restaurant or whether the friends are from work or long-standing old chums. What we wear will help to shape how we feel in the restaurant as well as how we are perceived and received: Are we given a good table? Do the waiters serve us well? Does the love-interest take the bait? As Bourdieu says: 'the social rank and specific power which agents are assigned in a particular field depend firstly on the specific capital they can mobilize, whatever their additional wealth in other types of capital' (1984: 113).

Bourdieu understands the logic of capital in strategic terms, but he weights the types of moves that can be played in the grounding of what he calls 'habitus'. Habitus is a complex concept and it is put to work in different ways in Bourdieu's theoretical architecture. Thus my comments on habitus can only be indicative. Nevertheless, Bourdieu talks of habitus as that which 'at every moment, structures new experiences in accordance with the structures produced by past experiences, which are modified by the new experiences within the limits defined by their power of selection, [which] brings about a unique integration, dominated by the earliest experiences, of the experiences statistically common to members of the same class' (1990: 60). Habitus is both a 'structuring structure' and a 'structured structure'. It refers to the generative structuring structure that is at the locus of cultural reproduction:

> The habitus is this generative and unifying principle which retranslates the intrinsic and relational characteristics of a position into a unitary lifestyle, that is, a unitary set of choices of persons, goods, practices ... [H]abitus are differentiated, but they are also differentiating. Being distinct and distinguished, they are also distinction operators, implementing different principles of differentiation or using differently the common principles of differentiation ... [H]abitus are also classificatory schemes, principles of classification, principles of vision and division, different tastes. (Bourdieu, 1998: 8)

Thus, my wearing a set of clothes in a meeting with friends in a restaurant is partly dependent on my relation to the accumulation of different forms of capital, the embodiment of their capital, my ability to mobilise that capital, my perception of the kind of restaurant and friends I am meeting, but also the interpretation of my clothes, my body, my status, my ability to read the situation by my friends, and their own location within their own habitus. Wearing a ball gown to a workers' cafe for lunch is just as much a potential mistake as wearing jeans to a black tie dinner. But one's ability to 'carry-it-off' is also dependent on one's habitus and one's accumulated cultural and economic capital. Paris Hilton certainly seemed to manage stilettos and a Gucci handbag in a backwater farm in the US.

Habitus, as it were, works not in a static, but a dynamic field. Social space is at once subjective and objective. It is not made up of fixed social positions, but of 'strategic emplacements, fortresses to be defended and captured in a field of struggles' (Bourdieu, 1984: 244). Moreover, our understanding (structured and structuring, classified and classifying) of any social space - whether as cultural scientist, restaurant goer, or music lover - is always reflexively caught up in this social space. Bourdieu argues that the social space in which habitus is located is one typified by struggle, force and transformation (cf. 1998: 31–4). Bourdieu talks about the specificity of any social space in terms of the notion of 'field'. Habitus is thus located within particular fields. Habitus is a kind of 'practical sense for what is to be done in a given situation' (1998: 25) 'a proleptic adjustment to the demands of a field' (1990: 66). Bourdieu talks about the relation between habitus and field, 'incorporated history and an objectified history' (1990: 66), through the analogy of the game:

> Produced by experience of the game, and therefore of the objective structures within which it is played out, the 'feel for the game' is what gives the game a subjective sense - a meaning and a *raison d'être*, but also a direction, an orientation, an impending outcome, for those who take part and therefore acknowledge what is at stake. (1990: 66)

Bourdieu continues:

> In a game, the field (the pitch or board on which it is played, the rules, the outcome at stake, etc.) is clearly seen for what it is, an arbitrary social construct, an artefact whose arbitrariness and artificiality are underlined by everything that defines its autonomy - explicit and specific rules, strictly delimited and extra-ordinary time and space. Entry into the game takes the form of a quasi-contract ... By contrast, in the social fields ... one does not embark on the game by conscious act, one is born into the game, with the game; and the relation of investment, *illusio*, investment, is made more total and unconditional by the fact that it is unaware of what it is. (1990: 67)

The practical sense through which habitus and field are coordinated is a precarious kind of game shaped by the dynamic relations between agency and structure. Culture, as with the social and the economic, provides the resource for particular fields of strategic struggle, particular fields of differentiation and distinction.

For Bourdieu, the point is not to apply the concepts of capital, habitus, and field in order to reify class and culture, but to demonstrate how their performance is strategic within particular, empirical structural dynamic conditions (i.e. to understand their application in practice). Thus, for example, when Bourdieu talks of the emergence of a new class fraction, the new bourgeoisie, he does so in terms of the emergent habitus that they occupy and in terms of the cultural, educational and economic capital that they have accumulated. He describes the new bourgeoisie in opposition to the old bourgeoisie; he describes them as mainly graduates, successful in their career as private sector executives, belonging to modern firms (1984: 304–5). The new bourgeoisie are central drivers of the new economy, not just in terms of their professional expertise, but also in terms of their embodiment of 'a hedonistic morality of consumption, based on credit, spending and enjoyment' (1984: 310). But correspondingly, the new bourgeoisie are also involved in professions associated with the selling and marketing of symbolic and cultural goods; they are involved in tourism, media, fashion and advertising. These are the 'new tastemakers'. In contrast to the flattening of culture and the economic that we saw in the work of Baudrillard, Bourdieu's analysis of the economy of culture in terms of distinction allows us to see how such a flattened culture can be seen as the world-view of a particular class fraction, namely the new bourgeoisie. The turn toward lifestyle and a postmodern aesthetic, to the dissolution of the boundary between the real and the simulation, is thus seen not as an enduring reality for all, but a particular way of classifying the world and classifying those who view it as such (cf. Featherstone, 1991).

What is important, then, in Bourdieu's analysis of the economy of culture is not that he reduces culture to an overarching economic model (i.e. an economism), but that he pluralises how we understand the economic (cf. Bourdieu, 1990, 1998). He states quite bluntly that '[e]conomism is a form of ethnocentrism' (1990: 112). In the context of a discussion about the anthropology of gift exchange, he says that 'the exchange of gifts (or women, or services, etc.) conceived as a paradigm of the economy of symbolic goods, is opposed to the equivalent exchanges of the economic economy as long as its basis is not a calculating subject, but rather an agent socially disposed to enter, without intention or calculation, into the game of exchange' (1998: 98). In contrast to Baudrillard, who reduces the symbolic to the logic of the economic, such that the system of exchange value and the 'overdetermination by the code' are seen as mutual reflections within the mirror of political economy (1975: 20), Bourdieu is keen to mark out the differences between different economies: '[t]he economic universe is made up of several economic worlds, endowed with specific "rationalities", at the same time assuming and demanding "reasonable" (more than rational) dispositions adjusted to the regularities inscribed in each of them, to the "practical reason" which characterizes them' (1998: 93). In this sense, then, although acknowledging the ubiquity of consumer cultures and market relations, we should be wary of reducing different 'economies' (cultural or otherwise) to 'the economic', to a single version of consumption or the market.

The Economic as Cultural

Many contemporary writers within, and beyond, cultural studies have increasingly begun to investigate and analyse the economic as itself cultural. For many of these writers, the context for the discussion has been an understanding of major shifts in economic organisation. These shifts are often referred to in terms of the move from industrialism to post-industrialism or Fordism to post-Fordism or modernity to late- or postmodernity. In order to do any justice to the accounts of these shifts, we would need to spend more time than is possible in this chapter. We would need, for example, to trace the different forms of industry from the spinning jenny in the cotton mills of the mid-eighteenth century to the development of scientific management and the accounts of the rationalisation of labour, space and time in the work of Frederick Taylor to the application of these technologies of labour and their further development in the factories of Henry Ford (the maker of the Model-T Ford motor car) and others in the 1920s. We would want to consider whether a dramatic shift occurred from one mode of production to another and we would want to think about the leading metaphor for explaining such change. Is change from Fordist forms of regulation to post-Fordist, from industrial to post-industrial or from modern to late- or postmodern? Equally each leading metaphor refers to a set of debates about when the change took place: in the 1950s, 1970s or 1980s? In all these accounts, the cultural has been construed as of central importance and very broadly we might say that there has been a shift in focus from Fordist, industrial and national economies and societies to post-Fordist, post-industrial, informational, technologically saturated, globalised economies and societies. But to focus on such a statement may be to miss what is actually important.

In an edited collection titled *Cultural Economy* (du Gay and Pryke, 2002), a number of writers, including Paul du Gay, Daniel Miller, Michael Pryke, and Don Slater discuss how cultural studies might understand the problem of economy. In their introductory essay, du Gay and Pryke use the notion of 'cultural economy' to capture the sense of an epochal shift that is suggested in the above debates, but also in phrases such as 'economies of signs', 'network society', 'information society' and 'knowledge economy'. The notion of 'cultural economy' is in some ways synonymous with these other terms, but also tries to refocus their emphasis onto the way in which the economic is seen increasingly as a cultural phenomenon. Du Gay and Pryke use the highly influential volume by Scott Lash and John Urry, *Economies of Signs and Space* (1994) to orient their argument. Lash and Urry argue that there is a greater interrelation and merging between the economy and culture.

On the one hand, culture is increasingly seen in economic terms. Art and culture, once conceived, in some quarters at least, as separate from commerce, are now understood importantly as economic. Art and culture are seen to constitute particular sectors of the economy (and hence increasingly talked about as 'cultural industries') and their legitimacy is increasingly understood in terms of economic efficiency, profit and loss, markets and so on. The language of the economy always a major factor in national film and television production is now also to be found, for example, in the museum sector, public art galleries, and the modus vivendi of the struggling artist.

On the other hand, we can see how the cultural industries - initially conceived to include the media industries, advertising, marketing and public relations, but conceived more so now to include leisure, tourism and the service industries generally - have become ever more important in economic terms. For example, governments from across the globe, north and south, have argued that the spread of interactive, broadband networks are central to the growth and competitiveness of national and regional economies. The ability to download movies from the internet, engage in networked game play, or facilitate interactive data services is not just a matter of entertainment, but of big business. Similarly, those producers of goods and services, not historically associated with the cultural industries, increasingly deploy 'culture' as a way of thinking about the making and selling of goods and services. Thus, the branding of a commodity has become a contentious, but central process in the selling and marketing of any major product. If Coca Cola is to sell its product globally, then it needs a product that is instantly recognisable in all international markets. Goods and services, from everyday household items to luxury products, are more and more thought of as 'cultural'. They are increasingly aestheticised and fashioned, whether in terms of the design or manufacture of the product or its marketing to niche, lifestyle consumer groups. More and more goods and services are cultural and culture (as aesthetic, style, fashion, design, image, etc.) becomes the means through which goods and services are increasingly conceived, produced and circulated.

Moreover, business organisation is itself increasingly understood as cultural. Not only the relations between business and consumer or between business and business, but also the relations within a business are seen as increasingly cultural. The culture of business is thus an important focus for contemporary economic organisations. This includes issues concerning, for example, management style, but also the work culture of managers, shop floor workers and those whose job it is to deal with clients or customers face-to-face or telephone-to-telephone. On all counts then, Lash and Urry talk about the way in which there is an increasing *de-differentiation of culture and economy*. The economy is cultural and culture is understood and governed as economic; the boundary between the two categories and domains is now blurred (1994: 64; see also Lash and Urry 1987).

Nevertheless, this argument goes well beyond the reaches of du Gay and Pryke's more restrained discussion concerning the 'culturalisation' of the economic. These two writers suggest that such claims, as made by Lash and Urry, but also Baudrillard and others, regarding a shift to a more symbolic, informational or cultural order are overplayed and reinforce a form of simplistic epochal transformation to the detriment of more nuanced and patient understandings of the way in which the 'economic' is constructed and governed as a cultural entity. Moreover, as the anthropologist Daniel Miller argues: 'while there is no denying the existence of a cultural turn as an approach to the study of economic institutions within social science, there is no reason to assume that this reflects changes in the political economy itself' (2002a: 174). In Miller's argument, one of the problems is that academic knowledges, such as those that herald a cultural turn or earlier neo-classical economics, are formed in the context of the university and might tend to misrepresent the reality of political-economic life, particularly with regard to the situated forms of local economic activity and life. These knowledges have authority and are taken up by institutions such as the International Monetary Fund, the World Bank and other global economic agencies and they are used to control local, predominantly southern hemisphere or 'third world' national economies. According to Miller they are abstractions and tend to ignore, for example, the institutional practice of firms that are more indicative of the reality of contemporary capitalism. It is at this level that Miller sees a place for a more detailed and substantive understanding of the culture of economic life. Thus, in relation to our understanding of a notion of the 'consumer', as against an abstracted 'rational choice consumer', Miller proposes one that has 'flesh' and 'blood':

> When it comes to the ethnographic encounter with actual consumption, the effective units of consumption are rarely individuals, their rationality is likely to be based around concepts of care and style, and most of the precise assumptions of economics as to the knowledge they have and how they use it bears no relation to any observable worlds. By the same token, anthropologists have had a terrible time finding any actual markets that accord with economic models. (2002a: 178)

Miller's account bears resemblance to epistemologies to be found in an earlier Marxism (cf. 2002b). Nevertheless, it points to a need to be cautious about simply accepting academic accounts of major social and economic transformation and getting caught up in debate as if the object of debate were 'real'.

Thus, although there is no reason to assume that these changes in academic focus (e.g. from industrial to post-industrial) necessarily 'reflect' changes in the political economy, there may, nevertheless, be good reason to think that change in discourses, more broadly, of the 'economy' and the 'economic' construct or perform new ways of understanding 'economic' practices and new ways of acting in relation to them (or to the practices that might come under this heading). The focus that du Gay and Pryke emphasise is one that shifts away from understanding a relation between culture and economy in terms of determination, to one of meaning and government or representation and intervention. In this sense, 'culture' constitutes a particular problem for understanding and action. Du Gay and Pryke state:

> The sets of processes and relations we have come to know as 'the economy' appear no longer as taken for granted as perhaps once they were ... [A]mong these proliferating uncertainties has emerged – or, better, re-emerged – a belief that something called 'culture' is both somehow critical to understanding what is happening to, as well as to practically intervening in, contemporary economic and organizational life. (2002a: 1)

The emphasis on meaning – for both academics, but also managers and others, understanding, for example, the meaning of work – is not secondary to actual economic entities existing out there in the real world. Markets and firms, for example, are not seen to exist externally or independently of the discourses that construct them. In this argument, culture is seen as primarily concerned with meaning production, but only inasmuch as culture is also performative or constructive. Du Gay and Pryke argue: 'economic discourses – not simply or primarily academic "economics", but those "hybrid" disciplines such as accounting, marketing, finance, and so forth – format and frame markets and economic and organizational relations, "making them up" rather than simply observing and describing them from a God's-eye vantage point' (2002: 2). The economic, then, is not external to these discourses. The 'economic' provides both a problem of understanding and meaning (namely, what is the economy, how do we conceptualise it, what lies within it, and so on) and an object of government (namely, what are the means through which that which has been defined can be ordered and acted upon): '[e]conomic discourse here is not simply a matter of beliefs, values and symbols but rather a form of representational and technological (i.e. "cultural") practice that constitutes the spaces within which economic action is formatted and framed' (2002: 2).

This move by du Gay and Pryke constitutes an important theoretical shift in our understanding of the 'cultural' nature of economic life. But there is still the nagging question as to what resources are drawn on in our interpretation of what counts as 'cultural'. Du Gay has argued that: 'economic processes and practices ... in all their plurality ... depend upon and have cultural "conditions of existence"'(1997: 4). There is a deep ambivalence that hangs over the phrase 'cultural conditions of existence'. A more critical reading of du Gay and Pryke's work might point to the problematic adoption of earlier definitions of culture as aesthetic or semiotic or as 'way of life'. There is a tendency, then, in du Gay and Pryke's understanding of 'culture' toward the a-historical, and toward a notion of culture as a universal of all societies. In this vein, Slater in his examination of advertising agencies argues that his concern 'is to bring market analysis into line with a perspective in which it is inconceivable that any social sphere could be "without culture" and still persist as a social order' (2002: 61).

In contrast to this reading, but in line with discussion in the previous chapters of this book, we can use du Gay and Pryke's analysis to argue that 'culture' just as much as the 'economic' needs to be placed under review. In identifying culture as a *problem*, rather than a concept or set of concepts, an analysis of cultural economy could look to the way in which actors, or agents (whether individual, collective, or institutional) themselves construct and perform the problem of culture and to the ways in which these actors draw on existing resources and definitions (regarding what culture means, how it might be put to work in particular contexts, and so on). Thus, although there are a stock of existing definitions of 'culture' and 'economy' and a series of historical and situated precedents for pursuing the problem of cultural economy, any new enterprising use of 'culture', for example, in relation to business practice, might be seen to constitute a new mobilisation and a new articulation. Such an understanding of the culture of economic life might allow for a rapprochement between social science approaches to culture and economy. Instead of assuming that economists have somehow taken the lead and snatched the 'economy' away from cultural studies, and that the task at hand is to 'capture' the economy back (see Slater, 2002), it is important to resist attempts to take such a unifying and imperial command of the situation. Instead, then, we might suggest that we stand back from the abstracted, a priori notions of culture and economy and move toward a more micro-analytic, interdisciplinary, hybrid understanding. In part Slater (2002: 60) suggests making this move, but he only takes the 'economic' to task and not the 'cultural'. It is important to do both and, in part, this means understanding the materiality of both.

The Cultural Life of Markets and Commodities

Much of this work, just discussed, on the cultural nature of economic life tries (whether it is successful or not is another matter) to move away from notions of material economy and immaterial (or symbolic) culture. Many authors make reference to material culture, but also to the ways in which agency is assigned to both the human and non-human and to the importance of micro-sociological and anthropological investigation. There is a clear attempt to refocus new sociological and cultural accounts of the economic as material-cultural practice; but whereas some writers tend to place the culture of the economy in the realm of meaning, others want to have a more post-social, material sense of the cultural connections (i.e. a notion of culture as material and not automatically concerned with meaning). A central aspect of this debate concerns the productive talk across cultural studies research and work developed in anthropology, sociology, and science and technology studies.

In neo-classical economic theory (such as that of the work of Alfred Marshall, 1842–1924) markets are seen to make visible a relation between buyers and sellers according to price. A monetary value is accorded to a product or service according to the balance between the supply of a product or service and its demand. Supply and demand constitute two distinct motives or forces.

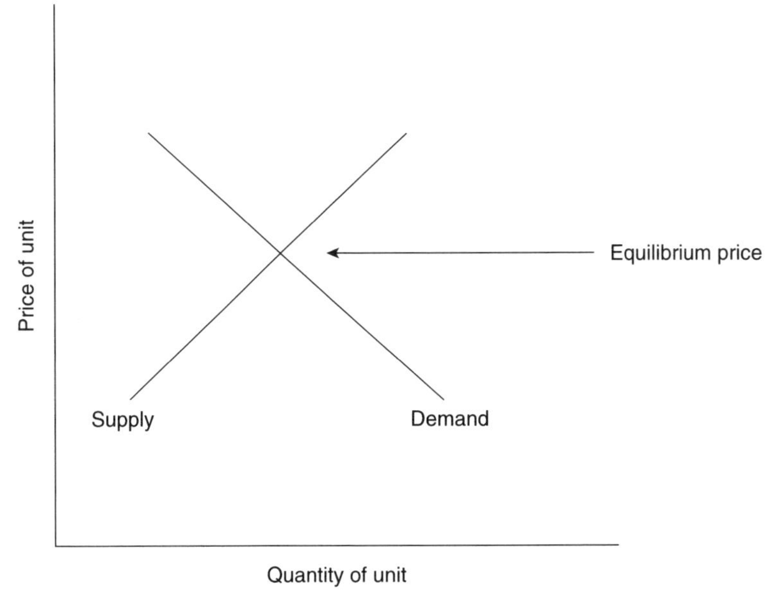

Thus in an ideal situation, according to this neo-classical model, the number of goods produced or services offered would not exceed that demanded at a particular price: price mediates the relation between producer and consumer. The market is the place where this mediation happens.

But markets are understandable not only from the perspective of neo-classical economic theory, but also from sociology, anthropology and cultural studies, in the sense that markets bring together calculative agencies or actors, material entities and forms and processes of organisation. What is strange about market relations, unlike some other forms of social and cultural relations, is that the agents that come together do so as complete strangers; moreover, once the transaction has been completed, the actors leave each other with no social attachments to the other actors involved over and above those that maintain the contractual nature of the exchange. When I go into my local supermarket and buy some cheese, bread and wine, I exchange money for these commodities, not on the basis of my social or cultural relations with the supermarket. I have no intimacy with the chain of stores from which I buy these goods. In fact, when a new store opens up down the road and offers the same products, but of better quality and for less money, I shift my allegiance to this new store and buy there from now on. I have no qualms about doing so. On the contrary, this seems perfectly natural for supermarket shopping in London, but equally in New York, Paris, Lisbon, New Delhi, Nairobi or for many places across the globe.

In addition, actors brought together in a market situation are deemed to have certain competencies: namely, optimal market conditions exist when all parties have optimal information. In order for this to happen, the actors involved are deemed to have certain cognitive competencies. It is typical for psychologists to locate such competencies in the mind of the actor, but equally typical for the social or cultural scientist to look to social and cultural context for an explanation. Moreover, just as certain cognitive competencies are seen to be beneficial to market situations, other social and cultural factors are seen to hinder the optimal workings of markets. In this sense, anthropologists and sociologists of economic life have been keen to point to the way in which markets and economic activities generally are always and necessarily located or embedded in social and cultural relations. For these commentators, there is never a pure abstracted market condition and the point of an anthropology or sociology of economic life is, in part, to constantly remind the economist of such a fact.

In contrast, sociologists such as Michel Callon have pointed to the way that market transactions are necessarily framed (1998a, b). For market exchanges to take place at all, they have to be framed so as to exclude certain elements from the transactional process. Thus, Callon argues, the buying and selling of a motor car is a result of a framing of the exchange in terms of three distinct components: the buyer, the seller and the car. In order for the property rights of the car to be exchanged, the buyer and seller need to be constructed and identified without any ambiguity. Without such clarity it would not be possible for the buyer to say, once the transaction has been completed, that they now own the car:

> To construct a market transaction, that is to say, to transform something into a commodity, and two agents into a seller and a consumer, it is necessary to cut the ties between the thing and the other objects or human beings one by one. It must be decontextualized, dissociated and detached. For the car to go from the producer-seller to the customer-buyer, it has to be disentangled ... If the thing remains entangled, the one who receives it is never quits and cannot escape from the web of relations. The framing is never over. The debt cannot be settled. (1998a: 19)

The framing of a market transaction thus involves the exclusion of certain entities and certain matters. In the discipline of economics this exclusion is often referred to in terms of the notion of externality. An externality is that which is not taken into account explicitly in any market transaction. Thus, for example, a chemical factory producing domestic detergents prices its products according to market conditions, labour costs and capital costs, such as buildings and factory equipment. But the price might very well not reflect the costs to the environment of the pollution that seeps out of the factory on a daily basis. These hidden environmental costs are referred to as externalities. Externalities can, of course, be beneficial. If you are a keen football fan and your house overlooks the Arsenal stadium, then you will be able to watch the game for free. The other supporters paying for tickets will effectively be subsidising your free spectatorship. Many cultural goods can be seen to produce externalities.

Callon is interested in the way in which a sociologist is able to contribute to this debate and to show how externalities are produced through framing, but more significantly how market transactions are necessarily framed. Commodities, in order to be bought and sold, have to be disentangled from both buyer and seller. But also they have to be disentangled from other commodities and other objects generally. For example, Callon describes a strawberry market in France. All the strawberries are placed in boxes side-by-side in order to differentiate the different producers, the different types, the different amounts and the different variations in quality and price. Moreover, this display of differences makes it possible for someone to take account of the differences, to log that information on a computer and then to circulate that information to all those retailers wanting to buy the strawberries. Callon calls this a 'space of calculability'. The space of the market is constructed through various techniques, knowledges and material practices. The commodities, then, in order to be sold, need to be disentangled from the producers and re-entangled within a space that allows the possibility of calculation: the information and material conditions needed in order to make buying and selling possible.

Other writers, such as Peter Miller and Nikolas Rose, have looked at the role of calculative technologies in the construction of economic relations (Miller, 1992; Miller and Rose, 1990; Rose, 1992a,1993). Markets are not abstract entities; but nor are they ideological; they are made through particular techniques and technologies that assemble people and things into ways of action or conduct. Markets, in this sense, have more to do with organisation and administration. Advanced liberal economies are highly complex forms of organisation and they work, not because we all, or most of us, subscribe to an ideology of Western liberal bourgeois capitalism, but because there are multiple knowledges, techniques, technologies and forms of organisation that make markets happen. We might add to the example of the strawberry market by also referring to the knowledges of marketing and accounting that would be required both to direct the selling of the strawberries to particular buyers and to the general public (i.e. the Wimbledon tennis tournament each year is a time for strawberries) and to take account of all the financial transactions that might take place between a seller and buyer or a chain of sellers and buyers. Markets that are highly complex, such as telecommunications, require highly complex forms of accounting and computing technology to take account of transactions. A simple mobile telephone call from one person subscribed to one network provider to another person subscribed to another network provider would need to take account of the billing system, the time spent on the call, the types of data transmitted (speech, text, image, e-mail) and the rental on the physical network for each of the providers. A simple telephone call is made possible through a range of complex knowledges and technologies.

The account of the role of calculative technologies, such as that given by Rose and Miller, in the construction of markets is one that is used by Callon in his discussion of market transactions, but it also feeds into broader discussions concerning the government of economic life: namely, the role of economic and financial disciplines in the government of individuals and populations. Accountancy, for example, is not simply a knowledge that makes visible the economic flows within and between economic actors; it is deployed as a tool for formulating and resolving particular problems of government. The production of budgets, the calculation of costs, the comparison between different budgets, the computation of rates of return, and so on, are managerial techniques that can be used in the government of people and things. For example, a Vice Chancellor of a university may believe that university departments function best when they have more direct control over their own affairs (i.e. in terms of hiring people, investing in certain types of research, investing in new equipment and buildings, and so on). Nevertheless, the Vice Chancellor may also want to make those departments 'responsible' in a way that supports the general objectives of the university. The making of devolved budgets visible to the government of the university and accountable in terms of these objectives thus provide ways of achieving these apparently contradictory paths: to govern through the freedom of others (Rose, 1993). Moreover, forms of conduct (such as writing books) that did not in the past have a financial value (in terms of investment and return) now have one and are made calculable and disciplined accordingly. The amount of time and money required to write a book that brings in a particular amount of money through government research funding is calculated. Academics that are given time to write and do not do so according to these marginal efficiencies are seen to be failing in their job. The accounting is made visible to other academics and the collegial framework becomes a form of collective discipline: if you don't produce the book in the time allotted, you not only fail for yourself, but also for the department and university.

In Callon's terms, such governmental technologies help to frame market transactions and thus facilitate the movement of a commodity from one owner to another. But whereas the sociological work on governmental technologies helps us understand the way in which markets might be framed, work in anthropology helps us to understand the entangling and disentangling of the commodity. The work of Arjun Appadurai and Igor Kopytoff is significant in this respect inasmuch as it proposes that commodities have 'life histories', 'careers' or 'biographies': Where does a commodity come from? What is its status? What is its life cycle? How does it change? In Appadurai and Kopytoff's account of the biographies of commodities, the distribution of knowledge and technology is of central importance, not only in terms of the technical, social, and aesthetic knowledge that facilitates production and consumption, but more generally 'the distribution of knowledge at various points in their careers' (Appadurai, 1986: 41). Clearly, as Callon admits, the biography of a commodity is such that even in market transactions whereupon a good is passed from a seller to a buyer, not every facet of the commodity's life up to this point can be excluded.

> [N]ot all the ties can be cut. Something passes from seller to the buyer: the car, which conveys with it the know-how and technology of the producer. All the property rights in the world cannot prevent this overflowing, except by eliminating the transaction itself. (1998a: 18)

As Callon says '[c]omplete framing is a contradiction in terms' (1998a: 18). Moreover, the overflowing of particular forms of knowledge and technical know-how is central to the commodity itself. As other writers have shown, the commodity is part of the package whereby the user is her or himself configured (cf. Woolgar, 1991). Thus, for example, the sale of a computer carries with it certain booklets, helplines and so on that assist in the configuring or disciplining of the user. Without that overflowing, there would be no preferred use. Nevertheless, whereas in situations with a high degree of discipline the use of a commodity, and hence its biography, may be controlled, in other situations the use and interpretation of a commodity may be more open. For example, a car needs to be driven in a certain way, on a particular side of the road, at particular speeds, avoiding certain objects and so on, whereas, in contrast, a film becomes successful, in part, because it is able to be interpreted in different ways and in different contexts. It might be seen, as Appadurai has argued, that 'as commodities travel greater distances (institutional, spatial, temporal), knowledge about them tends to become partial, contradictory, and differentiated' (1986: 56). It is well-documented how cultural goods, such as television programmes, become interpreted and used very differently in contexts distant from the sites of origination and production (cf. Ang, 1996; Hall, 1980). The 'decoding' of a commodity relies on knowledge and technical know-how, but another dimension to this is that knowledge is itself increasingly commoditised (cf. Appadurai, 1986: 54). The reception of a Hollywood film is not limited to the film itself but also to the whole merchandising enterprise that goes along with it, plus the various interviews and photo opportunities in the style magazines and popular tabloids. Kopytoff has argued that commodities in complex societies generally refer to no clear hierarchy of loyalties and to changing contexts of use and interpretation:

> The biography of things in complex societies reveals a similar pattern [to that of the social identity of a person]. In the homogenized world of commodities, an eventful biography of a thing becomes the story of the various singularizations of it, of classifications and reclassifications in an uncertain world of categories whose importance shifts with very minor change in context. As with persons, the drama here lies in the uncertainties of valuation and of identity. (1986: 90)

Thus, by following and tracking the biography of a commodity, it is possible to trace the variations of use and interpretation. The overflowings may not be pertinent to a market transaction, but they are central to the specificity of a commodity and hence to one's reason for attaching oneself (or not) to or becoming attached (or not) to such an object. As Kopytoff suggests:

> The biography of a car in Africa would reveal a wealth of cultural data: the way it was acquired, how and from whom the money was assembled to pay for it, the relationship of the seller to the buyer, the uses to which the car is regularly put, the identity of its frequent passengers and of those who borrow it, the frequency of borrowing, the garages to which it is taken and the owner's relation to the mechanics, the movement of the car from hand to hand over the years, and in the end, when the car collapses, the final disposition of its remains. All of these details would reveal an entirely different biography from that of a middle-class American, or Navajo, or French peasant car. (1986: 67)

This brings us firmly back to the question of culture and its relation to the economic. In Callon's account social and cultural context are seen as overbearing abstract entities that demand too much. He is critical of the claims that society or culture are the starting points or frame for economic activity and organisation (1998a: 30). For Callon, it is economics (albeit one that is also assembled from the more hybrid disciplines of accountancy, marketing, management studies and so on, as well as 'pure' economics) that performs the economy.

Equally, economic performances are local affairs. The construction of markets is not universal. Markets are made and remade in relation to various and local entanglements. This is also the point that is made by du Gay and Pryke in their discussion of cultural economy. But they depart from Callon's analysis by asserting that the performativity of the economic and its capacity to lead in the government of others (i.e. to both represent and intervene) is essentially 'cultural' (2002: 2). These two contrasting positions on the question of 'culture', though, can begin to be settled from a more situated reflexive understanding. Kopytoff is suggestive in this respect:

> But all such biographies - economic, technical, social - may or may not be culturally informed. What would make a biography cultural is not what it deals with, but how and from what perspective. A culturally informed economic biography of an object would look at it as a culturally constructed entity, endowed with culturally specific meanings and classified and reclassified into cultural constituted categories. (1986: 68)

But rather than construe singularisation as a facet of culture, as Kopytoff does, we must take the singularity of an object as an open question with regard to its disciplinary perspective. Nonetheless, the problem with Callon is that he cedes too much to the economist in the performance of the economy: why doesn't he see that what has traditionally been conceived as cultural now plays a significant part in our understanding of economic life. Equally, though, Pryke and du Gay assert the cultural nature of the economic, rather than leave it open to empirical investigation: namely, why not presume that performance and representation are not necessarily cultural and instead look at how performances of the economy become cultural in those performances?

What is clear, though, from this discussion is that, first, the relation between economy and culture is complex and that any attempt to reduce one to the other is problematic. Although it is noticeable how many attempts there have been that do just that and although the language of causality has lost its favour, the language of construction, making and performativity takes up that role. If culture performs the economy, how is this not a reiteration of linear causal model albeit one that prioritises the cultural over the economic? Secondly, the work of Callon, Appadurai, Kopytoff and others show how the question of culture and economy cannot be reduced to a question of meaning. Things, as well as people, are seen to have agency. Cultural economic relations are not simply, or even primarily, about meaning, but about use, connection and organisation. Thirdly, the shift toward micro-sociological accounts leaves the field wide open with regard to broader political economic, once-called structural interpretations, of the cultural-economic. And finally, the move to a more variated understanding of cultural-economic relations can fall back on a relativist understanding of the cultural (i.e. as with the nineteenth century play-off between culture and civilisation). Given these problems, recent understanding of the relation between culture and economy within cultural studies and associated disciplines offer the possibility of a more humble relation to both objects of concern and importantly, as a consequence, a more sympathetic, and possibly enlightened, rapprochement across the disciplines genuinely concerned with understanding cultural economy.

Chapter Summary

- Much of the history of culture has been constructed in terms of a divide between the economic and the cultural.
- Western Marxism, following Marx and Engels, has been preoccupied with the question of the determination of culture by the economic.
- Althusser presents an idea of structural causality that sees structure only in its effects and only inasmuch as it is overdetermined by other structures within a social formation.
- Other Marxist and political economists in cultural studies have used a weaker sense of determination in terms of 'setting limits'.
- More recent debates about consumer culture have refocused the relation between culture and economy not in terms of production, but in terms of consumption. Of importance are the writings of Jean Baudrillard and Pierre Bourdieu.
- Baudrillard argues that the logic of the sign is equivalent to the logic of the commodity and as a consequence production is subsumed by consumption and use value is subsumed by exchange value. Culture is understood through the logic of economic relations of exchange.
- In contrast Bourdieu also talks about the economy of culture, but in terms of the distribution of cultural capital and the different forms of habitus through which distinction (and hence power) is produced and reproduced. Bourdieu stresses that although we can talk of an economy of culture we should be wary of reducing all economies to the model of the economic economy.
- A number of writers have argued that there have been major shifts in economic and social organisation. Of prime importance to us are the collapsing boundaries between culture and the economic in the sense that culture becomes more economic, but also the economy becomes more cultural:
    - cultural industries are more broadly defined;
    - culture comes to define relations between as well as within business organisation.
- Lash and Urry talk about this in terms of the de-differentiation of the economic and cultural.
- A number of writers are critical of the claims of epochal change and talk more about the shift in academic focus since the 1980s onwards to more cultural aspects of the economic, these writers talk about the 'performance' of the economic through cultural discourses and practices.
- Michel Callon, Arjun Appadurai and Igor Kopytoff discuss the materiality of markets and commodities in terms of networks and biographies. Although the cultural is comprehended differently in the writings of these different thinkers, they all help to understand markets and commodity relations as singular expressions across particular actors and technologies.

EIGHT World: Between Globe and Empire

In many ways the discourse of globalisation comes to the fore in the context of broader debates concerning massive changes to national economies and relations of international trade. In this context it was often talked about - in the strategic meetings called by chief executives of transnational corporations such as Shell, BP, Vodafone and Deutsche Bank or by the premiers and heads of state of national government - alongside the notions of liberalisation and the rapid development of new technology. The processes of globalisation were seen to sit alongside those political programmes that called for the freeing-up of markets, for the opening up of public forms of organisation to privatised logics and for the withering away of the centralised state. Economic liberalism was seen as the lever that could tip heavy, centralised, bureaucratic and undemocratic forms of governance into the soft kiss of democracy and capitalism. The neo-liberals who called for both liberalisation and globalisation in the same breath argued that such moves were inevitable as a consequence of the openness of new communications technology with regard to border controls and blindness with regard to national legislation (cf. de Sola Pool, 1983; Veljanovski, 1989). First satellite television and broadband telecommunications networks, then the internet seemingly made a mockery of the nation-state. In the last days of the Cold War the mantra - 'technologise, liberalise, globalise' - seemingly lauded the inevitable cracking open of the centralised bureaucracies of state socialism: how could the Soviet Bloc and Communist China resist the temptations of the 'free market'?

Although the neo-liberal argument provided a major narrative to some significant economic, political, social and cultural trends, it nevertheless overly focused on the decline of centralised state administrations and the sovereignty of the nation-state. In fact, the increased movement of ideas, cultures, technologies and peoples seemed to signal something much more extensive and broad-ranging than had initially been anticipated. For those, such as ourselves, interested in the changing nature of culture, the global offers itself as a significant and fundamental problem. The rearticulation of culture as *geo-cultural*, namely as that which has an extension beyond the socio-politics of the nation-state, has meant a need to revisit some of the core problematics of cultural analysis in terms of the changing nature of culture, but also in terms of its half-visible history in the context of European and US empire. In this chapter we initially look at some of the major aspects of the debate about globalisation and at how global processes might be seen to impact on our understanding of culture. We then look at the formative relation between culture and empire and at some possible implications in studying culture in conditions of empire and post-empire. And finally we add a note of scepticism by considering the question of scale, namely the question that it might be a mistake to think about the global as if it were somehow *bigger* than the local.

One World?

The inevitabilities of capitalism, in terms of its search for new markets and its inherently imperial tendencies, were noted by Lenin in 1917 (1986) but in the latter part of the twentieth century writers such as Ernst Mandel (1978), Immanuel Wallerstein (1974, 1980), Frederic Jameson (1984), Anthony Giddens (1990) and David Harvey (1989) have developed an understanding of late or advanced capitalism and its tendency toward globalisation. Of course, there are major differences between these writers, but if we initially look at the bare bones of Wallerstein's argument, we can get a sense of a general argument about global capitalism as a world economic system. Wallerstein's understanding of a capitalist world system is one that emerges in the sixteenth century and has developed to the extent that it can be properly called a system, with its own forms of organisation and regulation. The world economic system integrates productive forces and relations from across the globe into a single division of labour; the correlative political framework is that of an interstate system within which individual national sovereign states have limited means of control. Wallerstein, following the work of Kondratieff, argues that economic systems are cyclical and the world economic system is no exception. The global capitalist economy has periods of expansion and contraction, highs and lows. As a consequence of its cyclical pattern, the world economy needs to expand its markets and to expand its productive base; it does so by expanding geographically. New corners of the world become new centres of production (such as the stitching of trainers in South East Asia) and new products and services are sold globally (such as a McDonalds in every high street). Global expansion is matched by capital accumulation. It is unsurprising, therefore, according to Wallerstein's argument, that peripheral and semi-peripheral states are the most exploited. Global capitalism is a system that is constantly innovating and re-organising; labour needs to constantly re-skill and labour is constantly moving at a global level to meet new skill demands (such as information technology workers from India moving to the US and Europe). The accumulation of capital, the reorganisation of production and the movement of labour serves to benefit some people located in certain parts of the globe more than others. The structure of the world system is inherently unequal. Moreover, the system is itself historical and thus it has a beginning and an end. At some point the system can expand and accumulate no more; at this point it collapses (Wallerstein, 1974, 1980, 1983, 1990). It follows from such an analysis of the global capitalist economy, that culture is - despite Wallerstein's protestations (1990) - largely epiphenomenal; it is seen to serve an ideological function, whether in the form of a series of divisions and hierarchies or an imagined one-world socialist culture and there is little sense of the complexities of culture that we might attain from the cultural sciences of cultural studies or anthropology (cf. Boyne, 1990).

Although Wallerstein's argument helps to put into the picture a general trope for understanding globalisation, there are clear differences between his mono-causal explanation and, for example, Giddens' multi-causal understanding of the dynamics at stake. Whereas Wallerstein prioritises the economic at the expense of other factors, Giddens stresses broader institutional changes including the changing nature of the nation-state and the role of the military. For example, transnational corporations, such as Microsoft and Sony, demonstrate massive economic power and they play a major role in technological and industrial development (especially in the area of communications) but they have no legitimate right to the means to violence. Or, for example, when individuals and corporations have become greedy for the natural resources of weak nations (especially in the continent of Africa) and have employed mercenary forces, those individuals and their operations can be, and have been, brought to heel within the jurisdictions of particular nation-states. Equally, the United Nations and the European Union are multinational organisations that act politically on a global scale. Yet these actors have no standing army and rely on the decisions of national governments for support in international conflicts and humanitarian operations. Nevertheless, when large-scale disasters strike or when conflicts are such that they demand an international military response, individual nation-states come together in multination forces to contain the problem. Of course, some military threats, due to technological advances such as nuclear weapons, are transnational by their very nature. The different dynamics between capitalism, industrialism, militarism, and the system of international relations between nation-states cannot be reduced to a single causal factor, but need to be understood in a manner that takes into account an inherent multi-causality. For Giddens, then, globalisation is understood in terms of the interconnected dimensions of these dynamics and in the context of the underlying conditions of modernity (Giddens, 1990).

By and large, most commentators accept that social and cultural relations in the contemporary world and across the whole of that world are shaped by factors, in part and in some shape or form, that can very crudely be called transnational. And most commentators talk about this transnationalism in terms of the notion of 'globalisation'. Equally though, earlier arguments from neo-liberals who exaggerated the absolute decline of the nation-state in the era of globalisation (e.g. in terms of the development of communications technology, such as the internet, that supposedly make national legislation, regulation and policing impossible) have rightly been corrected. This correction has come in part from the scepticism of Paul Hirst and Grahame Thompson (1996) or writers such as Linda Weiss (1997, 1998) and has produced a more attenuated understanding of globalisation. Hirst and Thompson caution against a 'strong version of globalisation' that 'requires a new view of the international economy' that 'subsumes and subordinates national-level processes' (1996: 4) and instead argue for an 'internationalization' that 'can be accommodated within a modified view of the world economic system, that still gives a major role to national-level policies and actors' and that is understood in terms of its longer historical perspective (1996: 4). In this sense the pressure of international trade and financial markets is not seen to open the floodgates to the anarchy of unrestrained self-interest. Markets are constructed, shaped and governed by a range of actors working at international, regional, local and national levels. The economy, in and of itself, does not contain the means to govern, regulate and organise itself. Legislation, regulation and politics are not thrown out of the window, but are importantly re-construed within the complexities of the current situation. Thus, for example, the opening of new satellite television markets in China and East Asia in the 1980s and 1990s went hand-in-hand with forms of regulation and political governance that made it possible to show programmes across national boundaries and to a large extent this meant negotiating with the national governments to hand. Hirst and Thompson talk of how different levels of government and policy making are stitched together or sutured. They maintain that '[t]he nation state is central to this process of "suturing": the policies and practices of states in distributing power upwards to the international level and downwards to sub-national agencies are the sutures that will hold the system of governance together' (1996: 184). Again, although there are clear differences of argument, Weiss holds that instead of seeing a diminution of the authority and power of nation-states, we are witnessing changing definitions and practices of the state itself. Thus, she argues that:

> [W]e can expect to see more and more of a different kind of state taking shape in the world arena, one that is reconstituting its power at the centre of alliances formed either within or outside the state. For these states, building state capacity, rather than discarding it, would seem to be the lesson of dynamic integration ... [T]he ability of nation-states to adapt to internationalization - so-called 'globalization' - will continue to heighten rather than diminish national differences in state capacity and the accompanying advantages of national economic coordination. (1997: 27)

In the broad terms in which we are looking at the debates here any stand-off between Giddens and those whom he calls the sceptics, such as Hirst and Thompson and Weiss, is minor. All see globalisation in a sense that takes account of different political, economic and social actors at different levels of the global, regional, national and local and see globalisation as emerging within conditions of modernity and not as an entirely new system (i.e. one congruent with the conditions of postmodernity). Although at times Giddens appears to wax lyrical about the radically new, self-enclosed system of the global economy (1998), he more consistently offers a sense of globalisation that is critical of the global as a self-regulating and organised system in and of itself (1990).

Global Culture

It is interesting to note that Giddens' more recent writings offer an understanding of globalisation that is more favourable to the power of culture and communications in the shaping of a global world (1998, 1999). Equally though there is a danger in simply turning to culture and communications as a solution to the question of how things have changed. The eating of an English muffin followed by an Asian curry, listening to US rap in Sydney Australia before e-mailing family in Trinidad might indicate the syncretic, mixed nature of much contemporary culture, but the image does little to explain how culture itself has changed. What concerns us, then, is the extent to which globalisation is a facet of contemporary practices of and discussions about culture. Why does globalisation matter for an understanding of culture?

An obvious place to start is with Marshall McLuhan who, in the early 1960s, argued that:

> Our specialist and fragmented civilization of centre-margin structure is suddenly experiencing an instantaneous reassembling of all its mechanized bits into an organic whole. This is the new world of the global village. The village ... had achieved a social and institutional extension of all human faculties ... The electronic age cannot sustain the very low gear of a centre-margin structure such as we associate with the past two thousand years of the Western world. (1964: 93)

The development of electronic media, such as television and telecommunications, brings about, according to McLuhan, an implosion of space and functional organisation. Many have understood McLuhan's notion of the 'global village' as if he were saying that, as a consequence of new communication technology, we are now living in a more homogenous and unitary world, a world community shaped in the image of the local village. As we shall discuss shortly, partly this is an issue concerning the reshaping of space and time in conditions of globalisation, but it is also a matter of the ability to imagine the world as a much smaller place. Most notably, in the 1960s as a consequence of space travel, we were able to see the world as a completely individuated entity, as a globe sitting in infinite space. Barbara Duden has talked about this in relation to shifts in our understanding of life itself (1993) and Sarah Franklin, Celia Lury and Jackie Stacey in a brilliant analysis of the interrelation between global nature and global culture in late modernity argue that:

> Since its appearance as an image, the blue planet has been deployed as a symbol of global unity, international collaboration and shared planetary interdependence. Instead of the horizon being the natural limit of humanity's expectations, a limit set by the curve of the earth and its movement around the sun, 'mankind' encountered a planet made visible as a whole, discrete entity. Space became a new location from which to view ourselves, and this *perspectival shift* has produced both a new context for universalisms and an added visual dimension by which the universe scales the order of things. (Frankin et al., 2000: 28)

These writers argue that because of space exploration we are able to see ourselves as transcendent of humankind and beyond the limited 'petty squabbles over land and property'. They argue that this global perspective makes possible 'the space of *panhumanity*, of a newly imagined and imagined form of global unity' (2000: 28).

Some have talked about this new perspective in terms of a 'global consciousness'. Although history demonstrates the fact that various 'civilisations' have had imperial conquests and shaped their territories according to commands from the centre, it is not until relatively recently that the whole world has been thought of as a single society. Roland Robertson, for example, talks about the shift from a world 'in itself' to a world 'for itself'. From the 1960s, he argues, we see the heightening of a global consciousness, a world that is aware of itself as one world (Robertson, 1990). From planet earth to Live 8, images of the world circulate around the world. The release of Nelson Mandela, the falling of the Berlin Wall, the tanks in Tiananmen Square, the Tsunami wave in South East Asia, these events and others circulate as images of our global consciousness. They, perhaps, make us realise that we belong to a global community. As McLuhan himself states: '[i]f the work of the city is the remaking or translating of man into a more suitable form than his nomadic ancestors achieved, then might not our current translation of our entire lives into the spiritual form of information seem to make of the entire globe, and of the human family, a single consciousness' (1964: 61). But this global consciousness is far from a unitary consciousness for itself. For McLuhan this consciousness is multiplicitous. In the opening pages of *The Medium is the Massage*, he quotes the scientist and philosopher A. N. Whitehead saying: '[i]nsistence on clarity at all costs is based on sheer superstition as to the mode in which human intelligence functions. Our reasonings grasp at straws for premises and float on gossamers for deductions' (Whitehead, 'Adventures in ideas' quoted in McLuhan and Fiore, 1967: 10). McLuhan talks about 'a collide-oscope of interfaced situations' in which there is no 'fixed unchangeable, point of view – the witless repetitive response to the unperceived' (McLuhan and Fiore, 1967: 10). Or he quotes James Joyce on the opening page of *War and Peace in the Global Village*: '[g]lobes make my head spin. By the time I locate the place, they've changed the boundaries' (McLuhan and Fiore, 1968: 1). Equally, for McLuhan, 'the old civic, state, and national groupings have become unworkable ... you can't *go* home again' (McLuhan and Fiore, 1967: 16). The 'global village' is not based on the model of any of those communities; moreover, minorities become visible within the same space, just as much as this space is one which is minoritarian: we are all minorities now (McLuhan and Fiore, 1967: 24).

Thus any global perspective is deeply ambivalent; any consciousness of panhumanity is plural; and there is certainly no single global culture. Despite the growth of global capitalism, of international relations, of global media and of an understanding of global risk (cf. Beck, 1992), we certainly do not all live in the same culture and the same community. Any sympathy for the panhuman following the devastation meted out by the Tsunami wave in South East Asia in December 2004 can be contrasted with the global divisions and fractures made visible by the attack on the Twin Towers in September 2001. As Anthony D. Smith states 'the idea of a "global culture" is a practical impossibility' (1990: 171). Across the globe there are differences of taste, lifestyle, habits and customs that militate against any understanding of global culture as a singular entity. We can see evidence that 'the partial mixing of cultures, the rise of lingua franca and of wider "Pan" nationalisms, though sometimes working in opposed directions, have created the possibility of "families of culture" which portend wider regional patchwork culture-areas' (Smith, 1990: 188). But we are far from any understanding of 'the kind of global culture and cosmopolitan ideal that can truly supersede a world of nations, each cultivating its distinctive historical character and rediscovering its national myths, memories and symbols in past golden ages and sacred landscapes' (Smith, 1990: 188).

Many academics believe not only that these stories and memories of the nation are cultivated, but also that the boundaries of the nation are themselves constituted through particular cultural technologies. Thus, Eric Hobsbawm and others have talked about 'the invention of tradition' (Hobsbawm and Ranger 1983). National rituals that seem timeless, such as the Queen of England's Speech at Christmas, are in fact relatively recent constructions. The broadcasting historian Paddy Scannell, for example, has shown how annual national events, such as Wimbledon tennis or the FA Cup Final, were made into 'national' events through their coverage on radio and later television broadcasting and how they construct the rhythms of a national calendrical time (Scannell, 1988). Benedict Anderson (1983) has talked with a view to the relation between print technology and capitalism, about the nation as an 'imagined community', namely that there is no prior 'national culture', but rather that any sense of the boundaries, limits and synchronicity of the nation are constructed through, for example, the co-location of peoples and places in the novelistic form or though the repetition and regularities of a national press. Other writers on the media have talked about how cultural technologies, such as radio, television and print, do not simply carry the content of a national culture, but are constitutive of that national time and space (cf. Donald, 1992; Schlesinger, 1991).

But if we accept this role of cultural technologies in the formation and construction of national identities and communities, then the major changes in regional and international media environments should signal changes at the level of the cultural construction of the nation. We might imagine then not necessarily that the 'nation' disappears in the face of a global culture, but that it is refigured within a different set of dynamics. For example, localised cultures that cannot be repackaged for international distribution might find survival in this new environment more difficult. The film *Bend It Like Beckham* reconfigures multi-ethnic and multi-faith 'Englishness', not simply to those resident in the UK, but to a global market. We need to be careful at this point because many commentators are too quick to suggest that there is now a global media system (cf. Robertson, 1990). If we look at the evidence we see, in contrast, a series of discriminated markets (Hoskins et al., 1997). A television programme, such as *Teletubbies*, might sell across the globe, but only to certain countries and not packaged in the same way. Some countries will have better trade contacts with some countries, but not others. Some cultural trade is only one-way (i.e. South Africa broadcasting US programmes, but the US not showing South African ones). Writing in 1989, but with a continuing validity for today, David Morley and Kevin Robins state that:

> What appears to be emerging in this process is a new articulation of spatial scales - of global, continental, national and the local spheres - associated with the increasing transnationalisation of accumulation. The worldwide organisation and integration of corporate activities is bringing about a more immediate and direct articulation of global and local spaces. Particular localities and cities are drawn into the logic of transnational networks. What appears to be developing through this process is a new global matrix of unevenly developed regions, cities and localities. (1989: 22)

There is, then, a greater international connectedness through interlinked media and communications networks, but also a high level of unevenness across these networks.

Any sense of culture in the context of globalisation, then, is problematised in respect of conventional notions of place and community. Giddens makes the distinction between 'place' and 'space' and argues that in conditions of modernity we see an increasing separation between the former and the latter. We see a radical transformation of social order from the medieval village to nineteenth century London to twenty-first century Mumbai. For Giddens, '"[p]lace" is best conceptualised by means of the idea of locale, which refers to the physical settings of social activity as situated geographically' (1990: 18). Place is understood in terms of conditions of co-presence, namely the way in which social interaction and relations occur face-to-face in physically close environments (such as the family or the village). Everyday communication is seen as predominantly oral. Trade, relations of authority, sociability and so on, by-and-large, take place with others who are physically close to you. These daily encounters might be understood as highly localised. In contrast, Giddens argues that in conditions of modernity social relations are increasingly typified not by the physical presence of others, but by their physical absence. Modern communication systems allow for social relations to be conducted at a distance. For example, the space of a typical conversation might now be divorced from place, from the co-presence of a face-to-face encounter; a conversation can be held over a telephone or on the internet with people at great physical distances from each other. Thus, Giddens talks about the separation of space from place in modernity:

> In conditions of modernity, place becomes increasingly *phantasmagoric*: that is to say, locales are thoroughly penetrated by and shaped in terms of social influences quite distant from them. What structures the locale is not simply that which is present on the scene; the 'visible form' of the locale conceals the distanciated relations which determine its nature. (1990: 19)

Giddens understands this process in terms of, what he calls, disembedding mechanisms. Modern social relations are increasingly typified by the fact of their having been 'lifted out' of their 'local context of interaction' and then restructured across time and space (1990: 21). A simple social relation of the exchange of goods between two people can now, for example, be stretched across symbolic tokens (such as money) and expert systems (such as a banking system, the internet, mobile telephones and so on). Moreover, for Giddens the stretching of social relations across distance allows for the reconstruction of both space and time. New forms of space and time can be constructed across territorial distance. He gives the example of a train schedule, but we might equally think of a television schedule as that which coordinates people (both producers and viewers) and machinery (television cameras as well as remote control devices) across time and space. The name Giddens gives to this complex process is 'time-space distanciation' (1984, 1990).

Manuel Castells, writing about the network society, talks of a similar set of processes. He describes how local practices are increasingly connected to global processes: '[t]he global city is not a place, but a process. A process by which centers of production and consumption of advanced services, and their ancillary local societies, are connected in a global network, while simultaneously downplaying the linkages with their hinterlands' (1996: 386). Castells argues that this global network of networks is constructed not in terms of the lifting and stretching of social relations, but in the transformation of social relations around a 'timeless time', such that 'time' can be constructed and reconstructed (e.g. the time of a modern global corporation might be geared around the time of other global trading partners rather than any notion of day-time, night-time, sleep-time and so on within one time zone) and around a 'space of flows': 'our society is constructed around flows: flows of capital, flows of information, flows of technology, flows of organizational interaction, flows of images, sounds, and symbols' (1996: 412). In Castells' argument timeless time is the consequence of the space of flows, a consequence of the material transformations that are typified by his notion of the 'network society'. But for Castells not all local places are caught up in these processes of globalisation: '[t]he relationships between the space of flows and the space of places, between simultaneous globalization and localization are not predetermined by their outcome' (1996: 425). Nevertheless, although the places in which people live are not directly caught up in the processes of globalisation, these people and places are affected by the space of flows precisely because it is in that global space of capital that power is located: '[e]xperience, by being related to places, becomes abstracted from power, and meaning is increasingly separated from knowledge' (1996: 428). Castells talks about a parallel universe between the fast-moving flow of capital and the more sedentary flow of place, the global and the local, the connected and the disconnected. For Giddens, as we have seen, there is a much more dialectical understanding of the relation between local and global, an understanding that is less pessimistic about the possibilities of the chasm of which Castells talks.

Another view of the inherently globalising forces of our contemporary world is put forward by David Harvey, who - as with Giddens and Castells - comments on the changing nature of time and space. Harvey argues that the history of capitalism can be characterised by the speeding up of the pace of life and that this is experienced as a collapsing of space. Harvey gives an example of the speed of the quickest vehicles and the time it would take to circumvent the globe at different historical periods. From the sixteenth to the mid-nineteenth century the average speed of a horse or a sailing ship was 10 miles per hour; from the mid-nineteenth to the early twentieth century steam trains could travel at 65 miles per hour; in the mid-twentieth century airplanes could fly at 400 miles per hour and in the 1960s jet aircraft could fly at 700 miles per hour. Over and above any quibbling about the actual speeds it might take to travel around the world, Harvey has a clear point that the world now seems much smaller as a consequence of the speed of transport. In the context of electronic communications, we can travel almost instantaneously, talking face-to-face with someone thousands of miles away (cf. Moores, 1993; Williams, 1974). Harvey refers to this process as 'time-space compression' (1989: 240) and in many ways this analysis borrows from McLuhan's argument about how the speeding up of modern society leads to an implosion of social relations and to greater globalisation (McLuhan, 1964). But Harvey offers an analysis that roots these transformations in the dynamic logic of capital: '[t]he dimensions of space and time have been subject to the persistent pressure of capital circulation and accumulation, culminating (particularly during the periodic crises of overaccumulation that have arisen since the mid-nineteenth century) in disconcerting and disruptive bouts of time-space compression' (1989: 327).

These different understandings of the dynamics of globalisation with regard to questions of time and space have different ramifications in terms of our understanding of the lines of fracture and unity in this modern world. More than any other writer, Arjun Appadurai has offered an account of the tensions between cultural homogenisation and heterogenisation: '[t]he new global cultural economy has to be understood as a complex, overlapping, disjunctive order' (1990: 296). Appadurai talks about the 'fundamental disjunctures between economy, culture and politics' in terms of certain forms of global cultural flow (1990: 296). He talks about these flows, not in the more homogenising manner of Castells, but in terms of five landscapes:

ethnoscapes, which concern the shifting of people as tourists, migrants, exiles, guestworkers and so on; technoscapes, by which he means the flows of technology, whether informational, mechanical or whatever; finanscapes, which refer to the flows of global capital through stock exchanges, futures markets and commodity speculation; mediascapes, by which he means the capabilities to produce and distribute media forms, such as television or radio or the press; and ideoscapes, which concern the flow of ideologies and political meanings and forms, such as democracy or fascism. Although the notion of 'scapes' is etymologically problematic, the idea that there are global cultural flows that are differentiated and that problematise existing concepts of nation, people and community is productive.

As Appadurai suggests 'people, machinery, money, images, and ideas now follow increasingly non-isomorphic paths'. Moreover, 'the sheer speed, scale and volume of each of these flows is now so great that the disjunctures have become central to the politics of global culture' (1990: 301). If we take the example of the flow of political ideas (ideoscape) that originate in one particular context, but circulate globally, then those ideas are distributed through particular media forms (mediascapes) and such distribution is possible because of prior distribution of particular communication technologies, such as television, the printing press, and the internet (technoscapes). These ideas are, then, received and discussed by particular people in particular contexts (ethnoscapes). The ideas travel, but they travel at different speeds, through different territories and space, and through different practices according to different temporalities. Thus, any political ideology that travels in this way is caught up in the dynamic tensions of global and local flows. Ideas about major events travel the world, by way of new communication technologies, in a quicker time than ever, but not everyone believes the same thing, not everyone is awake at the same time, not everyone eats at the same time not everyone works at the same time and not everyone shops at the same time. News travels fast, but only as fast as 'the people' will allow and put up with. The everyday practices that help structure our lives pull against any simplistic construction of community.

However, we should not simply settle for Appadurai's discussion of the different global cultural flows, but understand them in the context of the dynamics of distanciation, the speed of flows and compression. Let's take, for example, the ethnoscape of a ragga artist and his support act moving from Jamaica for a tour in the UK. Once in the UK, he is met by a campaign against his lyrics. Some political groups object to his tour because of the nature of his lyrics. They argue that his lyrics are homophobic and constitute a form of 'hate speech'. Others, though, object that the artist is being unfairly treated, that he is being victimised because he is a black artist, and that other non-black artists are not similarly treated for their homophobic lyrics. At the centre of the debate is not just the artist, but the whole genre of music. Moreover, the mainstream press and television media also discuss the issue in terms of the artist being from Jamaica and thus construct the issue in terms of a series of stereotypes about ethnicity and black hyper-masculinity. Hence, the mediascape is also constructed through the flow of ideoscapes both in the UK and Jamaica, and internationally. The unities of the ethnos (the ragga artist as 'Jamaican'), of the music (ragga) and the ideologies (freedom of speech, hate speech, discrimination) are distinct and yet interconnected. But the very fact of the connections across these flows leads to their stretching and warping. Thus, the ethnos of 'Jamaica' is not located within a particular territorial locale, but is itself constructed and constituted in the mediascapes and ideoscapes that flow across different locales. Ethnos is not fixed in the firm ground of 'place', but is itself stretched and compressed in a series of flows that can properly be called a transnational warping. We understand these flows, then, as both disjunctures and warpings.

Empire

Perhaps the most significant context for understanding globalisation is that of empire. It is through an understanding of empire that we can get to grips with the accumulated differentiations and regimes of power that since the sixteenth century have been associated with European imperial expansion and modernity, and with the economic, political and cultural conquests of the imperial ambitions of the US since the mid-twentieth century, but also with the significance of the image as itself an imperial sign. In ancient Republican Rome, the one who held the *imperium* was the one who had the entitlement to give orders and to command the military. From the reign of Augustus onward, the Roman empire (i.e. the territory under Roman command) was under the command of the emperor. The notion of empire is presented, then, in the context of a particular type of ordered domain. Edward Said in his *Culture and Imperialism* bluntly states that '[t]he main battle in imperialism is over land, of course; but when it came to who owned the land, who had the right to settle and work on it, who kept it going, who won it back, and who now plans its future – these issues were reflected, contested, and even for a time decided in narrative' (1993: xiii). Command over and narration of territory, of the earth, is central to understanding the complex articulation of culture and globalisation as a process of power and imagination.

Communications and cultural studies scholars have long understood the relation between culture and empire in terms of what is often referred to as 'cultural imperialism'. One of the major exponents of the idea, Herbert Schiller, stated that:

> For a quarter of a century, one doctrine - the idea that no barriers should prevent the flow of information among nations - dominated international thinking about communications and cultural relations. The genesis and extension of the free flow of information concept are roughly coterminous with the brief and hectic interval of US global hegemony, an epoch already on the wane. As we look back, it is now evident that the historical coincidence of these two phenomena - the policy of free flow of information and the imperial ascendancy of the United States - was not fortuitous. The first element was one of a very few indispensable prerequisites for the latter. (1979: 345)

Schiller has been consistent throughout most of his long and established work. In 1991, he stated that: '[m]edia-cultural imperialism is a sub-set of the *general* system of imperialism. It is not free-standing; the media-cultural component in a developed, corporate economy supports the economic objectives of the decisive industrial-financial sectors' (1991: 14). The media, in this analysis, are the leading-edge not only of cultural change and consolidation, but also economic colonisation. The US media are seen as little more than the marketing arm of US economic interests. There are a number of problems with this kind of thesis, most notably that it conflates media penetration with cultural change and it assumes that a national culture once disseminated outside of the territorial confines of that nation is able to act in the interests of that nation. Nevertheless, this is a thesis - in a very broad sense (cf. Tomlinson, 1991) - that has been propounded by a range of writers (such as Armand Mattelart, Dallas Smythe and Thomas Guback) and it is a position that was prominent in the 1970s.

Ariel Dorfman and Armand Mattelart's *How to Read Donald Duck*, originally written in 1971, quickly became, as the publishers state, a 'classic work on cultural imperialism and children's literature' (1984). Dorfman and Mattelart were both academics in Chile and the book about the Disney comics, written under Salvadore Allende's Popular Unity government, was seen as part of a process of decolonisation. The right-wing and pro-US press denounced the book as a form of brainwashing of the young. By 11 September 1973, the Chilean military had ousted Allende, taken over the country, put Augusto Pinochet in command and started the slaughter of many left-wing radicals and others. The US financially and militarily supported the coup. *How to Read Donald Duck* is in many ways prescient of the troubles that were to follow. In a chapter entitled 'From the Noble Savage to the Third World' they state:

> Walt took virgin territories of the US and built upon them his Disneyland palaces, his magic kingdoms. His view of the world at large is framed by the same perspective; it is a world already colonized, with phantom inhabitants who have to conform to Disney's notions of it. Each foreign country is used as

> a kind of model within the process of invasion by Disney-nature. And even if some foreign country like Cuba or Vietnam should dare to enter into open conflict with the United States, the Disney comics brand-mark is immediately stamped upon it, in order to make the revolutionary struggle appear banal. While the Marines make revolutionaries run the gauntlet of bullets, Disney makes them run a gauntlet of magazines. There are two forms of killing: by machine guns and saccharine. (1984: 48)

The Disney comics presented Latin American countries as backward and barbaric. Aztecland (clearly Mexico) is a land of volcanoes and peasant Indians. The peasants are superstitious and afraid of the magic of Western technology: 'good and inoffensive savages unto eternity' (1984: 48). These simple natives are ruled by corrupt kings and it is only the foreigners who can bring civilisation and development. Dorfman and Mattelart argue:

> In order to assure the redemptive powers of present-day imperialism, it is only necessary to measure it against old-style colonialism and robbery. Example: Enter a pair of crooks determined to cheat the natives of their natural gas resources. They are unmasked by the ducks, who are henceforth regarded as friends. (1984: 54)

The ducks are of course in cahoots with a big gas company, the Great Uncle Company (owned by Scrooge McDuck, Donald's uncle) yet the natives are happy with this form of exploitation. US capitalism, the imperialism of a new economic order, is seen to surpass the barbarities and injustices of European colonialism. There is something attractive about the analysis of Dorfman and Mattelart, the oppressive, yet well-defined, enemy, the meek but righteous native, the clarity of the terms of the analysis and the clear goals toward social justice. And yet more may be at stake than at first appears.

The problem of culture and empire does not simply rest on the role of the image in the service of imperialism (i.e. in the sense that agencies and forces external to culture adopt and use cultural resources for the purpose of changing lifestyles, ideological manipulation and so on), but on the way in which the relation between the image and the earth are understood in terms of an empire of the sign, namely in terms of how any global order is one that is subject to the order of the image, as the form that travels across space and time and that reconstructs those times and spaces in its own logic.

In a series of interviews for French television in 1987, Paul Virilio, Jean Baudrillard and Stuart Hall all refer to the imperialism of the image. Virilio states:

> A reflection on the imperialism of the image. From now on everything passes through the image. The image has priority over the thing, the object, and sometimes even the physically-present being. Just as real time, instantaneousness, had priority over space. Therefore the image is invasive and ubiquitous. Its role is not to be in the domain of art, the military domain or the technical domain, it is to be everywhere, to be reality. The new generation of the real. (Virilio, 1988: 7)

Although from a very different perspective, Baudrillard declares that: '[e]ffectively, everything can be an object of communication. Communication is completely generalised; it is no longer only discourse, but everything, which is an object of communication ... There is a kind of imperialism of communication' (Baudrillard, 1988: 8). It is not simply an epistemological fact that reality is (supposedly) constituted through culture, but also an empirical fact. The dispersion of the image across the earth constitutes an empirical encroachment or colonisation of the world. In Baudrillard's terms the media function at all costs to encode the world within their logic. In this sense, we might read Baudrillard's analysis of Disneyland in the US, not only in the context of a question of the epistemology of the real (i.e. that all is now simulation) and of the status of 'America' as the place of dissimulation (i.e. as if the logic of simulation could be contained within the imagined community of the nation), but also in terms of how the iconic figures of US cultural imperialism (such as Disney) actually serve to occlude just how far the earth has been colonised by the image:

> Disneyland is there to conceal the fact that it is the 'real' country, all of 'real' America, which *is* Disneyland ... Disneyland is presented as imaginary in order to make us believe that the rest is real, when in fact all of Los Angeles and the America surrounding it are no longer real, but of the order of the hyperreal and of simulation. (1983a: 25)

Thus, the classic critique of cultural imperialism, that we see in Dorfman and Mattelart, inasmuch as it poses such a stark opposition between the West and the Rest, might well actually further conceal the extensiveness of an imperialism of the image.

Hall agrees with this argument in part, but suggests a more ambivalent reading inasmuch as '[t]here is a deep underlying trend in post-modern culture, whatever you call it, towards difference, diversity, pluralisation; towards a kind of homogenised fragmentation' (Hall, 1988a: 11–2). Disney doesn't, in any simple way, represent US interests. Disney, as with the US itself, is not a unitary phenomenon. Disney is like a gargantuan machine that devours stories from different cultural traditions from across time and space. The Italian story of Pinocchio, the Danish stories from the Brothers Grimm, the native American figure of Pocahontas, all these stories and more are taken from their 'originary' context (and we should be wary of this notion of origin as the place of authenticity) and reworked in order to sell them to a global market. Disney is the creator of worlds; uniform in style – maybe, but US – hardly. What seems to be clearly emerging is that cultural differentiation is no longer dominated by national differentiation (although that is a factor) but by differentiations across transnational spaces. Disney might be almost everywhere, but it is read differently in different places (cf. Drotner, 2001, 2002). Mitsuhiro

Yoshimoto, for example, talks about Disneyland Tokyo in terms of how Tokyo is a hybrid culture; cultural bits and pieces are taken from across the globe and from different forms and styles, and then reprocessed in a quintessential Tokyo style (1994). In this sense, Tokyo Disney doesn't represent the 'Americanisation' of Japan, but an expression of Tokyo cultural identity. Thus many writers within media and cultural studies have argued that there is a dialectic between the global and the local. Although media images and texts might circulate widely across the globe, these images and texts are used and interpreted in local contexts (cf. Morley, 1991; Morley and Silverstone, 1991). Most notably in Tamar Liebes and Eliha Katz's work on the cross-national reception of the 1980s US soap opera *Dallas* it was found that different viewers read the programme according to very localised contexts of interpretation (1990). There was not simply one *Dallas*.

But this version of the global circulation of the image and the localisation of reception seems to replay a dynamic discussed earlier with regard to a global space of flows and a localisation of place. Although the relation between local reception and global flow may be understood in terms of a relation between localised creativity and global constraint, we can also see how this relation is constructed in terms of the stasis of place as against the movement of global space. Castells construes this as an issue concerning the movement and speed of global capital and the dominant managerial elites as against the relative immobility of labour and ordinary people more generally. In the conclusion to the first volume of *The Network Society*, he offers a bleak analysis:

> At its core, capital is global. As a rule, labor is local. Informationalism, in its historical reality, leads to the concentration and globalization of capital, precisely by using the decentralizing power of networks. Labor is disaggregated in its performance, fragmented in its organization, diversified in its existence, divided in its collective action. Networks converge toward a meta-network of capital that integrates capitalist interests at the global level and across sectors and realms of activity: not without conflict, but under the same overarching logic. Labor loses its collective identity, becomes increasingly individualized in its capacities, in its working conditions, and in its interests and projects ... [C]apitalist relationships of production still persist ... [C]apital and labor increasingly tend to exist in different spaces and times: the space of flows and the space of places, instant time of computerized networks versus clock time of everyday life ... [T]hey live by each other, but do not relate to each other ... (1996: 475)

Although drawing from much of the same intellectual resources and although the narrative of the argument is in some ways similar, Hardt and Negri, in their recent analysis of Empire and of the role of the multitude as a global revolutionary subject, turn Castells' logic on its head. For them labour, production and ordinary people are not fixed and immobile; they are not located in places; they are not left to simply use and redraw and make sense of the straws thrown down to them from on high. Hardt and Negri talk of a radical shift, in conditions of contemporary capitalism, away from an imperial sovereignty predicated on the nation-state, on the people and on the hierarchies and differences between peoples. They argue that the old European colonialisms were predicated on marking a difference between centre and periphery and between self and other:

> The boundaries defined by the modern system of nation-states were fundamental to European colonialism and economic expansion: the territorial boundaries of the nation delimited the center of power from which rule was exerted over external foreign territories through a system of channels and barriers that alternatively facilitated and obstructed the flows of production and circulation. Imperialism was really an extension of the sovereignty of the European nation-states beyond their own boundaries. Eventually nearly all the world's territories could be parceled out and the entire world map could be coded in European colors: red for British territory, blue for French, green for Portuguese, and so forth. Wherever modern sovereignty took root, it constructed a Leviathan that overarched its social domain and imposed hierarchical territorial boundaries, both to police the purity of its own identity and to exclude all that was other. (Hardt and Negri, 2000: xii)

European colonialism has been understood in terms of a dialectic between a white, metropolitan self and a racialised, native other. The racialised other has been both excluded from the centres of European power and authority and then held up as a mirror in which the European can recognise himself as not-raced, not-native and not-barbarian (Hardt and Negri, 2000: 114–36). For Hardt and Negri this old world order is typified by divisions not only between self and other, but also between inside and outside. Colonial power was seen to operate through the mechanisms of exclusion and inclusion. But, equally, resistance was seen to be always outside of power, untainted by it and always at a distance from it. In contrast, then, the condition of postmodernity is typified by a different sort of order, an order that Hardt and Negri, somewhat confusingly, refer to not as imperialism or colonialism, but 'Empire':

> In contrast to imperialism, Empire establishes no territorial center of power and does not rely on fixed boundaries or barriers. It is a *decentred* and *deterritorializing* apparatus of rule that progressively incorporates the entire global realm within its open, expanding frontiers. Empire manages hybrid identities, flexible hierarchies, and plural exchanges through modulating networks of command. The distinct national colors of the imperialist map of the world have merged and blended in the imperial global rainbow. (2000: xii–xiii)

Empire, according to Hardt and Negri, is typified not by negativity and despair, but by a profound optimism, hope and radical democracy. Empire is typified as a space that is completely inclusive; it is a global space that has no outside. There is no domain that falls outside of Empire. Empire signals the complete ascendancy of capital: 'there is no outside to the world market: the entire globe is its domain' (2000: 190). Equally, there is no centralised administration from which power emanates, from which commands are issued and acted upon, from which armies spill to overthrow and contain the hostile hinterlands. The power of Empire is everywhere. There is no logic of self and other, no master and slave, no dialectic of recognition; there is only the government of hybrid, mixed identities. For Hardt and Negri, the power of Empire is not linked to a particular place, such as a nation or community. The space of Empire is not striated; it is a smooth space: '[i]n this smooth space of Empire, there is no *place* of power – it is both everywhere and nowhere. Empire is an *ou-topia* or really a *non-place*' (2000: 190). Hardt and Negri, in thus typifying Empire as a space completely vacated of any identifying signs, are keen not to identify it with US empire: '[*t*]he *United States does not, and indeed no nation-state can today, form the center of an imperialist project*. Imperialism is over. No nation will be world leader in the way modern European nations were' (2000: xiv). And yet, although Hardt and Negri might argue that the US does not sit at the command centre of this new global power, we can nevertheless see how the centrality of a conception of US polity and the very model of network power mark Empire out as 'American' in some form or other. Hardt and Negri's vision of the space of Empire as a space without contours is perhaps one caught in the glare of the torch of Manhattan citizenship, the standard bearer of freedom without limits, the openness and inclusiveness of the US ideal. As they say: '[t]he contemporary idea of Empire is born through the global expansion of the internal US constitutional project' (Hardt and Negri, 2000: 182).

Nevertheless, although it is possible to critique Hardt and Negri's argument on the grounds of their romanticisation of US democracy (cf. Meikskins Wood, 2003) and a misreading of the role of the US in contemporary geopolitics (Laffey and Weldes, 2004) what concerns us here is the principal part played by the underdogs in this global drama. In Hardt and Negri's account, it is not the ruling class or capital that takes the lead and shapes the future from the front. On the contrary, in Hardt and Negri's account, capital simply follows in the dance of the multitude, of the productive class, of immaterial labour. As a consequence of the social and cultural innovations in the 1970s that were both highly localised and idealistically international (i.e. in the forms of collective organisation, new forms of revolt, Third World struggles, refusals to work, and so on) capital was forced to reinvent itself, to become post-Fordist and postmodern, to become flexible, transversal and global. The 1970s saw the end of the factory system at the same time as the US economic model spread across the globe. The US model offered hope in the face of the old imperial order, just as much as it brought about new forms of control.

The spread of transnational capital was coexistent with the process of decolonisation: a shift from colonial to economic order. But, according to Hardt and Negri, such was the desire for liberation expressed by the multitude that no order of the superpowers (neither the US nor the USSR) could contain it. Hardt and Negri argue that: '[t]he new transversal mobility of disciplined labor power is significant because it indicates a real and powerful search for freedom and the formation of new, nomadic desires that cannot be contained and controlled with the disciplinary regime' (Hardt and Negri, 2000: 253). It is thus the global mobility of populations, of the multitude, that has forced capital to change. Hardt and Negri – although aware of the awful human costs potentially involved in the movements of peoples – laud mobility, escape and migration as forms of refusal by the multitude:

> The multitude's resistance to bondage – the struggle against the slavery of belonging to a nation, an identity, and a people, and thus the desertion from sovereignty and the limits it places on subjectivity – is entirely positive. Nomadism and miscegenation appear here as figures of virtue, as the first ethical practices on the terrain of Empire. From this perspective the objective space of capitalist globalization breaks down ... Today's celebrations of the local can be regressive and even fascistic when they oppose circulations and mixture, and thus reinforce the walls of nation, ethnicity, race, people, and the like ... The concrete universal is what allows the multitude to pass from place to place and make its place its own ... Through circulation the common human species is composed, a multicolored Orpheus of infinite power; through circulation the human community is constituted ... [T]he desire of the multitude is not the cosmopolitical state but a common species ... [T]he bodies are mixed and the nomads speak a common tongue. (2000: 361–2)

The ideal – of a common humanity, mixed, together and not contained or constrained – is in many ways praiseworthy. And yet, perhaps it too easily assumes too much and too little. Can we really say that Empire is everywhere, that there is no outside to its power, that the residues of European colonialism are not felt, and that both class and gendered conflicts have simply fallen by the way? Can we really talk of forms of organisation devoid of government in the sense that a new global order can be predicated on a 'common species' but not a 'cosmopolitical state' (cf. Held, 1995)?

Despite these obvious problems, Hardt and Negri's analysis – once stripped of its geopolitical pretensions – helps us in understanding the relation between culture and globalisation. The turning of the tables of space and place, power and resistance, is clearly important for cultural studies and it helps to reframe (or at least to make us rethink) some of the orthodoxies in the field. It helps us to think positively about the mobility of peoples, to frame mobility positively in the necessity of historical circumstance – which is not to say that migration or exile are positive in themselves. But we should be wary of the ascription of a totalising global space, the smooth space of Empire. If anything, the contrast between Castells and Hardt and Negri's analyses allows us to refuse any generalised account of the global as a space of either capital or the multitude. Moreover, the contrast between these two different analyses allows us to think of the mix between capital and populations in the specific constructions of particular transnational or translocal spaces; spaces that cut across traditional boundaries and yet carry the traces of particularities (history, memory, and so on). Thus, rather than construct transnational cultures as timeless, with no memory, overly technical, and so on (cf. Castells, 1996, 2001; Smith, 1990), we might see them as heavily encoded with the particularities of culture.

Paul Gilroy in his brilliant understanding of the 'black Atlantic' begins to unhook the twin weights of nation and ethnos and argues that 'the theorisation of creolisation, metissage, mestizaje, and hybridity ... are rather unsatisfactory ways of naming the processes of cultural mutation and restless (dis)continuity that exceed racial discourse and avoid capture by its agents' (1993b: 2). He talks of hybridity, not as with Hardt and Negri to offer a deracinated smooth space, but to accent the transnational with the contours of historical memory. Gilroy states that:

> The image of the ship – a living, micro-cultural, micro-political system in motion – is especially important for historical and theoretical reasons ... Ships immediately focus attention on the middle passage, on the various projects for redemptive return to an African homeland, on the circulation of ideas and activists as well as the movement of key cultural and political artefacts: tracts, books, gramophone records, and choirs. (1993b: 4)

The actual ships caught up in the movement and enslavement of African populations, but also the vehicles that carry ideas and artefacts across the vast space of the Atlantic, from Africa, Europe, and America (both North and South) help to frame the material and symbolic place that Gilroy calls the 'black Atlantic': 'the Atlantic as one single, complex unit of analysis ... of the modern world ... an explicitly transnational intercultural perspective' (1993b: 15). This diasporic space is one that emerges from the brutal fact of slavery and yet delivers the musical joys of Jazzie B and Soul II Soul:

> A concern with the Atlantic as a cultural and political system has been forced on black historiography and intellectual history by the economic and historical matrix in which plantation slavery – 'capitalism with its clothes off' – was one special moment. The fractal patterns of cultural and political exchange and transformation that we try and specify through manifestly inadequate theoretical terms like creolisation and syncretism indicate how both ethnicities and political cultures have been made anew in ways that are significant not simply for the peoples of the Caribbean but for Europe, for Africa, especially Liberia and Sierra Leone, and of course, for black America. (Gilroy, 1993a: 15)

This black Atlantic space is one that is between the local and global, between space and place, between the ports that form the hubs of its intricate network of cultural connections. The formation of transnational cultures does not signal the dissolution of either the traces of older colonial orders or domestic ones; rather, we see their reconfiguration in terms of the particularisation of new spaces. These spaces are varied, whether, for example, they take the form of South East Asian families in Southall, West London watching Hindi videoed-television programmes (cf. Gillespie, 1995), or Trinidadian families dispersed across the globe using e-mail on an 'intimate, regular, day-to-day basis' to shape and facilitate family ties (Miller and Slater, 2000). It is these spaces and times that are perhaps more symptomatic of contemporary empire.

Returning to Scale

The sixteenth century English philosopher Francis Bacon in an essay 'Of Empire' states the following:

> It is a miserable state of mind to have few things to desire and many things to fear; and yet that commonly is the case of kings; who being at the highest, want matter of desire, which makes their minds more languishing; and have many representations of perils and shadows, which makes their minds less clear ... For multitude of jealousies, and lack of some predominant desire that should marshal and put in order all the rest, maketh any man's heart hard to find or sound. Hence it comes likewise that princes many times make themselves desires, and set their hearts upon toys: sometimes upon a building; sometimes upon erecting of an order ... This seemeth incredible unto those that know not the principle, *that the mind of man is more cheered and refreshed by profiting in small things than by standing at a stay in great.* (Bacon, 1906: 57)

In the rush to explain the new and to make sense of rapid changes, it is easy to become caught up by the fascination of the object, a new plaything. At times of massive accumulations of power, it is important not to confuse the image of the world with the world itself. The Latin 'globus' captures the sense of a spherical fireball in the sky, a star from the celestial heavens, or metaphorically a blazing crowd, fiery in their anger; it doesn't in the classical period refer to the 'whole world'. In many ways the earth is not 'global'. Equally, it is hard to say that there are any really 'global' cultures, as the relations of culture across and below national boundaries are not spherical in shape; they are shaped and warped in different ways, not simply in the manner of a globe. Even the sophistication of the image conjured up by the philosopher Michel Serres in his *The Natural Contract* falls into the same problem:

> Flying high enough to see her whole, we find ourselves tethered to her by the totality of our knowledge, the sum of our technologies, the collection of our communications; by torrents of signals, by the complete set of imaginable umbilical cords, living and artificial, visible and invisible, concrete or purely formal. By casting off from her so far, we pull on these cords to the point that we comprehend

> them all. Astronaut humanity is floating in space like a fetus in amniotic fluid, tied to the placenta of Mother-Earth by all the nutritive passages. (1995: 122)

The image of the blue planet is captivating; the spacemen and women, the angels, and maybe a few other extra-terrestrials have the vantage of seeing the earth from such a globular perspective; but for many we are not cast-off so far away from others; our ships are not so large, nor do they have such power to cast us into another world (cf. Serres, 1995).

McLuhan in a piece on the 'Wheel, Bicycle, and Airplane' offers the following story of the globe:

> An airline executive who is much aware of the implosive character of world aviation asked a corresponding executive of each airline in the world to send him a pebble from outside his office. His idea was to build a little cairn of pebbles from all parts of the world. When asked, 'So what?' he said that in one spot one could touch every part of the world because of aviation. (1964: 185)

McLuhan talks of this in terms of the 'mosaic principle' such that technology supposedly allows us to both see and touch the world at a distance. The executive builds a shrine, an icon of the earth; he touches things carried from far away, things that carry the traces of other places; but what he touches are pebbles, not that which is far away. The shrine of the global should not be confused with the touching of things at a distance; the latter does not take the form of the former. Even so, the former might help to conquer space and time at a distance.

John Law and Bruno Latour take examples of European colonialism in the late eighteenth century (Latour, 1987, 1990; Law, 1986). For example, Latour looks at the French expansion into the East Pacific. In 1787 the captain of the Astrolabe landed in a place unknown to him and his crew. As this territory was unknown to the West and as there were no European maps nor any maps that he knew of, he had no idea whether the land on which he was standing was an island or part of a peninsula. But he was lucky, for he met up with some natives from the land who informed him that the place was indeed an island and they proceeded to draw a map for him. The map was far from accurate, drawn as it was in haste and on the sand. But it was enough for the captain of the Astrolabe to copy and to take back to France. As more ships travelled to this island, on the coast of China, a better picture emerged of it and the surrounding lands. Moreover, samples of the local soils, plant life, animals and descriptions of local customs and practices were taken back to the European centres from where new maps and knowledges accumulated of this far away place. The things that were carried back needed to be mobile or made mobile and they had to maintain their form in the passage from the island to Europe. Plants needed to be preserved, just as cartographic inscriptions needed to maintain their exact measurements. Law and Hetherington comment of this colonial problematic, but draw on the example of the imperial Portuguese expansion:

> [T]he ship, its crew and its surroundings (or the navigator, his tables and instruments, and the sun or the stars) need to be seen as a *continuous network*. If the different parts stay in place, if their relations with their neighbours hold them in role, then the network as a whole generates knowledges... [K]nowledge, objects and people (or 'subjects') are *relational effects* or *emergent phenomena* ... For if the Portuguese were able to control the spice trade for nearly a century, if they were able to bombard the inhabitants of Calicut into submission, if they were able to get to India and get back, then this is because they succeeded by luck or good judgement in generating an array, a global network, within which immutable mobiles might circulate. Such that if a command was given in Lisbon, then war might be fought in India ... [M]aking action and knowledge at a distance not only makes action, knowledge and global symmetry ... it also *makes distance or space*, performs these into being. (2000: 38–9)

Clearly, if the materials disintegrated or warped in the journey from one place to another, then no reliable knowledge could be constructed, or at least no reliable knowledge of the distance or closeness, difference or sameness, between the island, or India, and Europe. The construction of the difference or sameness, distance or closeness between the island, or India, and Europe was predicated on the construction of a stable means of passage and of the accompanying stability of time and space. For a cartographer to draw any map, above and beyond that which is immediately visible to the naked eye, they need to know with exactitude how to measure time as well as space. Time and space, speed and distance are all bundled together. You can't have one without the other.

Just as McLuhan's airline executive needs his pebbles to see his world before him and to command that world accordingly, so the European colonisers needed their maps and networks to act at a distance. To present this image of the world, though, is precisely to see the world as just that, a series of *particular* constructions. Thus, Law and Hetherington argue that:

> [T]o talk of 'globalisation' is at best a risky short cut and at worst seriously misleading. It is a risky short cut because it implies some kind of totality, some kind of global system and some kind of overall space-time box within which ... phenomena ... are located. (2000: 48)

Hetherington, in other articles (cf. Hetherington and Hinchliffe, 2000), argues that space is folded to allow for creases in the folds to touch each other and thus leap across vast, but also small, distances. He talks about this in terms of a notion of 'crumpled spaces'. This notion is certainly provocative for thinking about the global, but it seems to imply that it is possible in principle to iron-out the wrinkles, such that the now flat ironed-out surface is one that is defined through a single system of measurement (i.e. all points on the surface are like the points on a geometric grid). But just as representations of 'the world' happen in specific places and cosmopolitanism happens in particular places, the actors producing these images and the places in which these images and networks are initiated cannot be lumped together into a single global grid that is either flattened or crumpled. The G8, IMF, WTO, UN, EU, NATO, Sony, Bertelsmann, Disney, but also the teenagers in their bedrooms, the surfers on the beach, the women harvesting the crops and so on and so on do not meet on a single grid and cannot be assembled within a single unit of measurement. As Serres states: '[t]he space without distance implies a subject without space. We no longer live in geometry, nor the Earth nor the measure, but a topology without measurement or distance, a qualitative space' (my translation 2001: 224). The cultural activities and spaces and times that comprise the earth cannot be measured through a single system of measurement. The earth cannot be reduced to a single scale. It is constituted through many scales; through different discourses, cultures, peoples; it is multiplicitous. Moreover, to repeat, just because the purview of our world is 'global', it does not mean that we are connected to everyone globally. It just means that we are connected to particular people and things, some near and some far. The people, the places and the things are particular, not universal. Thus, if we aggregate all the particulars, we do so in a particular place, with particular technologies, particular ways of imaging and imagining this global collection of things. There is not one place in which all the connections sit; there are only numerous places and actors that offer the pretence of such a vision. Nevertheless, we can now connect to people and things further away than we could in the distant past. We live in a world with numerous connections, but the greater connectedness does not bring us any closer to others at a distance; in many ways it makes those who were once my neighbours seem further away.

Chapter Summary

- Debates about globalisation initially become of concern due to economic questions about the impact of liberalisation and new technology.
- A number of writers talk about globalisation in terms of a global economic system. Some talk of this in terms of the determinacy of the economic (e.g. Wallerstein) others refer to a number of causal factors (e.g. Giddens).
- Although there is a large consensus that globalisation is a significant phenomenon, there are questions as to its nature and its extensiveness.
- The issue of global culture is first raised by Marshall McLuhan in terms of the notion of a global village. But most writers would argue that there is no single global culture, even if we might be able to frame a certain global perspective. McLuhan was critical of both claims.

- The focus on globalisation has meant that the question of the 'nation' is now posed in terms of the constitution of a national culture and its circulation, not simply within the context of the nation.
- A number of writers have suggested that we are witnessing major shifts in our experience of space and time. Notions of time-space distanciation, time-space compression, global timeless flows, and various 'scapes' are put forward as means of explaining global experiences. The point is not to pick one perspective over another, but to look at how culture and people are warped in processes of globalisation.
- The major context for understanding globalisation in modernity is empire, both European and US. Contemporary explanations mark a shift from earlier models of cultural imperialism. Hardt and Negri talk about the multitude as facilitating modern empire from below. Gilroy looks to the formation of transnational cultural spaces, particularly the 'black Atlantic'.
- It is important not to get carried away with the scale of the global, but rather to look at how the 'global' is itself mobilised in very local ways.

NINE Ethics: By Way of a Conclusion

Over the course of this book, we've covered a lot of ground. We've considered questions about semiosis, power and popular culture and we've pursued issues concerning identity, body, economy and the global. We started the book by asking a fundamental, but complex, question about the matter of culture. We've tried to understand and address this question in terms of: how semiosis involves both symbolic and indexical dimensions; how power is orchestrated through particular techniques and technologies of government; how common cultures are often heterogeneous and post-national; how identity is constructed, not only through language, but also through object worlds; how cultural bodies are agentic, non-unitary and dispersed through nature, society, and technology; how the distribution of cultural resources is a significant aspect of any cultural economy, but also how that economy is arranged as a network; and finally, how contemporary culture must be understood in the context of empire and the global. Across all these discussions, we have maintained that culture is not co-extensive with the nation, with a people, with language or with the state. Thus, I talk about the need to begin to think about the new and different diagrams, shapes and lines of power through which cultural distinction is now understood.

In many ways across all this discussion, I have tried to give a sense of how culture acts as a complex *medium*. It is at once material in its composition, but also it is productive of particular kinds of material outcomes. It is seen to be made up of signs, discourses, ideologies, people, bodies, institutions, practices and technologies. It is seen to be productive of identities, subjectivities, objects, societies, peoples, nations, economies and worlds. Moreover, it is a medium that is highly active, engaged and extensive. It is able to work in very local and particular places as well as very large and global spaces. It is able to cross over from different types of materiality, from words to physiological bodies to bricks-and-mortar to telecommunication cables and so on. It is able to raise the spirits of a person and to repress the hopes of a whole population. From a single song it can travel the world, into people's hearts and emotions, and make them feel as if they belong together. In this book, then, I have attempted to touch upon some of these different aspects of the matter of culture. In the face of such claims about the power of culture, we would be foolish to act either hastily or without reason. Whatever the case, it would seem wise to think ethically: namely, if culture matters why does it matter?

Ethics and Culture

Nick Couldry in the opening of his excellent text on contemporary cultural studies states:

> We cannot oversimplify the cultural experiences of others, without caricaturing our own. Cultural studies in this sense involves an ethic of reciprocity, a mutual practice of both speaking and listening, which is inextricably tied to taking seriously the complexity of cultures. It is here that ethics (and politics) converge with method; for it is method that provides the basic tools with which we can empirically research that complexity in a systematic and accountable way. (2000: 5)

Ethics has, since Aristotle's *Nicomachean Ethics*, been concerned with the 'good life', not in the sense of ascertaining the meaning of goodness, but in the sense of conducting enquiries in order to be good. Ethics, then, as distinct from the formation of moral codes (i.e. of laws of behaviour, of what we must and mustn't do) concerns how we conduct our lives in order to be good. But instead of only reading the 'good life' in terms of forms of virtuous living (i.e. as automatically ethical in a modern sense of the word) we should also remember that the 'good' concerns both happiness and excellence. The good life also carries the connotations of the life lived well and the life better than other lives. But this is neither a chapter on Aristotelian ethics nor on the philosophy of ethics more generally. It is, by way of a conclusion, an attempt to bring together some of the thoughts contained in this book in the context not only of the materialism of cultural matters, but of their worth.

Couldry brings together ethics with politics and method in the form of a dialogism. Cultural studies concerns the empirical understanding of 'culture' in the sense that the orientation of the researcher and the claims made therein are situated within culture, just as much as the object of research is placed on an equal footing that deserves not just to be known (as an object of knowledge) but to be respected and listened to as well. As we have seen throughout this book, a strand of the history and pre-history of cultural studies has, contrary to the dialogism of Couldry, been positively antagonistic to the convergence of an ethics and a politics of culture. Thus, if we were to investigate a genealogy of the ethical within cultural studies, namely if we were to ask how ethical relations become constructed within cultural studies as problems of significance, then we would in the first instance point to Arnold's understanding of culture as what is best, the ability to know what is best, the mental and spiritual application of what is best and the pursuit of what is best. In the opening chapter on 'Sweetness and Light' in *Culture and Anarchy*, Arnold declares that:

> Culture is then properly described not as having its origin in curiosity, but as having its origin in the love of perfection; it is *a study of perfection*. It moves by the force, not merely or primarily of the scientific passion for pure knowledge, but also of the moral and social passion for doing good ... [T]here is no better motto which it can have than these words of Bishop Wilson: 'To make reason and the will of God prevail!' (1960: 44-5)

Arnold prefaces these word by locating such 'love of perfection' in the context of motives that are social, concerning 'the love of our neighbour, the impulses towards action, help, and beneficence, the desire for removing human error, clearing human confusion, and diminishing human misery, the noble aspiration to leave the world better and happier than we found it' (1960: 44). For Arnold, such an ethics is not predicated on particular persons caring for less fortunate others, rather culture is seen as itself eminently democratic and egalitarian:

> Culture ... is not satisfied till we *all* come to a perfect man; it knows that the sweetness and light of the few must be imperfect until the raw and unkindled masses of humanity are touched with sweetness and light ... It does not try to teach down to the level of inferior classes; it does not try to win them for this or that sect of its own, with ready-made judgements and watchwords. It seeks to do away with classes; to make the best that has been thought and known in the world current everywhere; to make all men live in an atmosphere of sweetness and light, where they may use ideas, as it uses them itself, freely - nourished and not bound by them. This is the *social idea*; and the men of culture are those true apostles of equality. (1960: 69-70)

But by and large, cultural studies has construed Arnold and the ethical as deeply conservative. To understand culture as both an ethical substance and goal (and moreover to understand this in the context of the transformation of a population and the extension of democracy) has been seen as ideologically reactionary. The valuation of certain forms of ethical personhood and of certain forms of culture against others in a hierarchy of ethical good and taste has been seen as inimical to the political project of cultural studies. For much of the history of cultural studies, an ethics of culture has been the object of political critique.

This is in many ways surprising given that Gramsci's understanding of hegemony is such that leadership is deeply ethical and the dialectic of cultural development is constructed in the context of the progress of the 'ethical state' and the ethical relation between intellectuals and the masses. The task of the intellectual is to search 'for the conditions necessary for the freedom of the will in a certain sense, aimed at a certain end, and the demonstration that these conditions exist' (Gramsci, 1971: 410). This ethical task, though, is not shaped according to the individual, but to the relation between the individual and the collective will. Gramsci says:

> Critical understanding of self takes place therefore through a struggle of political 'hegemonies' and of opposing directions, first in the ethical field and then in that of politics proper, in order to arrive at the working out at a higher level of one's own conception of reality. Consciousness of being part of a particular hegemonic force (that is to say, political consciousness) is the first stage towards a further progressive self-consciousness in which theory and practice will finally be one. (1971: 333)

In the context of hegemony, one's understanding of the world is not simply scientific, but also political, and the bridging of these domains takes place through particular ethical techniques inasmuch as ethics is practical philosophy. The construction of 'critical understanding' thus implies the construction of oneself as different and apart from the mass of people inasmuch as the masses are caught up in the logic of common sense. Thus Gramsci talks of 'an ethic in conformity with a conception of reality that has gone beyond common sense and has become, if only within narrow limits, a critical conception'. Moreover, the formation of '[c]ritical self-consciousness means, historically and politically, the creation of an *elite* of intellectuals' (1971: 333–4). In a move resonant of Arnold, Gramsci states that:

> The intellectual stratum develops both quantitatively and qualitatively, but every leap forward towards a new breadth and complexity of the intellectual stratum is tied to an analogous movement on the part of the mass of the 'simple', who raise themselves to higher levels of culture and at the same time extend their circle of influence towards the stratum of specialised intellectuals, producing outstanding individuals and groups of greater or less importance. (1971: 334–5).

Although the gap between intellectuals and the masses widens at times, the movement of hegemony is toward its overcoming and future unity. This kind of understanding between ethics and politics has in part been concealed within cultural studies by the foregrounding of an ethics of suspicion in the sense of a constant critique of power. We see this in the early ideology critiques as well as in the take up of Foucauldian conceptions of power and knowledge and the construction of subjectivities. And by and large this ethics of suspicion has gone by the name of politics, not ethics.

More recently though, in the work of Ian Hunter and others, the relation between ethics and culture has been investigated in the context of a Foucauldian genealogy of an aesthetics of existence and technologies of the self. Hunter draws on Foucault's later work on the aesthetics of existence, but whereas Foucault looks to ancient Greece and Rome and then to Enlightenment modernity for techniques of the self that contribute to the practices of freedom, Hunter looks to Romantic aesthetic philosophy, to the administration of schooling, and to the emergence of literary education in the nineteenth and early twentieth centuries (1988a, b). In Hunter's work from the Romantics to much of contemporary cultural studies, he argues that particular technologies and techniques of the self have been invented and deployed in relation to how individuals construct themselves and recognise themselves as particular types of individuals living particular kinds of lives. Thus, Hunter argues that 'what Romantic aesthetics provides is not a *theory* of culture and society but an *aesthetico-ethical exercise* aimed at producing a particular kind of relation to self and, through this, the ethical demeanour and standing of a particular category of person' (1988b: 109). Hunter typifies Romanticism in terms of an ethical imperative to resolve the dualities between, for example, thought and feeling, freedom and necessity, and didacticism and spontaneity. For Hunter, the techniques of cultural criticism are understood in terms of their facilitating the construction of the critic as a particular type of person or character as a 'moral exemplar' (i.e. as a pedagogic model of good character and sensibility) and in terms of their contribution, not to a theory of culture and society, but to an array of techniques for questioning and shaping the self (1988a, b).

In this sense, then, given even our brief comments on Arnold and Gramsci above, we can see how – despite offering different theoretical and political positions with regard to the problematic of industrial modernity, an understanding of class and the formation of modern democracy – both thinkers share a similarity with regard to the ethical shaping of the self (i.e. in terms of an ethical resolution of contradictions in society). Hunter sees the formation of dualities within an ethical substance (e.g. between thought and feeling) and the resolution of, for example, cultural difference (i.e. between classes) as an ethical achievement; but we might want to add that for both Arnold and Gramsci (as with others) the shaping of an ethical self is made possible only in conjunction with the transformative potential of a community external to that self. Ethical reflection, understandings of cultural difference, and attempts to achieve the development of culture on the path to social unity are not seen as purely 'internal' matters of the self, but explicitly matters concerning the relations between self and others. Thus, a pastoral ethical relation between pastor and flock (as in Christian theology) is figured as a context for the resolution of the dialectic between intellectual and masses, but only inasmuch as an ethics of the intellectual is seen necessarily to require a series of real relations with those others external to oneself, who are in need of being led and who provide the recognition of any achievement in one's ethical objectives.

Moreover, if we are to take seriously this genealogy of the relation between ethics and culture, one that is, importantly, mapped out initially by Hunter, then we need also to look at some more recent sources from within cultural studies. In doing so, we might be able to frame the relation between ethics and culture less as a series of historical descriptions and more positively as a field of resources (i.e. as techniques that we might actually use ourselves in understanding some thorny problems concerning ethics and culture).

Political Community, Cultural Medium

In many ways 'community' is the most overused word in cultural studies, but it is also perhaps the most problematic. Williams, in the conclusion to his great work *Culture and Society*, talks about the problem of community in modern post-war Britain and particularly in the context of mass communications such as television:

> [A] transmission is always an offering, and ... this fact must determine its mood: it is not an attempt to dominate, but to communicate, to achieve reception and response. Active reception, and living response, depend in their turn on an effective community of experience, and their quality, as certainly, depends on a recognition of practical equality. The inequalities of many kinds which still divide our community make effective communication difficult or impossible. We lack a genuinely common experience, save in certain rare and dangerous moments of crisis. What we are paying for this lack, in every kind of currency, is now sufficiently evident. We need a common culture, not for the sake of an abstraction, but because we shall not survive without it. (1958: 317)

Here Williams is talking of a common culture as the basis of community and social solidarity, but he is not talking about an 'equal culture' as such, rather he is talking about an 'equality of opportunity' for which a common culture could provide the ground (1958: 317–19). Gilroy, as with other more recent critics, has rightly castigated Williams for his failure to examine the context and conditions for such a 'common culture'. Gilroy states:

> Any satisfaction to be experienced from the recent spectacular growth of cultural studies as an academic project should not obscure its conspicuous problems with ethnocentrism and nationalism. Understanding these difficulties might commence with a critical evaluation of the ways in which notions of ethnicity have been mobilised, often by default rather than by design, as part of the distinctive hermeneutics of cultural studies or with the unthinking assumption that cultures always flow into patterns congruent with the borders of essentially homogenous nation states. (1993a: 5)

In part the problem is one of the homogeneity that might be presumed in the notion of community, in part it is the stasis of ethnos that the term 'community' colludes in presenting. The lines of inclusion and exclusion that community might be seen to produce are ones that historically have sought to construct racialised others, as well as others (on the lines of religion, disability, sexuality and gender) as non-citizens and non-humans. In that sense, cultural community, as with political community, bears the traces of those who have been excluded, but it also faces the problem of those within its borders, of difference within.

Thus Jeffrey Weeks, in a discussion of the Muslim protests against the author Salman Rushdie after the publication of his book *Satanic Verses*, declares:

> On the one hand we have a call to respect absolutely the rights of a specific community to organise its own way of life, regardless of the traditions of the wider community as a whole ... On the other hand, there is a despair of the challenge of diversity ... Neither position really deals with the fundamental issues. One in effect insists that it is impossible to evaluate different traditions. The other hopes that the claims of other traditions may dissolve into a greater whole. (1990: 97)

Weeks argues that both positions are flawed as they both construe difference as absolute. Instead Weeks suggests that identities and their supporting social solidarities are in flux, change over time and cannot be 'frozen by any moral system'. And yet, Weeks then goes on to argue for a political community that will 'necessarily embody a notion of the common good and of justice, in order to regulate the variety of rights and demands'. He adds that such a community must be such that 'differences can be aired and negotiated, and unavoidable conflicts mediated, in a democratic fashion'. He continues by describing this negotiation 'as a process of continuous debate and mutual education ... to broaden the democratic imagination through the acceptance of human variety and difference' (1990: 99). Such a conception of political community – as living through and with difference – would in some ways mark a rapprochement between Williams and Gilroy. It would though fall at first base, if those for whom such a community offered the possibility of negotiating difference rejected outright the values of negotiation, compromise, and democracy as thoroughly foreign. In that sense, the offer of political community as a solution to the problem of cultural difference is only tenable if it is itself not seen as 'cultural' or if it is accepted for what it is, namely a necessary imposition, a necessary discipline. In a world in which culture is hybrid, collective and not tied to place, it is politics that must introduce the discipline of democracy and it is politics that must re-invent the *polis*, the political community. In such a world, culture takes a supporting role to the demands of politics. Or to put it differently, the culture of political culture is repressed for the sake of a liveable *polis*.

But, political community is itself questioned, as culture is made visible as more than human, as it takes on the demands of the non-human, of the environment, of nature, of the earth. Many would now question any neat divide between human and non-human in the creation and construction of things cultural. The work of Haraway, Latour and others such as Michel Serres, would be central to such a rethinking of culture. And, although 'community' is always an open question, the extension of culture certainly begins to force the door of the *polis*. Should a radical democratic conception of community take into consideration the rights of foxes, gorillas, but also Gaia (the planet Earth itself)? The disciplines of ethnology and primate anthropology have long assumed that certain animals have, and live in, a culture (cf. Haraway, 1989). We know, for example, that many animals are sensate creatures; many are only a few genomes away from human; and many have well-formed languages and are social in nature. Many animals bear the traces of what we might consider as culture. Some research, also, raises the question as to whether some animals might 'do politics' (cf. Stengers, 2000). If the response is that some animals, such as baboons, do politics, then the second question is whether they do so in 'our' political community or only in 'theirs'? Of course, a question of this magnitude is not for a book such as this to even begin to answer.

Nevertheless, some writers, whether wittingly or not, help us to open up this problematic in such a way, perhaps, as to be helpful for cultural studies. Michel Serres, in his *The Natural Contract* (1995) makes reference to a painting by the Spanish eighteenth century artist Francisco Goya. The painting is of two men, two peasants, fighting with sticks in some quicksand. Serres explains that with every blow the peasants give each other, the deeper in the mud they sink. The image of the men fighting is an image that typifies the Hegelian struggle between two forces, two humans, a struggle for recognition and mastery, a struggle to dominate, to become either master or slave. But Serres suggests that such a reading of the picture is blind to the mud, to the earth, not as a passive context for the struggle, but as part of the struggle itself, the third party in the picture. For Serres, then, the notion of culture needs to accept nature as part of itself, but equally we need to redefine a new contract, not social, but natural:

> The word *politics* must now be considered inaccurate, because it refers only to the *polis*, the city-state, the spaces of publicity, the administrative organisation of groups. Yet those who live in cities, once known as bourgeois, know nothing of the world. From now on, those who govern must go outside of the human sciences, outside the streets and walls of the city, become physicists, emerge from the social contract, invent a new natural contract by giving back to the word *nature* its original meaning of our natal and native conditions, the conditions in which we are born – or ought to be reborn tomorrow. (1995: 43–4)

We might argue that Serres' concern about politics is overstated and that his proposition of a 'natural contract' is actually deeply political, inasmuch as it reinvents the boundaries of political culture. In this sense, Serres' argument for a natural contract is just one move in a broader series of arguments about *cosmopolis* (i.e. a politics of the earth, cosmos and order (cf. Featherstone, 2002)). The condition – whether or not declared as such – for thinking such a politics is culture and its contemporary extension. We are born and grow – plants as well as people, microbes as well as animals – through culture, in its older pre-modern, as well as its newer late-modern, sense. And the medium through which governors become physicists, through which the social and the natural sciences talk to each other and through which all talk to their 'publics', or constituencies, is culture.

Just as Serres deconstructs the notion of human community and conflict, by making visible the agency of nature in both struggle and community; so too does Latour by bringing not just animals and people, but also 'things' back into politics. In *We Have Never Been Modern* (1993) and later writings, Latour talks of reinventing 'the Constitution' and about a 'Parliament of things'. In this post-social political world, objects are undisciplined; they block, they disappear, they refuse, they have objectity: '[n]atural objects are naturally *recalcitrant*; the last thing that one scientist will say about them is that they are fully masterable' (2000: 115). Latour doesn't make it his task to 'convene' such a Parliament (1993: 145). Instead it is sufficient for him to have made visible an extended notion of culture (or in his term 'natures-cultures'). Any understanding of an extended notion of political community is itself predicated on an extended notion of culture to include humans and non-humans. But such a conception of the changed, or changing, ontology of community has profound implications for how we think of ourselves within a community. How do we help ourselves without the help of other things? The medium, or the culture, of community is not passively lived; it is itself vibrant, agentic and vital. Those things that we happily accepted as tools and technologies for communicating and mediating, that helped us (humans) talk to other humans, now must be understood as compatriots or colleagues. Thus, if we push Latour's argument, whether politician or physicist or cultural studies scholar, we don't simply speak *to* an audience; we speak *through* an audience. The medium through which the speech occurs doesn't passively accept the message communicated; the speaker, audience and medium are collectively assembled in the event of speaking. We don't speak through a telephone; we speak with it, to another. Of course, the degree to which some objects *act up* rather than others is such that they should not be seen as ontologically separate from people, but that sociologically speaking they have patterns and degrees of consistency, just as humans do. Such a conception of the medium of culture and the politics of community clearly has wide-ranging implications for any ethics of culture and cultural studies. Cultural artefacts, cultural stories, cultural practices and cultural technologies constitute part of the active culture and 'we' are dispersed across that constituency. Culture is more than the ground or soil within which we humans grow.

An Ethics of Community

If we do indeed live in a world in which things object, in which objects don't happily accept their representation, but equally in which people similarly don't allow themselves to be passively represented, then any sense of an ethics that assumes that culture is the means to pacify that crowd of beings would be woefully mistaken. Culture is what names their living complexity. Any sense of leadership on the model of the pastoral, such that the pastor is separate from their flock, but leads them into heaven, must now take account of a notion of culture as that which mediates any ethical relation. Moreover, culture mediates or translates in a very lively way. If any of us are getting to heaven then we, as with the pastor, all walk on the ladder of culture. From the position of the pastor, or any one who cares, it is no longer possible to imagine that we can simply recognise our ethical responsibility to the other (cf. Levinas, 1969, 1985) as if that relationship to the other was not in its very being mediated by culture, as if it were not mediated by channels of communication, as if it were not mediated by things and as if it were not noisy. Or in the case of Serres, both noisy and muddy!

Let's briefly go back to Williams. In his discussion of the 'idea of community' he considers a notion of public service:

> The stress has been confirmed by the generations of training which substantiate the ethical practice of our professions, and of our public and civil service. As against the practice of laissez-faire, and of self-service, this has been a major achievement which has done much for the peace and welfare of our society. (1958: 328)

The ethical practice of the public servant acts as a bulwark against self-interest and against the unsteady hand of the market. Nevertheless, Williams argues that the ethical practice of the public servant works 'to maintain and confirm the status quo' which has denied an equity among men and women and which has been based on 'existing distributions of property, remuneration, education and respect'; '[t]he real personal unselfishness, which ratified the description as service, seemed to me to exist within a larger selfishness, which was only not seen because it was idealized as the necessary form of a civilization, or rationalized as a natural distribution corresponding to worth, effort and intelligence' (1958: 329). So, in opposition to the notion of public service, Williams turns to the idea of solidarity: '[i]n its definition of the common interest as true self-interest, in its finding of individual verification primarily in the community, the idea of solidarity is potentially the real basis of society' (1958: 332). The notion of solidarity, and its attendant notion of a 'common culture', provides the basis for a critique of any institutional and structured division or stratification. Moreover, it provides the means to overcome that representational gap between, for example, public servant and people, or leader and led, or intellectual and masses, inasmuch as it offers a form of governance based on 'active mutual responsibility' (1958: 330).

Such an argument has some similarities with Hardt and Negri's argument about the multitude, concerning its coming into being through the common space produced by immaterial labour. Hardt and Negri argue that the multitude 'is based on the *communication* among singularities and emerges through the collaborative social processes of production' (2004: 204). Although Hardt and Negri might scoff at the phrasing, such an understanding of the multitude can be seen in terms of a self-productive ethical community. It might seem, then, that any ethics of a common culture of the multitude is internal to itself. It is not an ethics that stands above the collective - as with Williams' public servant - acting on behalf of the public, but unable to escape from the social, economic, political, and cultural divisions that makes possible such a seemingly neutral and beneficent servant of the people. This is an ethics immanent to, not transcendent of, community; an ethics in which all the flock are pastors; all care for all.

If this is so, then all mechanisms of representation and accountability are equally damned. Paradoxically, all representatives of the public interest, in whatever form (from public servants, to politicians, to 'representations', to consumer research) make visible both the distance between those who represent and those represented and also the desire to close that ontological and epistemological gap. It is a condition of those who serve the public - in whatever form - to do so faithfully and in the best interests of that constituency. Thus, when we refer to a television production team or an artist as 'ethical', we do so because these people can be seen to remain true to their ethical goals, for example, of producing a culture, rich and diverse, commensurate with the cultures of the population. We can read Williams' notion of 'active mutual responsibility' and Hardt and Negri's understanding of multitude in this light, namely that they are figured in such a way as to close the gap between producer and consumer, between representative and represented. The issue is both whether this is a reasonable and appropriate ethical objective and also whether these writers propose sufficient techniques or technologies for thinking through and actualising the overcoming of this gap.

As we have seen in this book, Haraway provides some useful starting points. Her criticism of the 'modest witness' standing in the 'culture of no culture' and her arguments regarding 'diffraction' and 'situated knowledge' can be seen alongside the discussion I am presenting above: namely she constructs a relation of cultural innovation and experimentation on the basis of an ethical affinity between subject and object, producer and consumer, knower and known. Such an ethics constructs the process of witnessing the diversity of culture-nature, not in terms of the passivity and inertness of the event, but its activity and productivity. Diffraction, as the building of alliances through the construction of elective affinities, concerns not simply the articulation of existing elements, but the creation of new patterns and experimentation. If these patterns formed through practices of diffraction are constituencies of things, then they are also communities of invention and innovation. Furthermore, these communities don't live *in* culture, but *through* it.

Haraway's concept of diffraction is presented originally as a means of understanding the relation of sociologists and cultural theorists of science and technology to 'representational' practices in such a way that any critical understanding of our own location in the production of knowledge, and hence our own location in the practices of power, does not revert to an endless loop of reflexivity (i.e. a recognition that one is caught in the practice of representation as much as the object represented, such that we get caught in an infinite regress of seeing oneself between two mirrors reflecting oneself infinitely). In this sense, Haraway's concept of diffraction is posed as an ethical concept, similar to that of Williams' notion of 'active mutual responsibility'. As agents of culture – when understood in the extensive sense as discussed throughout this book – we act as co-creators and co-producers of community.

Latour put a similar, but slightly different spin on this. He argues that '[b]y insisting so much on hermeneutic loops, social scientists have got too easily out of the loop – leaving in the dark the myriad of *non-human* actants, so essential to the very definition of humanity' (2000: 116). Latour calls upon Dewey's definition of the vocation of the social sciences to represent the social – for us also the cultural – to the public:

> That is, not to define the unknown structure of our actions (as if the social scientist knew *more* than the actor) but in *re*-presenting the social to itself because neither the 'public', his [Dewey's] word for what we would now call risk society, nor the social scientist knows for sure in what sort of experience we are engaged. The good social sciences, in this view, are not those who play the game of the (imagined) natural sciences in inventing infrastructures, but those who are able to modify the representations the public has of itself *fast enough* so that we can be sure that the greatest number of *objections* have been made to this representation. Then the social sciences will begin to imitate the natural ones. Nay, they might begin to bring the 'things' back to what they pertain: this assembly in charge of composing the common world that should rightly be called politics. (2000: 119)

Although Latour rightly refers to this Parliament of things as a matter of politics and the building of political community, one's relation to that assembly, one's relation to knowledge, one's address to a public and one's engagement in constant innovation is surely also ethical in the sense that Williams talks about as 'active mutual responsibility'.

This said, any ethics poses not just the question of engagement (as Haraway and Latour suggest), but also separation, distance and recognition of one's limited power to act. It is in this sense, that recent understandings of cultural studies as a discipline have become more sanguine about the ability of any academic discipline not simply to know the world, but to change it. It is noticeable that the quotation from Couldry at the beginning of this chapter synthesises ethics and politics not in some grand scheme for changing societal structures of power, but in the context of method: namely, it poses a politics that is both appropriate and discrete, a politics that knows its limits. This is not to suggest that somehow cultural studies should not intervene in a whole array of different arenas, from the small to the large, but that it must do so with some 'realism' in mind. Any ethics of cultural studies – as an ethics of reciprocity in the manner that Couldry discusses in relation to the question of method (2000: 5) – should be clear that there is a difference between the disciplined knowledge of culture and the world of culture itself. Furthermore, in talking about the ethics of cultural studies and culture, we should not presume that all of the discipline should be occupied by such concerns. The question of ethics should not dominate the field of study in the way that a concern with politics has dominated cultural studies for much of its history. Good research does not necessarily include an explicit reflection or discussion of ethical matters. This said, good research should nevertheless stand corrected by others if it is unethical.

Undoing Community

Before finally concluding, we should make it clear that any ethics of culture might just as well be oriented to the undoing, as much as the building, of community. Where a collective is oppressive, where a community is stifling, or where a culture does not suit our tastes, we think not of working with others but of getting away from them. We think of escape; we think of flight. We should pause here and reflect. What understanding of 'community' do we have when we talk of leaving and escape? And what sense of flight do we have? In the context of the discussion throughout this book, any understanding of community cannot be seen to be predicated on a collapse of culture and place nor can it be assumed that community is like a walled garden.

Communities don't exist *in* particular places nor are they built on the model of a walled city or prison. There was maybe a time when social existence was governed through carceral technologies, when city planners thought only of defending their community from attack through the elaborate structures of military arithmetic or when designers of penal institutions thought only of how to keep people in and away from other 'normal' communities. There was maybe a time when 'to belong' to a culture meant that one lived *in* a community, in a particular place alongside others who equally belonged. Escaping from these communities meant literally or metaphorically jumping over the wall, to a freedom outside. In this sense, also, to be free meant to not belong. But in late modernity our understandings of community, culture and freedom have radically changed.

Foucault's work on ethics, toward the later stages of his life, helps us to think further about this problem. In particular John Rajchman's reading of this work is of major assistance and, in itself, a major innovation:

> Community ... was about the bonds we may have with one another, affective and political; it was about who we are and may be. In stressing 'subjectivity' and 'subjectivization' he did not intend to abandon a social or collective ethic in favor of an individual or private one ... [H]e wanted to rethink the great question of 'community': the question of how and why people band together, of how and why they are bound to one another. (1991: 99)

Rajchman argues that Foucault distinguished between three different types of community. First, a 'given community' is one that a particular system of recognition makes available to us. It is not a constraint upon us except by virtue of the fact that we know no better than what it presents to us. Secondly, there is the notion of a 'tacit community' such that we actively support such a community. We help to maintain its functioning through our actions and we do so because of its 'self-evidence'. Thirdly, Rajchman talks about a 'critical community' as one in which one no longer accepts the system of identification within which others define themselves. This is a community of refusal, interruption and reversal. Although, given our discussion earlier in the book, we might argue that belonging or not belonging is much more than (dis)identification, we can accept, more generally, that critical community occurs through problematisation: '[i]t is the sort of community or bond we may have in so far as we are free' (1991: 102). Rajchman argues that 'the "critical community" of Foucault's ethic was not a "transcendental" one, but the community of the specific moments of critical "transcendence" in the forms which make a particular kind of "subjectivity" possible' (Rajchman, 1991: 103). A critical community is, thus, one that supports the freedom of self in the sense that community and self and belonging and freedom are not mutually exclusive ideas or practices. Foucault refers to a 'critical ontology of self' and to genealogy as the method for disclosing the historical field of problematisations through which the real might open itself up to an undoing. For Foucault, a critical ontology of the self is understood as a practice of freedom:

> Freedom is a *practice*. So there may, in fact, always be a certain number of projects whose aim is to modify some constraints, to loosen, or even to break them, but none of these projects can, simply by its nature, assure that people will have freedom automatically, that it will be established by the project itself. The freedom of men is never assured by the institutions and laws that are intended to guarantee them. This is why almost all of these laws and institutions are quite capable of being turned around. Not because they are ambiguous, but simply because 'freedom' is what must be exercised ... The guarantee of freedom is freedom. (1984: 245)

But given Foucault's understanding of bio-power – as a productivity, not a negativity – we cannot present freedom and critical community as a removal of oneself from the problem or a removal of a problem from self and community. In that sense, Foucault disavows the possibility of seeing freedom and change simply as the removal of one bad apple from the cart or the removal of one good apple from a cartload of bad ones. And in that sense too, power is not simply defined in terms of its capacity to include or exclude. To define a community along those lines would imply a very flat and carceral sense of communal space.

For Foucault, then, if our obligation is an obligation to be free, it is not predicated on 'belonging'. We cannot escape from the necessity of belonging: 'being a subject is to belong' (cf. Macherey, 1992: 192). Thus, in his 1984 lecture on Kant and the Enlightenment, Foucault says:

> [I]t can be seen that for the philosopher to ask the question about *belonging* to this present is by no means any longer to ask the question of his belonging to a doctrine or to a tradition; nor is it any longer the simple question of his belonging to a human community in general, but of his *belonging to a certain 'us'*, to an us which is related to a cultural ensemble characteristic of its own present state. (quoted in Macherey, 1992: 182)

We should understand the reference to 'cultural ensemble' in the context of the rich sense of culture as discussed throughout this book. To return more centrally to the problem of flight, then, any sense of escape is not akin to jumping over the wall, but maybe of retracing and remaking our being. I mean this in two senses. First, Foucault's critical ontology of the self is oriented to an undoing of the being of the present in the sense that freedom can be seen, to borrow Levinas' idea, as 'otherwise than being' (1985, 1998a, b) an undoing of being for the sake of being, or what Jean Luc Nancy calls the 'freedom of freedom' (Nancy, 1993). Foucault's critical ontology of the self, then, is not a freedom between two or more possibilities, as in a rejection of one 'conservative' 'normative' community in favour of a belonging to 'a certain us', a 'non-normative community'. Freedom, for Foucault, is not the freedom to choose between one or more existing entities, for example, between different television channels. Rather, the practice of freedom implies the possibility of a community of possibility (in Rajchman's understanding of 'critical community') but only in the sense that this community is not a community of being, but of otherwise than being or *between being*. However awkward this may sound, I can't make it any clearer. Secondly, if freedom is not akin to jumping over the wall, then it's about building bridges and its about equipping ourselves for the journey. In the context of what we've argued above and throughout the book, the ability to leave requires the help of others (both human and non-human). We never leave on our own. We can only be free with others. Moreover, these others cannot be completely distanced from myself before I have freed myself. If, for example, leaving home requires that I pack a bag of clothes, gather some money and buy a train ticket, then these things travel with me and support my flight, but only inasmuch as they form a bridge between my home and elsewhere. What kind of community, then, is able to facilitate such lines of flight? This is, of necessity, an open question.

Casting Off

At the close of *The Natural Contract* Serres invokes the image of a sailor casting off. But for Serres, casting off is not a clean metaphor; it is cluttered with noise. Serres talks of casting off initially in terms of the literal meanings of 'object', namely to throw away and 'subject', namely to throw under:

> Casting off throws us elsewhere, or toward and into another world, so that this relation causes a craft or piece of gear, an 'object', to appear: in the literal sense, a thing cast before us. Of course it must have left our bodies, to be lying before us like that! ... Sometimes the whole organism hurls itself outward, the functions of its organs casting off to become tools. The projection comes from the subject, once again well named. In contrast to animals, enclosed in the stable armour of their instincts, let us call man this animal whose body leaks, its organs becoming objects. (1995: 118)

Our movement away from somewhere and our movement toward somewhere doesn't entail the disconnection of ourselves from that initial place, but rather the casting of our bodies between where we are going and where we have been. Those on land, those satellite systems, those maps, those makers of ships are not transposed to mind when the craft sets sail, but also in their bodies. One heroic sailor has said of these others, '[t]here was always a team of people behind me, in mind if not in body' (MacArthur, The *Guardian*, 9 February 2005); but maybe it should have read 'in body, if not always in mind'. To cast off, to sail away is thus a complex and entangled endeavour:

> To cast off means that the boat and its sailors entrust themselves to their technologies and their social contract, for they leave the port fully armed, head to toe, with proud yards and boom aimed toward the future ... I have no more gear on my craft ... I have gone naked. Reduced to bare leftovers. I am even missing much of the indispensable baggage for living comfortably. I live in shipwreck alert. Always in dire straits, untied, lying to, ready to founder. (1995: 123–4)

From Plato, Descartes, Haraway, Gilroy and Serres, the sailor, the one who governs a boat or ship, is presented as a central figure for understanding our connectedness to the world and our ability to govern ourselves and others in the face of that world. The steersman, by his ancient Greek name, is called the cybernaut. The strengths of the cybernaut are not that she arches her compass on a fixed world, but that she stays afloat in all weathers in order to travel to meet other places and peoples. If my discussion of community is in any way significant for thinking through an ethics of our contemporary cultural world, it is not because the world can be reduced to these words, but because an ethics of culture holds in place, hand firmly on the rudder, the principle of irreduction. As the brilliant and wonderful Belgian philosopher of science and culture, Isabel Stengers has said:

> The principle of irreduction prescribes a retreat from this claim to know and to judge ... Irreduction thus signifies a certain distrust of all the 'words' that lead quasi-automatically to the temptation to explain by reducing, or to construct a difference between two terms that reduces them to a relation of irreducible opposition. In other words ... it is a matter of learning to use words that do not bestow, as if it were their vocation, the power to *unveil* (the truth behind appearances) or to *denounce* (the appearances that veil the truth). We must be clear that this does not mean we will reach a world where everyone would be beautiful and kind. (2000: 15–16)

Far from constructing big divides between human and machine, art and industry, and so on and wanting to resolve these divisions, the principle of irreduction suggests an ethics in-between. This is far from an ethics of uncertainty or relativity. To steer a boat one needs a map, to read the co-ordinates of one's position, a sextet to find one's position, a radio to hear the weather reports. Each of these help in the government of the boat, but they don't dictate what is to be done. What is to be done and our relation to that doing occurs precisely in that field of irreduction. The storm blows up, the sea changes. I don't only look to the map to sail a boat. I pay attention to the world. I get affected by the buffeting of the waters. And I'm guided by hope.

Bibliography

Adorno, Theodor (1991) *The Culture Industry*. London: Routledge.

Adorno, Theodor and Horkheimer, Max (1979) *Dialectic of Enlightenment*. London: Allen Lane.

Aglietta, Michel (1979) *A Theory of Capitalist Regulation*. London: Verso.

Ahmed, Sarah (1999) 'She'll wake up one of these days and find she's turned into a nigger: passing through hybridity' in Bell, Vikki (ed.) *Performativity and Belonging*. London: Sage.

Ali, Suki (2003) *Mixed-Race, Post-Race: Gender, New Ethnicities and Cultural Practices*. Oxford: Berg.

Althusser, Louis (1969) *For Marx*. London: Verso.

Althusser, Louis (1971) *Lenin and Philosophy and Other Essays*. London: Monthly Review Press.

Althusser, Louis and Balibar, Etienne (1979) *Reading Capital*. London: Verso.

Amin, Ash (1994) *Post-Fordism: A Reader*. Oxford: Blackwell.

Anderson, Benedict (1983) *Imagined Communities: Reflections on the Origins and Spread of Nationalism*. London: Verso.

Ang, Ien (1992) 'Dismantling "cultural studies"', *Cultural Studies*, 6(3): 311–21.

Ang, Ien (1996) *Living Room Wars: Rethinking Media Audiences for a Postmodern World*. London: Routledge.

Appadurai, Arjun (1986) 'Introduction: commodities and the politics of value' in Appadurai, Arjun (ed.) *The Social Life of Things: Commodities in Cultural Perspective*. Cambridge: Cambridge University Press.

Appadurai, Arjun (1990) 'Disjuncture and difference in the global cultural eonomy' in Featherstone, Mike (ed.) *Global Culture: Nationalism, Globalization and Modernity*. London: Sage.

Appadurai, Arjun (1996) *Modernity at Large: Cultural Dimensions of Globalization*. Minneapolis: University of Minnesota Press.

Arnold, Matthew (1960 [1869]) *Culture and Anarchy*. Cambridge: Cambridge University Press.

Austin, J. L. (1962) *How to Do Things with Words*. Oxford: Oxford University Press.

Bacon, Francis (1906) 'Of empire', *Essays*. London: J. M. Dent and Sons.

Bakhtin, Mikhail (1968) *Rabelais and his World*. Cambridge, MA: MIT Press.

Bakhtin, Mikhail (1981) *The Dialogic Imagination*. Austin, TX: University of Texas Press.

Bakhtin, Mikhail (1984) *Problems of Dostoevsky's Poetics*. Minneapolis: University of Minnesota Press.

Balibar, Etienne and Wallerstein, Immanuel (eds) (1991) *Race, Nation and Class: Ambiguous Identities*. London: Verso.

Barnes, Barry (2001) 'The macro/micro problem and the problem of structure and agency' in Ritzer, George and Smart, Barry (eds) *Handbook of Social Theory*. London: Sage.

Barthes, Roland (1968) *Elements of Semiology*. New York: Hill and Wang.

Barthes, Roland (1973) *Mythologies*. London: Palladin.

Barthes, Roland (1974) *S/Z*. New York: Hill and Wang.
Barthes, Roland (1977) *Image, Music, Text*. London: Fontana.
Barthes, Roland (1990) *A Lover's Discourse: Fragments*. London: Penguin.
Baudrillard Jean (1975) *The Mirror of Production*. St. Louis, MO: Telos Press.
Baudrillard, Jean (1981) *For a Critique of the Political Economy of the Sign*. St. Louis, MO: Telos Press.
Baudrillard, Jean (1983a) *Simulations*. New York: Semiotexte.
Baudrillard, Jean (1983b) *In the Shadow of the Silent Majorities*. New York: Semiotexte.
Baudrillard, Jean (1988) Interview in *Block* 14: 8–10.
Baudrillard, Jean (1989) *America*. London: Verso.
Beck, Ulrich (1992) *Risk Society: Towards a New Modernity*. London: Sage.
Belsey, Catherine (1980) *Critical Practice*. London: Methuen.
Benjamin, Walter (1973) *Illuminations*. London: Fontana.
Bennett, Tony (1986a) 'Popular culture and "the turn to Gramsci"' in Bennett, Tony, Mercer, Colin and Woollacott, Janet (eds) *Popular Culture and Social Relations*. Milton Keynes: Open University Press.
Bennett, Tony (1986b) 'The politics of the "popular" and popular culture' in Bennett, Tony, Mercer, Colin and Woollacott, Janet (eds) *Popular Culture and Social Relations*. Milton Keynes: Open University Press.
Bennett, Tony (1992a) 'Putting policy into cultural studies' in Grossberg, Lawrence, Nelson, Cary and Treichler, Pauler (eds) *Cultural Studies*. London: Macmillan.
Bennett, Tony (1992b) 'Useful culture', *Cultural Studies*, 6(3): 395–408.
Bennett, Tony (1998) *Culture: A Reformer's Science*. London: Sage.
Bennett, Tony, Mercer, Colin and Woollacott, Janet (eds) (1986) *Popular Culture and Social Relations*. Milton Keynes: Open University Press.
Benveniste, Emile (1971) *Problems in General Linguistics*. Miami: University of Miami Press.
Bhabha, Homi (1983) 'The other question', *Screen*, 24(4): 18–36.
Bhabha, Homi (1985) 'Signs taken for wonders: questions of ambivalence and authority under a tree outside Delhi, May 1817' in Barker, Francis (ed.) *Europe and its Others, Volume 1*. Colchester: University of Essex.
Bhabha, Homi (1988) 'The commitment to theory', *New Formations*, 5: 5–23.
Bhabha, Homi (1990a) 'The third space' in Rutherford, Jonathan (ed.) *Identity: Community, Culture, Difference*. London: Lawrence and Wishart.
Bhabha, Homi (ed.) (1990b) *Nation and Narration*. London: Routledge.
Bhabha, Homi (1994) Interview in *The Times Higher*, 17. 11 February.
Bhabha, Homi (1996) 'Culture's in-between' in Hall, Stuart and du Gay, Paul (eds) *Questions of Cultural Identity*. London: Sage.
Billig, Michael (1997) 'From codes to utterances: cultural studies, discourse and psychology' in Ferguson, Marjorie and Golding, Peter (eds), *Cultural Studies in Question*. London: Sage.
Bourdieu, Pierre (1984) *Distinction: A Social Critique of the Judgement of Taste*. Cambridge, MA: Harvard University Press.
Bourdieu, Pierre (1990) *The Logic of Practice*. Cambridge: Polity Press.
Bourdieu, Pierre (1998) *Practical Reason*. Cambridge: Polity Press.
Boyne, Roy (1990) 'Culture and the world-system' in Featherstone, Mike (ed.) *Global Culture: Nationalism, Globalization and Modernity*. London: Sage.
Braidotti, Rosi (1994) *Nomadic Subjects: Embodiment and Sexual Difference in Contemporary Feminist Theory*. New York: Columbia University Press.
Brown, Steve D. (2002) 'Michel Serres: science, translation and the logic of the parasite', *Theory, Culture and Society*, 19(3): 1–27.
Brunsden, Charlotte (1981) '*Crossroads*: notes on soap opera', *Screen*, 22(4): 32–7.
Butler, Judith (1990) *Gender Trouble: Feminism and the Subversion of Identity*. London: Routledge.

Butler, Judith (1991) 'Imitation and gender insubordination' in Fuss, Diana (ed.) *Inside/Out: Lesbian Theories, Gay Theories*. London: Routledge.

Butler, Judith (1993) *Bodies that Matter: On the Discursive Limits of Sex*. New York: Routledge.

Callinicos, Alex (2003) 'Toni Negri in perspective' in Balakrishnan, Gopal (ed.) *Debating Empire*. London: Verso.

Callon, Michel (1986) 'Some elements of a sociology of translation: domestication of scallops and the fishermen of St. Brieuc Bay' in Law, John (ed.) *Power, Action and Belief: A New Sociology of Knowledge?* London: RKP.

Callon, Michel (1992) 'Techno-economic networks and irreversibility' in Law, John (ed.) *A Sociology of Monsters: Essays on Power, Technology and Domination*. Oxford: Blackwell.

Callon, Michel (1998a) 'Introduction: the embeddedness of economic markets in economics' in Callon, Michel (ed.) *The Laws of the Markets*. Oxford: Blackwell.

Callon, Michel (1998b) 'An essay on framing and overflowing: economic externalities revisited by sociology' in Callon, Michel (ed.) *The Laws of the Markets*. Oxford: Blackwell.

Callon, Michel and Latour, Bruno (1981) 'Unscrewing the big Leviathan: how actors macro-structure reality and how sociologists help them to do so' in Knorr-Cetina, Karin and Cicourel, Aaron V. (eds) *Advances in Social Theory and Methodology: Toward an Integration of Micro- and Macro-Sociologics*. London: RKP.

Campbell, Kirsten (2004) 'The promise of feminist reflexivities: developing Donna Haraway's project for feminist science studies', *Hypatia: A Journal of Feminist Philosophy*, 19(1): 162–82.

Canguilhem, Georges (2000) *A Vital Rationalist: Selected Writings from Georges Canguilhem*. New York: Zone Books.

Cartwright, Lisa (1995) *Screening the Body: Tracing Medicine's Visual Culture*. Minneapolis: University of Minnesota Press.

Castañeda, Claudia (2002) *Figurations: Child, Bodies, Worlds*. London: Duke University Press.

Castells, Manuel (1996) *The Rise of the Network Society*. Oxford: Blackwell.

Castells, Manuel (2001) *The Internet Galaxy: Reflections on the Internet, Business, and Society*. Oxford: Oxford University Press.

Clynes, Manfred and Kline, Nathan (1960) 'Cyborgs and space', *Astronautics*. 26–27th September, pp. 26-7 and pp. 74-5. Reprinted in Gray, Chris Hables (1995) (eds) *The Cybora Handbook*. New York: Routledge.

Coleridge, Samuel Taylor (1972) *On the Constitution of the Church and State*. London: Dent.

Couldry, Nick (2000) *Inside Culture: Re-Imaging the Method of Cultural Studies*. London: Sage.

Cunningham, Stuart (1992) *Framing Culture*. Sydney: Allen and Unwin.

Curran, James (1977) 'Capitalism and control of the press, 1800-1975' in Curran, James and Gurevitch, Michael (eds) *Mass Communication and Society*. London: Edward Arnold.

de Certeau, Michel (1984) *The Practice of Everyday Life*. Berkeley: University of California Press.

Deleuze, Gilles (1983) *Nietzsche and Philosophy*. London: Athlone Press.

Deleuze, Gilles (1988) *Foucault*. Minneapolis: University of Minnesota Press.

Deleuze, Gilles (1992) 'What is a *dispositif*?' in Armstrong, Timothy, J. (ed.) *Michel Foucault: Philosopher*. London: Harvester Wheatsheaf.

Deleuze, Gilles (1993) *The Fold: Leibniz and the Baroque*. Minneapolis: University of Minnesota Press.

Deleuze, Gilles (1994) *Difference and Repetition*. London: Athlone Press.

Deleuze, Gilles and Guattari, Felix (1983a) 'Rhizome', *On the Line*. New York: Semiotexte.

Deleuze, Gilles and Guattari, Felix (1983b) *Anti-Oedipus: Capitalism and Schizophrenia*. Minneapolis: University of Minnesota Press.

Deleuze, Gilles and Guattari, Felix (1988) *A Thousand Plateaus: Capitalism and Schizophrenia*. London: Athlone Press.

Derrida, Jacques (1976) *Of Grammatology*. Baltimore, MD: Johns Hopkins University Press.

Derrida, Jacques (1978a) 'Differance' in *Margins of Philosophy*. London: Routledge.

Derrida, Jacques (1978b) 'Structure, sign and play in the discourse of the human sciences' in *Writing and Difference*. London: Routledge.
Derrida, Jacques (1987) *Positions*. London: Athlone Press.
Descartes, Rene (1968) *Discourse on Method and The Meditations*. Harmondsworth: Penguin.
Descombes, Vincent (1980) *Modern French Philosophy*. Cambridge: Cambridge University Press.
de Sola Pool, Ithiel (1983) *Technologies of Freedom*. Cambridge, MA: Harvard University Press.
Donald, James (1992) *Sentimental Education*. London: Verso.
Donzelot, Jacques (1979) *The Policing of Families*. London: Hutchinson.
Donzelot, Jacques (1991) 'The mobilisation of society' in Burchell, Graham, Gordon, Colin and Miller, Peter (eds) *The Foucault Effect: Studies in Governmentality*. London: Harvester Wheatsheaf.
Dorfman, Ariel and Mattelart, Armand (1984) *How to Read Donald Duck: Imperialist Ideology in the Disney Comic*. New York: International General.
Drotner, Kirsten (2001) 'Denmark: "Donald seems so Danish": Disney and the formation of cultural identity' in Wasko, Janet, Phillips, Mark and Meehan, Eileen (eds) *Dazzled by Disney: the Global Disney Audiences Project*. London: Leicester University Press.
Drotner, Kirsten (2002) 'Disney discourses or mundane globalization', paper presented at the Second Plenary Conference of the European Science Foundation's 'Changing Media, Changing Europe' Programme, Copenhagen, Denmark.
du Bois, W.E.B. (1989) *The Souls of Black Folk*. New York: Bantam Press.
Duden, Barbara (1993) *Disembodying Women: Perspectives on Pregnancy and the Unborn*. Cambridge, MA: Harvard University Press.
du Gay, Paul (1997) 'Introduction' in du Gay, Paul (ed.) *Production of Culture/Cultures of Production*. London: Sage.
du Gay, Paul and Pryke, Michael (2002) 'Cultural economy: an introduction' in du Gay, Paul and Pryke, Michael (eds) *Cultural Economy*. London: Sage.
Durkheim, Emile (1982) *The Rules of Sociological Method*. Basingstoke: Macmillan.
Eagleton, Terry (2000) *The Idea of Culture*. Oxford: Blackwell.
Eco, Umberto (1976) *A Theory of Semiotics*. Bloomington, IL: Indiana University Press.
Eco, Umberto (1984) *Semiotics and the Philosophy of Language*. London: Macmillan.
Elias, Norbert (1994) *The Civilizing Process*. Oxford: Blackwell.
Eliot, T. S. (1948) *Notes Towards the Definition of Culture*. London: Faber and Faber.
Fanon, Frantz (1967) *The Wretched of the Earth*. London: Penguin.
Fanon, Frantz (1986) *Black Skin, White Masks*. London: Pluto Press.
Featherstone, Mike (1991) *Consumer Culture and Postmodernism*. London: Sage.
Featherstone, Mike (ed.) (2002) Special Issue on Cosmopolis. *Theory, Culture and Society*, 19(1–2).
Fiske, John (1987) *Television Culture*. London: Macmillan.
Fiske, John (1989) *Understanding Popular Culture*. Sydney: Allen and Unwin.
Fitzpatrick, Peter (2004) 'The immanence of *Empire*' in Passavant, Paul A. and Dean, Jodi (eds) *Empire's New Clothes*. New York: Routledge.
Foucault, Michel (1970) *The Order of Things: An Archaeology of the Human Sciences*. London: Tavistock.
Foucault, Michel (1972 [1969]) *The Archaeology of Knowledge*. London: Tavistock.
Foucault, Michel (1977a) 'Theatrum philosophicum' in Bouchard, Donald F. (ed.) *Language, Counter-Memory, Practice: Selected Essays and Interviews by Michel Foucault*. New York: Cornell University Press.
Foucault, Michel (1977b) *Discipline and Punish*. Harmondsworth: Penguin.
Foucault, Michel (1979) *History of Sexuality, Vol. 1*. Harmondsworth: Penguin.
Foucault, Michel (1980) 'The Confession of the Flesh' in Gordon, Colin (ed.) *Michel Foucault: Power/Knowledge*. Brighton: Harvester Press.

Foucault, Michel (1981) 'Omnes et singulatim: towards a critique of "political reason" in *The Tanner Lectures on Human Values, Vol. 2*, Utah: University of Utah Press.

Foucault, Michel (1982) 'The subject and power' in Dreyfus, Hubert and Rabinow, Paul (eds) *Michel Foucault: Beyond Structuralism and Hermeneutics*. Brighton: Harvester Press.

Foucault, Michel (1984) 'Space, knowledge and power' in Rabinow, Paul (ed.) *The Foucault Reader*. New York: Random House.

Foucault, Michel (1986) *The Uses of Pleasure: The History of Sexuality, Vol. 2*. London: Viking.

Foucault, Michel (1988) *The Care of the Self: The History of Sexuality, Vol. 3*. Harmondsworth: Penguin.

Foucault, Michel (1989) 'Introduction' to Canguilhem, Georges *The Normal and the Pathological*. New York: Zone Books.

Foucault, Michel (1991) 'Governmentality' in Burchell, Graham, Gordon, Colin and Miller, Peter (eds) *The Foucault Effect: Studies in Governmentality*. London: Harvester Wheatsheaf.

Franklin, Sarah (1991) 'Fetal fascinations: new dimensions to the medical scientific construction of fetal personhood' in Franklin, Sarah, Lury, Celia and Stacey, Jackie (eds) *Off-Centre: Feminism and Cultural Studies*. London: Harper Collins.

Franklin, Sarah (2000) 'Life itself: global nature and the genetic imaginary' in Franklin, Sarah, Lury, Celia and Stacey, Jackie *Global Nature, Global Culture*. London: Sage.

Franklin, Sarah (2003a) 'Culturing biology: cell lines for the second millennium' http//comp.lanc.ac.uk/sociology/soc084sf.htm

Franklin, Sarah (2003b) 'Biologization revisited: kinship theory in the context of new biologies' http//comp.lanc.ac.uk/sociology/IHT/eofcpaper.htm

Franklin, Sarah and Roberts, Celia (2001) 'Innovative health technologies: the social life of the embryo', http//comp.lanc.ac.uk/sociology/IHT/eofcpaper.htm

Franklin, Sarah, Lury, Celia and Stacey, Jackie (2000) *Global Nature, Global Culture*. London: Sage.

Gans, Herbert, J. (1974) *Popular Culture and High Culture*. New York: Basic Books.

Garfinkel, Howard (1985) *Studies in Ethnomethodology*. Cambridge: Polity Press.

Gellner, Ernest (1983) *Nations and Nationalism*. Oxford: Blackwell.

Geertz, Clifford (1973) *The Interpretation of Cultures*. New York: Basic Books.

Giddens, Anthony (1984) *The Constitution of Society*. Cambridge: Polity Press.

Giddens, Anthony (1990) *The Consequences of Modernity*. Cambridge: Polity Press.

Giddens, Anthony (1991) *Modernity and Self-Identity: Self and Society in the Late Modern Age*. Cambridge: Polity Press.

Giddens, Anthony (1998) *The Third Way: The Renewal of Social Democracy*. Cambridge: Polity Press.

Giddens, Anthony (1999) *Runaway World: How Globalisation is Reshaping Our Lives*. London: Profile Books.

Gillespie, Marie (1995) *Television, Ethnicity and Cultural Change*. London: Routledge.

Gilroy, Paul (1993a) *The Black Atlantic*. London: Verso.

Gilroy, Paul (1993b) *Small Acts: Thoughts on the Politics of Black Cultures*. London: Serpents Tail.

Gilroy, Paul (1995) *Status of Difference: From Epidermalisation to Nano-Politics*. London: Critical Urban Studies Occasional Papers, Goldsmiths College.

Golding, Peter and Murdock, Graham (1991) 'Culture, communications and political economy' in Curran, James and Gurevitch Michael (eds) *Mass Media and Society*. London: Edward Arnold.

Goodeve, Thyrza Nichols (2000) in Haraway, Donna (ed.) *How Like a Leaf: An Interview with Thyrza Nichols Goodeve*. New York: Routledge.

Gordon, Colin (1991) 'Governmental rationality: an introduction' in Burchell, Graham, Gordon, Colin and Miller, Peter (eds) *The Foucault Effect: Studies in Governmentality*. London: Harvester Wheatsheaf.

Gramsci, Antonio (1971) *Selections from the Prison Notebooks*. London: Lawrence and Wishart.

Gramsci, Antonio (1978) *Selections from Political Writings, 1921-26*. London: Lawrence and Wishart.
Greimas, A. J. (1984) *Structural Semantics: An Attempt at Method*. Nebraska: University of Nebraska Press.
Greimas, A. J. (1987) 'Actants, Actors, and Figures' in Greimas, A. J. (ed.) *On Meaning: Selected Writings in Semiotic Theory*. Minneapolis: University of Minnesota Press.
Guattari, Felix (1984) *Molecular Revolution: Psychiatry and Politics*. Harmondsworth: Penguin.
Hacking, Ian (1991) 'How should we do a history of statistics?' in Burchell, Graham, Gordon, Colin and Miller, Peter (eds) *The Foucault Effect: Studies in Governmentality*. London: Harvester Wheatsheaf.
Hall, Stuart (1980) 'Encoding/decoding' in Hall, Stuart, Hobson, Dorothy, Lowe, Andrew and Willis, Paul (eds) *Culture, Media, Language*. London: Hutchinson.
Hall, Stuart (1981) 'Notes on deconstructing the popular' in Samuel, Ralph (ed.) *People's History and Socialist Theory*. London: RKP.
Hall, Stuart (1987) 'Minimal selves' in Appignesi, Lisa (ed.) *Identity, the Real Me: Post-Modernism and the Question of Identity*. London: ICA.
Hall, Stuart (1988a) Interview in *Block* 14: 11-14.
Hall, Stuart (1988b) 'New ethnicities' in Mercer, Kobena (ed.) *Black Film, British Cinema*. London: ICA.
Hall, Stuart (1990) 'Cultural identity and diaspora' in Rutherford, Jonathan (ed.) *Identity: Community, Culture, Difference*. London: Lawrence and Wishart.
Hall, Stuart (1996) 'Introduction: who needs "identity"?' in Hall, Stuart and du Gay, Paul (eds) *Questions of Cultural Identity*. London: Sage.
Hall, Stuart (1997a) 'The work of representation' in Hall, Stuart (ed.) *Representation: Cultural Representation and Signifying Practices*. London: Sage.
Hall, Stuart (1997b) 'The spectacle of the "other"' in Hall, Stuart (ed.) *Representation: Cultural Representation and Signifying Practices*. London: Sage.
Hall, Stuart and Jacques, Martin (eds) (1989) *New Times: The Changing Face of Politics in the 1990s*. London: Lawrence and Wishart.
Hall, Stuart and Whannel, Paddy (1964) *The Popular Arts*. London: Hutchinson.
Hall, Stuart, Critcher Chas, Jefferson Tony, Clarke, John and Roberts, Brian (1978) *Policing the Crisis: Mugging, the State, and Law and Order*. London: Macmillan.
Hannerz, Ulf (1990) 'Cosmopolitians and locals in world culture' in Featherstone, Mike (ed.) *Global Culture: Nationalism, Globalization and Modernity*. London: Sage.
Haraway, Donna (1989) *Primate Visions: Gender, Race, and Nature in the World of Modern Science*. London: Routledge.
Haraway, Donna (1991a) 'A manifesto for cyborgs' in Haraway, Donna, *Simians, Cyborgs and Women*. London: Free Association Press.
Haraway, Donna (1991b) 'Situated knowledges: the science question in feminism and the principle of partial perspective' in Haraway, Donna, *Simians, Cyborgs and Women*. London: Free Association Press.
Haraway, Donna (1997) *Modest_Witness@Second_Millennium.FemaleMan_Meets_OncoMouse*. New York: Routledge.
Haraway, Donna (2000) *How Like a Leaf: An Interview with Thyrza Nichols Goodeve*. New York: Routledge.
Hardt, Michael (2004) Interview in Passavant, Paul A. and Dean, Jodi (eds) *Empire's New Clothes*. New York: Routledge.
Hardt, Michael and Negri, Antonio (2000) *Empire*. Cambridge, MA: Harvard University Press.
Hardt, Michael and Negri, Antonio (2004) *Multitude: War and Democracy in the Age of Empire*. New York: Penguin.
Harvey, David (1989) *The Condition of Postmodernity*. Oxford: Blackwell.
Hegel, G. W. F. (1977) *Phenomenology of Spirit*. Oxford: Oxford University Press.

Held, David (1989) *Political Theory and the Modern State*. Cambridge: Polity Press.

Held, David (1995) *Democracy and the Global Order: From the Modern State to Cosmopolitan Governance*. Cambridge: Polity Press.

Hetherington, Kevin (1998) *Expressions of Identity: Space, Performance, Politics*. London: Sage

Hetherington, Kevin and Hinchliffe, Steve (eds) (2000) *Crumpled Spaces and Society*. London: Routledge.

Hirst, Paul (1976) 'Althusser and the theory of ideology', *Economy and Society*, 5(4): 385-412.

Hirst, Paul and Zeitlin, J. (1991) 'Flexible specialisation versus post-Fordism', *Economy and Society*, 20(1): 1-56.

Hirst, Paul and Thompson, Grahame (1996) *Globalization in Question: The International Economy and the Possibilities of Governance*. Cambridge: Polity Press.

Hobbes, Thomas (1968) *Leviathan*. Harmondsworth: Pelican Press.

Hobsbawm, Eric and Ranger, Terence (eds) (1983) *The Invention of Tradition*. Cambridge: Cambridge University Press.

Hoggart, Richard (1958 [1957]) *The Uses of Literacy*. Harmondsworth: Penguin.

Holquist, Michael (1990) *Dialogism: Bakhtin and His World*. London: Routledge.

hooks, bel (1991) *Yearning: Race, Gender and Cultural Politics*. Boston, MA: South End Press.

hooks, bel (1992) *Black Looks: Race and Representation*. Boston, MA: South End Press.

Hoskins, Colin, McFadyen and Finn, Adam (1997) *Global Television and Film: An Introduction to the Economics of the Business*. Oxford: Oxford University Press.

Hunter, Ian (1984) 'After representation: recent discussions on the relation between language and literature', *Economy and Society* 13(4): 397-430.

Hunter, Ian (1988a) *Culture and Government: The Emergence of Literary Education*. London: Macmillan.

Hunter, Ian (1988b) 'Setting limits to culture', *New Formations*, 4: 103-23.

Huyssen, Andreas (1986) *After the Great Divide*. Indiana: Indiana University Press.

Jakobson, Roman and Halle, Morris (2002) *Fundamentals of Language*. Hague: Mouton de Gruyter.

Jameson, Frederic (1984) 'Postmodernism, or the cultural logic of late capitalism', *New Left Review*, 146: 59-92.

Kant, Immanuel (1952) *The Critique of Judgement*. Oxford: Clarendon Press.

Kember, Sarah (2003) *Cyberfeminism and Artificial Life*. London: Routledge.

Knorr-Cetina, Karin (2001) 'Postsocial relations: theorizing sociality in a postsocial environment' in Ritzer, George and Smart, Barry (eds) *Handbook of Social Theory*. London: Sage.

Knorr-Cetina, Karin and Bruegger, Ure (2002) 'Trader's engagement with markets: a postsocial relationship', *Theory, Culture and Society*, 19(5-6): 161-86.

Kojeve, Alexandre (1980) *Introduction to the Reading of Hegel: Lectures on the Phenomenology of Spirit*. London: Cornell University Press.

Kopytoff, Igor (1986) 'The cultural biography of things: commoditization as process' in Appadurai, Arjun (ed.) *The Social Life of Things: Commodities in Cultural Perspective*. Cambridge: Cambridge University Press.

Kristeva, Julia (1982) *Desire in Language: A Semiotic Approach to Literature and Art*. Oxford: Blackwell.

Kristeva, Julia (1984a) *Revolution in Poetic Language*. New York: Columbia University Press.

Kristeva, Julia (1984b) *Powers of Horror*. New York: Columbia University Press.

Kumar, Krishan (1995) *From Post-Industrial to Post-Modern Society: New Theories of the Contemporary World*. Oxford: Blackwell.

Kuper, Adam (2000) *Culture: The Anthropologists Account*. Cambridge, MA: Harvard University Press.

Lacan, Jacques (1977) *The Four Fundamental Concepts of Psycho-Analysis*. Harmondsworth: Penguin.

Lacan, Jacques (1980) *Ecrits: A Selection*. London: Tavistock Press.

Laclau, Ernesto (1977) *Politics and Ideology in Marxist Theory*. London: Verso.

Laclau, Ernesto (1990) *New Reflections on the Revolution of Our Time*. London: Verso.

Laclau, Ernesto (2004) 'Can immanence explain social struggles?' in Passavant, Paul A. and Dean, Jodi (eds) *Empire's New Clothes*. New York: Routledge.
Laclau, Ernesto and Mouffe, Chantal (1985) *Hegemony and Socialist Strategy*. London: Verso.
Laffey, Mark and Weldes, Jutta (2004) 'Representing the international: sovereignty after modernity' in Passavant, Paul A. and Dean, Jodi (eds) *Empire's New Clothes*. New York: Routledge.
Laplanche, Jean and Pontalis, Jean-Bertrand (1982) 'Fantasy and the origins of sexuality' in Burgin, Victor and Kaplan, Cora (eds) *Formations of Fantasy*. London: Macmillan.
Lash, Scott, and Urry, John (1987) *The End of Organized Capitalism*. Cambridge: Polity Press.
Lash, Scott and Urry, John (1994) *Economies of Signs and Space*. London: Sage.
Latour, Bruno (1987) *Science in Action*. Milton Keynes: Open University Press.
Latour, Bruno (1988) '*The Prince* for Machines as well as machinations' in Elliott, Brian (ed.) *Technology and Social Process*. Edinburgh: Edinburgh University Press.
Latour, Bruno (1990) 'Drawing things together' in Lynch, Michael and Woolgar, Steve (eds) *Representation in Scientific Practice*. Cambridge, MA: MIT Press.
Latour, Bruno (1993) *We Have Never Been Modern*. London: Harvester Wheatsheaf.
Latour, Bruno (2000) 'When things strike back: a possible contribution of science studies', *British Journal of Sociology*, 51(1): 107-23.
Latour, Bruno and Woolgar, Steve (1979) *Laboratory Life: The Social Construction of Scientific Facts*. London: Sage.
Law, John (1986) 'On the methods of long-distance control vessels navigation and the Portuguese route to India Bay' in Law, John (ed.) *Power, Action and Belief: A New Sociology of Knowledge?* London: RKP.
Law, John (1997) 'Traduction/trahison: notes on ANT', University of Lancaster, http//comp.lanc.ac.uk/sociology/stslaw2.html
Law, John and Hassard, John (1999) *Actor Network Theory and After*. Oxford: Blackwell.
Law, John and Hetherington, Kevin (2000) 'Materialities, spatialities, globalities' in Bryson, John, Daniels, Peter, Henry, Nick and Pollard, Jane (eds) *Knowledge, Space, Economy*. London: Routledge.
Lenin, V. I. (1969) *What is to be Done?* London: Central Books.
Lenin, V. I. (1965 [1917]) *The State and Revolution*. Peking: Foreign Languages Press.
Lenin, V. I. (1986) *Imperialism, the Highest Stage of Capitalism*. Moscow: Progress Publishers.
Levinas, Emmanuel (1969) *Totality and Infinity: An Essay on Exteriority*. Pittsburgh, PA: Duquesne University Press.
Levinas, Emmanuel (1985) *Ethics and Infinity*. Pittsburgh, PA: Duquesne University Press.
Levinas, Emmanuel (1998a) *Otherwise than Being, or Beyond Essence*. Pittsburgh, PA: Duquesne University Press.
Levinas, Emmanuel (1998b) *Entre Nous: On Thinking-of-the-Other*. London: Athlone Press.
Liebes, Tamar and Katz, Elihu (1990) *The Export of Meaning: Cross-Cultural Readings of Dallas*. Oxford: Oxford University Press.
Lowell, Robert (1974) *Robert Lowell's Poems: A Selection*. London: Faber and Faber.
Lukes, Steven (1974) *Power: A Radical View*. Basingstoke: Palgrave.
Lury, Celia (1996) *Consumer Culture*. Cambridge: Polity Press.
Lynch, Michael (1993) *Scientific Practice and Ordinary Action: Ethnomethodology and Social Studies of Science*. Cambridge: Cambridge University Press.
Lynch, Michael and Woolgar, Steve (eds) (1990) *Representation in Scientific Practice*. Cambridge, MA: MIT Press.
Macheray, Pierre (1992) 'Towards a natural history of norms' in Armstrong, Timothy, J. (ed.) *Michel Foucault: Philosopher*. London: Harvester Wheatsheaf.
Machiavelli, Niccolo (2003) *The Prince*. London: Penguin.
Mandel, Ernest (1978) *Late Capitalism*. London: Verso.

Marcuse, Herbert (1968) 'On the affirmative concept of culture' in *Negations: Essays in Critical Theory*. London: Allen Lane.

Marx, Karl (1971) *The Poverty of Philosophy*. New York: International.

Marx, Karl (1976) *Preface to A Contribution to the Critique of Political Economy*. Peking: Foreign Languages Press.

Marx, Karl (1999) *Capital*. Oxford: Oxford University Press.

Marx, Karl and Engels, Frederick (1970) *The German Ideology*. London: Lawrence and Wishart.

Mattelart, Armand, Delcourt, Xavier and Mattelart, Michelle (1984) *International Image Markets*. London: Comedia.

McGuigan, Jim (1992) *Cultural Populism*. London: Routledge.

McGrew, Anthony (1992) 'A global society?' in Hall, Stuart, Held, David and McGrew, Anthony (eds) *Modernity and Its Futures*. Cambridge: Polity.

McLuhan, Marshall (1964) *Understanding Media: The Extension of Man*. London: RKP.

McLuhan, Marshall and Fiore, Quentin (1967) *The Medium is the Massage: An Inventory of Effects*. New York: Gingko Press.

McLuhan, Marshall and Fiore, Quentin (1968) *War and Peace in the Global Village*. New York: Gingko Press.

Meiksins Wood, Ellen (2003) 'A manifesto for global capitalism?' in Balakrishnan, Gopal (ed.) *Debating Empire*. London: Verso.

Merrington, John (1978) 'Theory and Practice in Gramsci's Marxism' in New Left Review (ed.) *Western Marxism: A Critical Introduction*. London: Verso.

Michael, Mike (2000) *Reconnecting Culture, Technology and Nature: From Society to Heterogeneity*. London: Routledge.

Miller, Daniel (2002a) 'The unintended political economy' in du Gay, Paul and Pryke, Michael (eds) *Cultural Economy*. London: Sage.

Miller, Daniel (2002b) 'Turning Callon the right way up', *Economy and Society*, 31: 218-33.

Miller, Daniel and Slater, Don (2000) *The Internet: An Ethnographic Approach*. Oxford: Berg.

Miller, Peter (1992) 'Accounting and objectivity: the invention of calculating selves and calculable spaces', *Annals of Scholarship*, 9(1-2): 61-86.

Miller, Peter and Rose, Nikolas (1990) 'Governing economic life', *Economy and Society*, 19(1): 1-31.

Modleski, Tania (1982) *Loving with a Vengeance: Mass Produced Fantasies for Women*. Hamden, CT: Archon Books.

Modleski, Tania (ed.) (1986) *Studies in Entertainment: Critical Approaches to Mass Culture*. Minneapolis: University of Minnesota Press.

Moores, Shaun (1993) 'Television, geography and "mobile privatization"', *European Journal of Communication*, 8(3): 365-79.

Morley, David (1991) 'Where the global meets the local', *Screen*, 32(1): 1-15.

Morley, David and Robins, Kevin. (1989) 'Spaces of identity', *Screen*, 30(4): 10-34.

Morley, David and Silverstone, Roger (1991) 'Domestic communication', *Media, Culture and Society*, 12(1): 31-55.

Murray, Robin (1989) 'Fordism and Post-Fordism' in Hall, Stuart and Jacques, Martin (eds) *New Times: The Changing Face of Politics in the 1990s*. London: Lawrence and Wishart.

Nancy, Jean-Luc (1993) *The Experience of Freedom*. Stanford: University of Stanford Press.

Nettleton, Sarah (1992) *Power, Pain and Dentistry*. Milton Keynes: Open University Press.

Nietzsche, Frederich (1998) *On the Genealogy of Morals*. Oxford: Oxford University Press.

O'Regan, Tom (1992) '(Mis)taking policy: notes on the cultural policy debate', *Cultural Studies*, 6(3): 409-23.

Oswell, David (2002) *Television, Childhood and the Home: A History of the Making of the Child Television Audience in Britain*. Oxford: Oxford University Press.

Pasquino, Paulo (1991) 'Theatrum politicum: the genealogy of capital - police and the state of prosperity' in Burchell, Graham, Gordon, Colin and Miller, Peter (eds) *The Foucault Effect: Studies in Governmentality*. London: Harvester Wheatsheaf.

Peirce, Charles Sanders (1992) *The Essential Peirce: Selected Philosophical Writings, Vol. 1 (1867-1893)*. Bloomington: Indiana University Press.

Peirce, Charles Sanders (1998) *The Essential Peirce: Selected Philosophical Writings, Vol. 2 (1893-1913)*. Bloomington: Indiana University Press.

Pels, Dick (2000) *The Intellectual as Stranger: Studies in Spokespersonship*. London: Routledge.

Philbrick, Nathaniel (2001) *In the Heart of the Sea: The Epic True Story that Inspired Moby Dick*. London: Harper Collins.

Prins, Bowkje (1995) 'The ethics of hybrid subjects', *Science, Technology and Human Values*, 20: 352-67.

Propp, Vladimir (1968) *The Morphology of the Folktale*. Austin, TX: University of Texas Press.

Rabinow, Paul (1992) 'Artificiality and enlightenment: from sociobiology to biosociality' in Crary, Jonathan and Kwinter, Sanford (eds) *Incorporations*. New York: Zone Books.

Rajchman John (1991) *Truth and Eros: Foucault, Lacan and the Question of Ethics*. London: Routledge.

Rajchman, John (2000) *The Deleuze Connections*. Cambridge, MA: MIT Press.

Ranciere, Jacques (2002) 'Peuple ou multitude: question d'Eric Alliez à Jacques Ranciere', *Multitudes*, 9: 95-100.

Robertson, Roland (1990) 'Mapping the global condition: globalization as the central concept' in Featherstone, Mike (ed.) *Global Culture: Nationalism, Globalization and Modernity*. London: Sage.

Rosaldo, Renato (1993) *Culture and Truth: The Remaking of Social Analysis*. Boston, MA: Beacon Press.

Rose, Nikolas (1989) *Governing the Soul: The Shaping of the Private Self*. London: Routledge.

Rose, Nikolas (1992a) 'Governing the enterprising self' in Heelas, Phil and Morris, Paul (eds) *The Values of the Enterprise Culture: The Moral Debate*. London: Routledge.

Rose, Nikolas (1992b) *Toward a Critical Sociology of Freedom*. London: Goldsmiths College, University of London.

Rose, Nikolas (1993) 'Government, authority and expertise in advanced liberalism', *Economy and Society*, 22(3): 283-99.

Rose, Nikolas (1996) 'Identity, genealogy, history' in Hall, Stuart and du Gay, Paul (eds) *Questions of Cultural Identity*. London: Sage.

Said, Edward (1979) *Orientalism*. Hamondsworth: Penguin.

Said, Edward (1985) 'Orientalism reconsidered' *Cultural Critique*, 1: 89-107.

Said, Edward (1993) *Culture and Imperialism*. London: Vintage.

Saussure, Ferdinand de (1974 [1915]) *Course in General Linguistics*. London: Fontana.

Scannell, Paddy (1988) 'Radio times: the temporal arrangements of broadcasting in the modern world' in Drummond, Phillip and Paterson, Richard (eds), *Television and Its Audiences*. London: British Film Institute Press.

Schiller, Herbert, I. (1979) 'Genesis of the free flow of information principles' in Matterlart, Armand and Siegelaub, Seth (eds) *Communication and Class Struggle: Volume 1 - Capitalism, Imperialism*. New York: International General.

Schiller, Herbert, I. (1991) 'Not yet the post-imperialist era', *Critical Studies in Mass Communications*, 8: 13-28.

Schlesinger, Philip (1991) *Media, State and Nation: Political Violence and Collective Identities*. London: Sage.

Serres, Michel (1982) *Hermes: Literature, Science, Philosophy*. Baltimore, MD: Johns Hopkins University Press.

Serres, Michel (1990) *Conversations on Science, Culture and Time*. Ann Arbor: University of Michigan Press.

Serres, Michel (1995) *The Natural Contract*. Ann Arbor: University of Michigan Press.

Serres, Michel (2001) *Hominescence*. Paris: Le Pommier.

Shapin, Steven (1994) *A Social History of Truth: Civility and Science in Seventeenth-Century England*. Chicago: University of Chicago Press.
Simon, Roger (1982) *Gramsci's Political Thought: An Introduction*. London: Lawrence and Wishart.
Slater, Don (1997) *Consumer Culture and Modernity*. Cambridge: Polity.
Slater, Don (2002) 'Capturing markets from the economists' in du Gay, Paul and Pryke, Michael (eds) *Cultural Economy*. London: Sage.
Smith, Anthony, D. (1990) 'Towards a global culture?' in Featherstone, Mike (ed.) *Global Culture: Nationalism, Globalization and Modernity*. London: Sage.
Soper, Kate (1986) *Humanism and Anti-Humanism*. London: Hutchinson.
Star, Susan Leigh and Griesemer, James R. (1989) 'Institutional ecology: "translations" and boundary objects: amateurs and professionals in Berkeley's Museum of Vertebrate Zoology, 1907–39', *Social Studies of Science*, 19: 387–420.
Stengers, Isabel (2000) *The Invention of Modern Science*. Minneapolis: University of Minnesota Press.
Stocking, George Jr. (1968) *Race, Culture and Evolution: Essays in the History of Anthropology*. New York: Free Press.
Storey, John (1993) *An Introductory Guide to Cultural Theory and Popular Culture*. London: Harvester Wheatsheaf.
Strathern, Marilyn (1991) *Partial Connections*. Savage, MD: Rowman and Littlefield.
Strathern, Marilyn (ed.) (1995) *Shifting Contexts: Transformations in Anthropological Knowledge*. London: Routledge.
Strathern, Marilyn (1996) 'Cutting the network', *Journal of the Royal Anthropological Institute*, 2: 517–35.
Strinati, Dominic (1995) *An Introduction to Theories of Popular Culture*. London: Routledge.
Thompson, E. P. (1978) *The Poverty of Theory*. London: Verso.
Todorov, Tzvetan (1984) *Mikhail Bakhtin: The Dialogical Principle*. Manchester: Manchester University Press.
Tomlinson, John (1991) *Cultural Imperialism: A Critical Introduction*. London: Pinter.
Tylor, E. B. (1874) *Primitive Culture*. London: John Murray.
Veljanovski, Cento (ed.) (1989) *Freedom in Broadcasting*. London: Institute of Economic Affairs.
Veyne, Paul (1992) 'Comment on Paper' in Armstrong, Timothy, J. (ed.) *Michel Foucault: Philosopher*. London: Harvester Wheatsheaf.
Virilio, Paul (1988) Interview in *Block* 14: 4–7.
Virno, Paulo (2004) *A Grammar of the Multitude*. New York: Semiotexte.
Voloshinov, Valerian (1973) *Marxism and the Philosophy of Language*. New York: Seminar Press.
Wagner, Peter (2001a) *Theorizing Modernity*. London: Sage.
Wagner, Peter (2001b) *A History and Theory of the Social Sciences*. London: Sage.
Wallerstein, Immanuel (1974) *The Modern World System, Vol. 1*. New York: Academic Press.
Wallerstein, Immanuel (1980) *The Modern World System, Vol. 2*. New York: Academic Press.
Wallerstein, Immanuel (1983) *Historical Capitalism*. London: Verso.
Wallerstein, Immanuel (1990) 'Culture as the ideological battleground of the modern world-system' in Featherstone, Mike (ed.) *Global Culture: Nationalism, Globalization and Modernity*. London: Sage.
Weber, Max (1930) *The Protestant Ethic and the Spirit of Capitalism*. London: Allen and Unwin.
Weeks, Jeffrey (1990) 'The value of difference' in Rutherford, Jonathan (ed.) *Identity: Community, Culture, Difference*. London: Lawrence and Wishart.
Weiss, Linda (1997) 'Globalization and the myth of the powerless state', *New Left Review*, 225: 3-27.
Weiss, Linda (1998) *The Myth of the Powerless State: Governing the Economy in a Global Era*. Cambridge: Polity Press.
Williams, Raymond (1958) *Culture and Society, 1780–1950*. London: Chatto and Windus.
Williams, Raymond (1965) *The Long Revolution*. Harmondsworth: Penguin.

Williams, Raymond (1974) *Television: Technology and Cultural Form*. London: Fontana.
Williams, Raymond (1976) *Keywords: A Vocabulary of Culture and Society*. London: Fontana.
Williams, Raymond (1977) *Marxism and Literature*. Oxford: Oxford University Press.
Williams, Raymond (1980) 'Base and superstructure in Marxist cultural theory' in Williams, Raymond *Problems in Materialism and Culture*. London: Verso.
Williams, Raymond (1997 [1958]) 'Culture is ordinary' in Gray, Ann and McGuigan, Jim. (eds) *Studying Culture: An Introductory Reader*. London: Edward Arnold.
Willis, Paul (1990) *Common Culture*. Buckingham: Open University Press.
Wittgenstein, Ludwig (1958) *Philosophical Investigations*. Oxford: Blackwell.
Wittgenstein, Ludwig (1977) *Remarks on Colour*. Oxford: Blackwell.
Wittgenstein, Ludwig (1980) *Remarks on the Philosophy of Psychology*. Oxford: Blackwell.
Wood, Gaby (2002) *Living Dolls: A Magical History of the Quest for Mechanical Life*. London: Faber and Faber.
Woolgar, Steve (1991) 'Configuring the user: the case of usability trials' in Law, John (ed.) *A Sociology of Monsters: Essays on Power, Technology and Domination*. Oxford: Blackwell.
Yoshimoto, Mitsuhiro (1994) 'Images of empire: Tokyo Disneyland and Japanese cultural imperialism' in Smoodin, Eric (ed.) *Disney Discourse: Producing the Magic Kingdom*. New York: Routledge.

Index

Entries in *italics* denote films, publications and foreign language terms.